ıuda.

Civil-Military
Relations in Israel

JAFFEE CENTER FOR STRATEGIC STUDIES
Tel Aviv University

Civil-Military Relations in Israel

Yehuda Ben Meir

Columbia University Press
New York

Columbia University Press
New York   Chichester, West Sussex

Library of Congress Cataloging-in-Publication Data
Ben Meir, Yehuda.
    Civil-military relations in Israel / Yehuda Ben Meir.
        p.   cm.
    "A study of the Jaffee Center for Strategic Studies, Tel Aviv
University."
    Includes bibliographical references and index.
    ISBN 0–231–09684–4
    1. Civil-military relations—Israel.   2. Israel—Politics and
government.   I. Merkaz le-meḥkarim esṭraṭegiyim 'al shem Yafeh.
II. Title.
JQ1825.P38C583   1995
322'.5'095694—dc20   94–33142
                                                           CIP

Casebound editions of Columbia University Press books
are printed on permanent and durable acid-free paper.

Printed in the United States of America

c 10 9 8 7 6 5 4 3 2 1

Contents

Preface

Researchers entering the complex, exciting, and difficult field of civil-military relations should do so with great trepidation. Many have gone before them—including some of the most brilliant, analytical, and inventive minds of our times—yet all have recognized that the study of civil-military relations is fraught with many pitfalls. If this is true for any scholar, how much more so for an Israeli bent on studying civil-military relations in Israel. There is no country in the world for whom the question of national security is as vital—indeed as existential—as it is for Israel. Israel remains today the only country whose neighbors openly call for its annihilation. For Israel, national security is a question not merely of national existence but of life and death for its citizens. Nowhere in the world is John Kennedy's statement that national security remains the sphere where "a mistake can kill us" more apposite than in Israel.

I myself, having been actively engaged for many years in national security decision making at the highest levels, am acutely aware that this research deals with a topic considered by many in Israel—and rightly so—as the "holy of holies." I have therefore undertaken this research with much care and great caution, maintaining the disinterested curiosity and objective neutrality that should be the hallmark of a good scientist and researcher—to the extent possible when dealing with a process that bears on one's life and well-being.

In *National Security Decision Making: The Israeli Case*, I demonstrated that a key problem and a major drawback in Israel's decision-making process is the disproportionate role played by the Israel Defense Forces (IDF) in shaping Israel's strategy. A wide consensus exists on this point, bringing together academic researchers as well as high-ranking IDF officers. The recommendations for an Israeli-style national security staff I presented in the book were the subject of an intense national debate and subsequently have been partially enacted by legislation. The present study of civil-military relations in the Israeli context should in many ways complement and reinforce the earlier study. I hope it, too, will have a positive impact on the instrumental aspects of Israeli national security.

In researching and writing this book, I have benefited from many others and am deeply grateful to them all. Those parts dealing with theoretical issues or with civil-military relations in other countries owe much to the writings and works of Samuel Huntington, Morris Janowitz, Samuel Finer, Amos Perlmutter, and Martin Edmonds, among others. I also owe much to those who pioneered the study of civil-military relations in Israel—above all, Edward Luttwak, Dan Horowitz, Amos Perlmutter, Moshe Lissak, and Yoram Peri. But this book is based primarily on a series of in-depth interviews with individuals who at different periods in Israel's history have been the key actors in civil-military relations. I wish to acknowledge the complete cooperation of all those interviewed, a detailed list of whom appears at the end of this book. I was at times surprised and even taken aback by their candidness, openness, and sincere desire to help. I only hope that the reader will be as appreciative of their efforts and cooperation as I am.

Finally, I would also like to thank all my colleagues at the Jaffee Center for Strategic Studies (JCSS) for their advice and many worthwhile suggestions, which greatly improved this work. Specifically, I would like to mention Moshe Grundman, director of the JCSS Information and Documentation Center; Alex Szilvassy, who spared no effort to make available to me any helpful material or publication; and Joseph Alpher, deputy head of the center, who offered invaluable assistance in the editing of this manuscript.

A special word of thanks to the former head of JCSS, Major General (Reserve) Aharon Yariv, whose untimely death has been a blow to all his colleagues and friends. It was he who originally encouraged me to undertake this assignment and who continued to give me intellectual guidance, support, and encouragement until its completion. Finally, while many have aided me in the preparation of this study, to all of whom I am greatly indebted, its drawbacks and limitations are my own, and, in the end, I alone bear responsibility for its contents.

Introduction

Simultaneously part of the Third World and part of the Western world, Israel is an ideal laboratory for the study of civil-military relations. The country shares with the Western nations a deeply rooted tradition of and solid commitment to democratic government. The constitutional principle of civilian supremacy over the armed forces is firmly and clearly grounded both in law and in custom. Yet Israel is the only Western democracy to be suspended in a perpetual state of war throughout its lifetime. Born in war, Israel has always faced a direct military threat to its existence: even today, after having fought six wars in forty-five years of independence, many of its Arab neighbors still refuse to recognize its right to exist. Forged by necessity from the instinct for survival, the Israeli army has become both a symbol of national unity and a dominant force highly involved in almost all facets of Israeli life. Such a reality must certainly pose challenges to healthy civil-military relations, and the way in which Israel has met these challenges is a source of fascination to anyone with an interest in modern civil-military relations. It is to this story that this book is primarily devoted.

Many scholars have asked why it is that, although the IDF occupies a far more central place in Israeli public life than the military in any other democracy, it nevertheless poses no threat to the state's democratic institutions. Some have tried to find the answer in the concept of "civilianization," asserting—absurd as it may sound—that the IDF is itself a civilian institution. Others have introduced the concept of a "schizophrenic society," claiming that Israel is characterized by a clear differentiation and demarcation between the security sphere and all the other civil spheres, the two arenas being subject to distinctly different rules.

In the last decade, a number of Israeli scholars have begun a reexamination of the Israeli pattern of civil-military relations, challenging many of the assumptions that until now have typified the research and writing on this subject. According to these scholars, the portrayal of the IDF as a classic or professional army in the Western sense is both oversimplistic and unrealistic; the IDF is far from being the "benign" or "civilian" institution it is made out to be. Although there is no question that, from a formal point of view, the Israeli government exercises civilian control over the IDF, new evidence, based especially on primary sources in Hebrew and on interviews with key actors in the system, seems to indicate that behind the scenes it is the IDF that calls the shots. An examination of certain recent events in Israel seems to support this contention.

On December 10, 1992, the Israeli government, headed by Prime Minister Rabin, decided to deport 415 Arab residents of the Administered Territories (the Gaza Strip and the West Bank), activists in the Hamas terror organization, which had taken responsibility for the kidnapping and brutal murder of an Israeli policeman the day before. The decision was clearly of major political importance, having serious, far-reaching consequences for the ongoing peace talks as well as for Israel's foreign relations. There was little question that such an unprecedented action would result in severe international criticism, as well as in Arab attempts to persuade the United Nations to take action against Israel. Moreover, its psychological effects on the Arab citizens of Israel (Israeli Arabs) could be quite grave and might even jeopardize the continued parliamentary support of the government by the five Arab members of the Knesset.

Under such circumstances, it stands to reason that Prime Minister Rabin, the moving spirit behind the deportation decision, would consult extensively with his civilian advisers, namely with key members of the cabinet, senior officials of the Foreign Ministry, legal experts, and the heads of the security services. Since the IDF bears the major responsibility for the territories, the prime minister would also consult with the army as the body that would have to implement the decision. Yet the nature of the decision would remain primarily civilian and political.

In reality, however, the driving force behind the deportations was none other the chief of the general staff (CGS) of the IDF, Lieutenant General Barak. Prime Minister Rabin informed a number of key ministers of the resolution he was about to bring to the cabinet only a short while before the cabinet meeting that approved the deportation; the discussion with these ministers lasted less than an hour. Foreign Minister Peres, abroad at the time, was not informed at all, nor was anyone at the Foreign Ministry privy to the secret. Indeed, it seems that even the head of the General Security Service (Shabak, also known as the Shin Bet, its Hebrew abbreviation) and his key people, as well as the attorney general, were consulted only after Rabin himself had already decided on the deportation.

On the other hand, CGS Barak was in on the process from the very beginning. Faced with tremendous public outrage at the kidnapping and brutal murder of the policeman—the culmination of a succession of terrorist attacks in Israel—Prime Minister Rabin turned to CGS Barak for advice as to a proper and effective response. It should be noted that for a long time Barak had been advocating large-scale deportation of terrorists for limited periods rather than permanent deportation of individuals. It would thus be fair to say that a major national security decision with far-reaching political ramifications—both domestic and foreign—was taken in effect by the prime minister (who also serves as defense minister) and the CGS. Formally, of course, it was a cabinet decision, and the government bears the ultimate collective responsibility for it; however, the true parents of the deportation were Prime Minister Rabin and CGS Barak.

Another example of the crucial influence wielded by the IDF in all areas of national security is the case of the Gulf War. During the five months between Saddam Hussein's invasion of Kuwait and the actual onset of hostilities between the allied coalition and Iraq, Israel's civilian leaders—especially Prime Minister Shamir and Defense Minister Arens—issued dire warnings to Saddam Hussein that if he implemented his threats to attack Israel with Scud missiles, he would face severe retaliation. It should be noted that since 1949, the Israeli home front had been immune to attack from the air—owing to both Israel's efficient air defense and the deterrent capability of the Israeli Air Force. In fact, the perception that no Israeli government would tolerate missile attacks on Israeli cities and that such attacks would trigger a massive response by the Israeli Air Force was considered by almost all Israelis as a central element in Israel's defense doctrine and national strategy.

As we all know now, things turned out quite differently. Israeli cities were indeed attacked for six weeks by Iraqi missiles, people were killed, and considerable damage was caused to property. Life in the country was seriously disrupted for six weeks, and the people had to adjust to a "routine emergency" regime. Israel suffered eighteen missile attacks in forty-two days, during which forty Scud missiles were fired at the country's major population centers. Yet throughout the Israeli Air Force remained on the ground or within Israeli airspace. No military action whatsoever was taken against Iraq.

The common perception is that although the IDF high command pressured the government to respond with airstrikes against Iraqi cities, or at least to allow the Israeli Air Force to attack and destroy the missile sites in western Iraq, the government decided to refrain from military action because of strong pressure from the United States, including personal appeals from Secretary of State Baker and President Bush. The truth, however, is rather more complex. No doubt the persistent entreaties of American leaders for Israeli restraint, lest the anti-Iraq coalition crumble or crack, had an important effect on Israel's leaders, but the major factor shaping Israel's policy in the Gulf War was the adamant position of none other than the IDF.

Contrary to what might be expected, the IDF was strongly opposed to any Israeli intervention in the Gulf War (as long as Iraqi attacks were confined to conventional weapons), and it was the IDF's opposition to military action that had the most effect on Prime Minister Shamir, Defense Minister Arens, and the Israeli cabinet. The IDF's attitude was formed and espoused by its three key officers: CGS Lieutenant General Dan Shomron, Deputy CGS Major General Barak (later to became the CGS), and Director of Military Intelligence Major General Shachak (later to become deputy CGS). Their stand was that Israel's long-range interests lay in enabling the American and coalition military action against Iraq to continue as long as possible, the result of which would be the destruction of Iraq's armed forces, her unconventional (nuclear, chemical, and biological) capability, and a large part of her civilian infrastructure. Any Israeli action that might lead to an abrupt or early end to the war would be detrimental to those interests.

Without doubt the IDF's position had a major impact on Israel's leaders. Indeed, before the crucial cabinet meeting of January 19, 1991—held after the second missile attack on Israel—CGS Shomron met privately with Prime Minister Shamir in order to impress upon him both the IDF's view and the great importance it attached to having that view adopted by the government.[1] Shomron was also reported to have allayed his fellow officers' concerns that the government might yield to public opinion by noting that never in Israel's history had the government ordered the IDF to undertake military action that it strongly opposed.

It would be simplistic and far from accurate to conclude from this that the IDF determines Israeli national security policy with the government acting merely as a rubber stamp. But where does the truth lie? Has there been an erosion or an increase in civilian control over the armed services during the past forty years? What are the precise relationships among the prime minister, the defense minister, the ministerial committee on national security, and the cabinet in term of ultimate authority over the armed forces? What are the advantages and disadvantages for Israel of precise and vigorous constitutional definitions of the civil-military relationship as opposed to the present flexible and general ones? Can a society experiencing protracted war, in which security is such a salient factor, preserve an instrumentalist army, i.e., one that does not penetrate civil institutional spheres? How healthy is the current system and what changes are necessary? This book attempts to find answers to these questions.

A key concept in any modern analysis of civil-military relations is that of civilian control. There is universal recognition that civilian control over the military is a sine qua non of democratic government and essential to understanding civil-military relations. Huntington claims that "the role of the military in society has been discussed frequently in terms of 'civilian control.'" Saying the same thing in the negative sense, Sweetman writes that "the ability and inclination of an army to intervene in politics has been viewed as the nub of civil-military relations." In the same vein, Lowell states that "from a formal, legalistic perspective, the problem in civil military relations lies primarily in the threat posed by a military establishment . . . to popular control of government and to individual liberty. The solution to the problem is perceived to lie in the maintenance of 'civil control' of the military."[2]

The handful of scholars who have studied Israeli civil-military relations, however, have offered different evaluations of civilian control in the Israeli context. Thus Perlmutter writes: "The rapid turnover of officers, . . . the economic and social integration of Zahal's [the Israel Defense Forces'] veterans, the nation's dependence upon the reserve system, the identity of political goals, and the Army's professionalism preclude Zahal's actual intervention in politics. In addition, the institutionalized legitimacy of the independent civilian political structures fur-

nishes an effective guarantee of civilian control." At the same time, Perlmutter, in line with his fusionist approach, emphasizes that: "The military in Israel—as a pressure group similar to those in other non-praeto-
rian states where the civilian is formally and informally supreme—will
nevertheless continue to challenge the civilian, especially in the realm of
defense and foreign affairs." Luttwak and Horowitz cite Israel's extensive
reserve system as a major factor causing military life to be pervaded by
civilian influences, i.e., the civilianization of the military. Lissak also
takes a positive view regarding the degree of civilian control in the Israeli
system. He lists a number of apparent paradoxes that add a special quality to civil-military relations in Israel. Peri, on the other hand, takes a less
positive and dimmer view of the status of civilian control in Israel. He
speaks of nominal civilian control but only weak instrumental control
and describes Israeli civil-military relations as being characterized by a
political-military partnership. In his opinion, while one can speak of
civilianization of the military in Israel, there is a definite militarization
of civil society as well.[3]

A major factor determining the extent of civilian control in Israel has
been the firm ideological commitment of the military to democratic government, complete with a deep and unshakable belief in the principle of
civilian supremacy. Israel may be a young country, but its society reflects
the age-old traditions and mentality of the Jewish people. Many scholars
credit Ben-Gurion's leadership and vision for the fact that, unlike so
many other new nations, the military did not become predominant and
never showed praetorian tendencies.[4] In my opinion the roots go much
deeper and can be traced back 3,500 years to the exodus from Egypt. Back
then the Jews had alrady been defined by the Almighty as a "stiff-necked
people" and ever since they have manifested a suspicion of, and at times
a disregard for, all forms of authority. Jews have always shown democratic and pluralistic tendencies ("two Jews—three opinions"), at times bordering on anarchy. Some go so far as to contend that the Jews are
ungovernable, a contention not without empirical support. Be that as it
may, the commitment of the IDF's officer corps to a free, pluralistic, and
democratic society reflects the cultural heritage of the people and society
of which they are part.

Given this, can the continuation of firm civilian control in Israeli civil-
military relations be taken for granted? Is it certain that civilian control,
at least in the formal sense, will continue to be a nonissue in Israeli society? At present the answer seems clearly to be yes, but if one looks toward

the more distant future there is room for some concern—for two major reasons. First, the composition of the Israeli officer corps is changing. Amos Perlmutter defines the IDF as a professional revolutionary army, emphasizing the ideological motivation of the soldier in such an army. He points out that revolutionary soldiers seldom aspire to be soldiers; rather, they become soldiers as loyal servants of the revolutionary movement. This quality originally was highly characteristic of the IDF and had a significant bearing on civil-military relations.[5] The cadre of IDF commanders was strongly imbued and indoctrinated from childhood with Zionist, democratic, and liberal values, i.e., with the revolutionary ideology of the Jewish national liberation movement. It is for this reason that one finds it so inconceivable that Dayan or Allon or Rabin or Gur or Eitan or Levy or Shomron or any CGS would ever seriously challenge civilian supremacy. This picture, however, is slowly but surely changing. Many young soldiers today see officership in the IDF as a key vehicle for socioeconomic mobility. It is less and less a calling and more and more a career; the IDF itself is becoming more and more corporate. There is room for doubt whether the chief of staff in ten or twenty years will have the same commitment to the principle of civilian control characteristic of chiefs of staff to date.

Alone, this development, though worrisome, does not seem to pose a direct challenge to civilian control. The principle of military subordination to civilian authority is so much a part of the IDF culture that anyone reaching the rank of CGS, or of any general staff position, would presumably have acquired a reasonable commitment to civilian control. But when the second factor enters the picture, there is cause for genuine concern.

The past two decades have seen a growing polarization within Israeli society, with public opinion characterized by a basic lack of consensus, or what is technically known as a "state of desensus." The country is divided between religious and nonreligious, Sephardim and Ashkenazim (Jews from Africa and Asia and Western Jews), supporters of Greater Israel and advocates of territorial compromise, right and left, doves and hawks, Likud supporters and Labor adherents. The massive influx of Russian immigrants in the 1990s poses a potential new division: newcomers versus old-timers. The most troublesome and even dangerous feature of this polarization is that these factors (ethnic group membership, religiosity, political leaning) are highly correlated; consequently, the country is divided into two hostile camps: the so-called national camp, composed mostly of religious and traditional Jews of African and Asian origin, who are hawkish, anti-Arab, and Likud supporters, and the so-called peace camp, composed of secular Jews of Western origin, who are dovish and Labor supporters.

As the debate over the future of the territories becomes more and more bitter, ever bordering on the violent, Israel may be quickly approaching the state of "a house divided against itself." At the same time, the Israeli political system is showing signs of a deep malaise, much strain and stress, and a basic structural weakness. Many observers characterize the Israeli political system as very sick, and some even see it as on the verge of paralysis. As a result of Israel's archaic system of proportional elections, its parliamentary system of government, and an electorate evenly split between right and left, effective government is growing more and more difficult. The political parties are at their lowest ebb ever; the public seems to have lost confidence in them. Given the changing nature of the IDF, and especially of its officer corps, one may wonder how such an army will react to severe social and economic instability coupled with the near paralysis of the civilian government. Former CGS Eitan claims that even in such a dire situation, i.e., one where the civilian government is barely functioning and the country is facing national paralysis, the IDF would not take over power unless it were given some sort of civilian legitimacy, such as a call by the Knesset to do so.[6] Nevertheless, there is still room for doubt and concern, and it is for this reason, among many others, that a book such as this is so vitally important for Israel's future.

I conducted twenty-one interviews with former prime ministers, defense ministers, chiefs of staff, heads of military intelligence, heads of the Mossad and of the General Security Service, senior military officers, senior advisers, and civil servants. As a rule—with one or two exceptions—individuals currently occupying the aforementioned positions were not interviewed. All living former prime ministers were interviewed, as were all former defense ministers (with the sole exceptions of former defense minister Mr. Sharon and former prime minister Mr. Shamir but including current prime minister and defense minister Rabin) and all former chiefs of staff of the IDF (with the sole exception of General Zur). A detailed list of all the interviewees and their government/military service records appears in appendix B at the end of this work.

The integrated cumulative information derived from these interviews offers a fascinating view of civil-military relations in Israel as they really are—a comprehensive review that has never before been documented to such an extent. Concrete and specific examples support and further define the overall picture. I have tried to document the source or sources on which each factual statement, assumption, assessment, or evaluation is based. In a small number of cases, the source of an example or observation has specifically requested to remain anonymous. In view of the sensitivity of some of the material, I have honored all such requests, identifying such sources merely as "personal communication." My own observations and knowledge, resulting from my experience and involvement in national security decision making, are referred to similarly, as they represent, in effect, personal communications between the author and himself.

Abbreviations

BKA	Bundeskanzleramt
CDS	Chief of the Defense Staff
CENTCOM	Central Command
CGS	chief of the general staff
CID	Ministerial Committee of Imperial Defence
CINC	Commander in Chief
CJCS	chairman of the Joint Chiefs of Staff
CNO	chief of naval operations
COS	chiefs of staff
COMDR ARCENT	the commander of the United States Army, service component of the Central Command
D-G	director-general
DMI	director of military intelligence
EUCOM	European Command
FADC	Foreign Affairs and Defense Committee
FA-HB	financial advisor–head of the budget
FCH	field corps headquarters
GFH	ground forces headquarters
HCJ	high court of justice
IAI	Israel Aircraft Industries
IDF	Israel Defense Forces (aka Zahal)
JCS	Joint Chiefs of Staff

MDC	ministerial defense committee
MNSC	ministerial national security committee
MOD	Ministry of Defense
NSU	national security unit
O/C	officer in command
OSD	Office of the Secretary of Defense
PLA	Chinese People's Liberation Army
PUS	permanent undersecretary
SGDN	Secrétariat Général de la Défense Nationale

Civil-Military
Relations in Israel

1 | The Scope of the Study: A Theoretical Model

Civil-military relations can be studied from a number of perspectives. The perspective any given study adopts determines both how the subject matter will be organized and which institutions will be examined. A common perspective emphasizes the relationship between civilians and soldiers, i.e., the uniformed services. Here the focus is on the interaction between the civilian masters operating within a civilian structure and the men and women in uniform who are subject to a military hierarchy and under civilian control. Another perspective involves looking at the relationship between the political echelon and the professional bureaucracy. In this perspective, the focus is on the interaction between the elected officials and the bureaucrats—between the formulators of policy and those who are entrusted with its execution and implementation. A third perspective, albeit a less prominent one, emphasizes the influence of professional and/or bureaucratic vested interests and pressure groups—primarily but not solely in the military—on the decision-making process.

A study that tried encompass all these perspectives would be overly ambitious. On the other hand, a study limited to a single perspective would omit many important insights and present an incomplete picture. To achieve a proper sense of balance, then, this study focuses primarily on the relationship between the civilian and the soldier but at the same time examines some relevant aspects of the relationship between the authority vested in the country's elected officials and the government bureaucracy, whether civilian or military. Aspects of the third perspective are also considered, albeit to a much lesser extent.

Having taken the first perspective as my primary guide, I decided to exclude the civilian intelligence and security services from the scope of the study. A detailed examination of these services and of the delicate and intricate relationship between the political decision makers and the espionage, intelligence, and security networks is appropriate subject matter for a study in and of itself. On the other hand, I decided to focus on the entire gamut of civilian-political authority, at all its levels. This study thus encompasses the executive, legislative, and judicial branches of government. Naturally, the executive branch exercises the primary responsibility for the activities of the military, but the military is also subject to legislative oversight and judicial review.

Western countries differ greatly as to the degree to which their legislatures are involved in military affairs. At one end of the spectrum is, of course, the United States, where Congress and the president share almost equal power over and responsibility for the armed forces. All students of American civil-military relations stress the checks-and-balances approach of the founding fathers that led to the Constitution dividing civilian control over the armed services between the executive and the Congress.[1] The president is the commander in chief, but only the Congress may declare war, raise and support armies, and make rules for the government and for regulation of the land and naval forces. In most Western European parliamentary democracies, on the other hand, civilian authority over the armed forces is invested almost entirely in the executive arm of the state, although parliamentary involvement in major national security decisions and in the supervision of the military establishment—mainly the committees dealing with foreign affairs and defense—is on the rise, though varying from country to country.

In Israel, the degree of parliamentary involvement with the armed forces could be a good test of Dan Horowitz's concept of a "schizophrenic society."[2] The Israeli parliament—the Knesset—is active in all civil spheres; if it is inactive in the security spheres, this would show that these two arenas are indeed, as Horowitz claims, subject to two distinct sets of rules. The degree of the courts' involvement with the military is another such test. The judicial system is an instrument of state, playing an important role in civilian affairs. Its activity or inactivity in the security sphere thus indicates whether these two arenas are or are not subject to different rules. Though this study of the relationship between the armed forces and the state will include the legislative and judicial branches of government, its primary concern will be the executive branch, which remains the key player. (The executive arm in Israel includes the government, or cabinet, which enjoys collective responsibility for running the affairs of state; the ministerial committee on national security—which acts on behalf of the cabinet; and the individual ministers who are responsible for those areas related to national security, namely, the prime minister, the minister of defense, and the foreign minister.)

In this book, the terms *political* and *civil* are used interchangeably. Nevertheless, there is a clear distinction between the two. "Political authority" refers to the elected officials of government: president, prime minister, member of the cabinet, and ministers of defense. "Civilian authority" refers to members of the civil service who are part of the civilian bureaucracy. Presidential appointments fall somewhere in the middle. The term *civil* (or *civilian*) *authority* will be used throughout this book in its wider context, i.e., as including both concepts, while "political authority" will be used only in the narrow sense, i.e., as referring to the elected officials of government.

The aim of this book is to give a detailed and broad overview of the actual ongoing relationship between the civilian and military authorities in Israel. The book deals primarily with the division of authority and the nature of the boundaries between the civil administration and the military command, but it will also examine such issues as the phenomenon of militarism and the conditions for the involvement of military officers in the process of political, economic, and social decision making. I have based the study on a theoretical model of civil-military relations that represents, in my view, a more modern approach to civil-military relations (see appendix A). Central to the model are a fusionist theory of administration, an emphasis on military involvement instead of military intervention, and a consideration of both sides—civilian and military—of the involvement equation. Sweetman writes that initially "the ability and inclination of an army to intervene in politics has been viewed as the nub of civil-military relations" but that today one should not focus only on the political context, i.e., consider civil-military relations only in terms of the containment of the armed forces, but rather on the wider overall national and public context.[3]

This theme has been repeated by many scholars in the past few years. Lovell writes that the traditional approach, which views the maintenance of civil control through a series of constitutional checks and balances as the ideal solution to the central problem of civil-military relations, tends to neglect important informal patterns of interaction and sources of power. Concern in the West today is not over possible military coups or unauthorized military intervention but rather about the growing influence of the military-industrial complex and the undue emphasis the civilian political leadership places on military solutions to diplomatic and political problems. The threat to popular control is not from military adventurism or the warrior caste but rather from mutual meddling and the blurring of civil-military areas of special competence. As far back as 1957, Huntington observed that "the problem in the modern state is not armed revolt, but the relation of the expert to the politician."[4]

Edmonds, reflecting the current up-to-date state-of-the-art approach, is most explicit about the need to substitute the notion of involvement for that of intervention, stating that "the first step in constructing a model of armed services 'intervention' in politics, therefore, is to get rid of the concept of intervention." He goes on to say that "the involvement of armed services in politics can be seen as a permanent condition; the critical consideration becomes, then, one of degree more than kind."[5]

The basic theoretical premise of this study is, then, that the military is constantly involved in the affairs of state as is the civilian authority in the affairs of the military and that this two-way influence is constant. The issue at stake is the extent of each sphere's influence and the areas in which it is most likely to be exercised. Most studies have concentrated on the relative influence of each sector in the area of foreign affairs and defense—national security. However, since World War II, and especially with the advent of the nuclear age, security and defense issues have become increasingly associated with domestic and civilian concerns, such as the state of the economy, scientific and technological research and development, employment, and education.[6] Figure 1 gives a schematic representation of a model of civil-military relations; the functions of state are divided into four areas.[7]

The column at the extreme right of the diagram would normally be subsumed under the label National Security, since the armed forces are an aspect—perhaps the main aspect—of a nation's security effort. The activities included in this area, however, relate to the actual functioning of the military and are seen by many as the proper domain of the professional soldier. In the same way, political affairs could be considered a subset of domestic affairs, all of which are clearly within the civilian domain. Again, however, because political affairs are considered strictly off limits to the military, I have singled it out as a separate area for consideration.

FIGURE 1

A Model of Civil-Military Relations

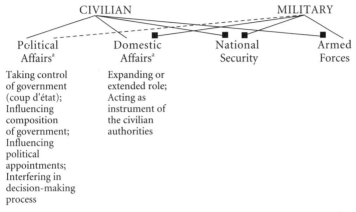

Dotted line represents prohibited involvement. Blackened squares show main areas of interest in civil-military relations.
[a]Possible expression or manifestation of military involvement.

The area of foreign affairs and defense, on the other hand, is the traditional gray area, where there is room for both military and civilian input.

Civilian and military involvement in all four of the areas defined in the figure should result, theoretically, in eight avenues of involvement. However, the principle of civilian supremacy dictates that these two echelons not be treated equally. Civilian involvement is legitimate in any and every area of the state, but there are still certain areas in which any military involvement is taboo. Specifically, military involvement in the political affairs and the electoral process of the state is illegitimate and prohibited (signified in the figure by the dotted line).

Civilian involvement in strictly civil areas and the involvement of the military leadership in the day-to-day functioning of the armed forces are the rule, and the reasons for this are self-evident—and consequently of less interest. The focus of interest in the study of civil-military relations is on the four points that form the crux of modern civil-military relations. These points (shown in figure 1 by the darkened squares) are: civilian involvement in the armed forces proper, military involvement in domestic affairs (either through role expansion by the military or through the use of the military by the civil authorities as an instrument to achieve certain ends), and involvement by both civilian and military echelons in the gray area of national security.

A comprehensive review of Israeli civil-military relations should cover all four points. Civilian and military involvement in the area of national security, as well as civilian involvement in the armed forces (an area that is, in effect, an integral part of national security), are inseparably intertwined and so must be considered each in relation to the other. Military involvement in domestic affairs, on the other hand, is not necessarily crucial in determining the country's civil-military relations. The use of the military by the Israeli government as an instrument to achieve domestic ends in Israel proper (as opposed to the Administered Territories) is almost nonexistent; the use of the IDF in labor disputes or in cases of public disorder is taboo—in all Israel's history, there has only been one instance of each. Since constraints of time and space make it impossible for all four points and for the entire gamut of issues to be dealt with in depth here, it seemed both wise and prudent to leave the thorough examination of the involvement of the Israeli military in domestic affairs for another study.

It should be noted, however, that the role expansion of the IDF beyond its purely military function is quite extensive and has been fairly well documented in many studies and accounts of Israeli civil-military relations.[8] The IDF has its own radio station—which broadcasts to the entire population, twenty-four hours a day, with extensive coverage of news and current affairs—as well as its own popular weekly magazine. It carries on paramilitary training in the high schools, maintains a number of premilitary vocational schools, and offers a series of educational programs for soldiers, primarily those from disadvantaged homes. The IDF is also intensively involved in settlement activity and is responsible for all security censorship.

The IDF's substantial role expansion and its extensive involvement in civilian spheres of activity have been characterized by many as a classic example of permeable boundaries leading to a militarized civility. This phenomenon merits a proper and more balanced appraisal, but, as stated above, it has been excluded from this study. Nevertheless, three important points should be made. First, there is no involvement whatsoever by the IDF in the area of political affairs, i.e., in the electoral process. Second, most of the role expansion has been forced on the military by the civilian authorities, and the IDF would be only too happy to be relieved of most, if not all, of these functions. A good example of this is CGS Ehud Barak's tenacious though unsuccessful campaign to close down the army radio. Finally, one can conclude from the material and evidence accumulated during this study that the IDF role expansion poses no danger or threat to civilian control and is not a major factor in Israeli civil-military relations.

Two exceptions to this conclusion need to be made. Both the IDF's role in civil defense and, especially, the military government and its civilian administration in the Administered Territories could potentially have far-reaching consequences for Israel's civil-military relations. The IDF's control of all civil defense activities is relevant primarily in time of war, but the military government in the territories is a glaring example of the day-to-day use of the military by the civilian government to achieve domestic and at times even political ends. One can conceive of certain developments in the territories that could give rise to a most grave crisis in Israel's civil-military relations.

The above notwithstanding, an attempt to include the issue of the IDF's role in the Administered Territories within this study would have been a mistake. In addition to the reasons already stated, two further arguments can be made: The issue is not basic or inherent but, by definition, temporary—it did not exist before 1967, and some day in the near or far future it will vanish. Moreover, the issue is fraught with political sensitivity and to tackle it would have endangered the objectivity of this study. Its exclusion, however, should not be seen as belittling its importance.

In order to examine, properly and in depth, military and civilian involvement in national security affairs (represented in the figure as "national security" and "armed forces"), there is a further need to identify the types of decision making involved and the individuals responsible for each. One can identify and delineate three distinct types or areas of decision making. According to Huntington, the first is concerned with strategic doctrine, force contingency plans, disposition and deployment of forces and resources, and defense policy and priorities, while the second addresses more practical and detailed questions of weapons acquisition, defense budgetary matters, and armed services' morale, organization, equipment, resources, and training. Edmonds points out that this model is satisfactory only in peacetime; in war, an additional area has to be included, namely, the overall conduct, control, and command of fighting units involved in combat—i.e., operations. He adds that the complex character of nuclear warfare "has made this area, once a responsibility that devolved largely onto the armed services, one that political leadership has increasingly assumed the authority to control."[9]

The military, by definition, is a hierarchical organization and thus can be represented by the officer who stands at its head. In the Israeli context, this is the chief of staff, whose office is defined by law as the "highest military command echelon."[10] The civilian arm of government, on the other hand, is more diffuse and lines of authority are less clear; one has to deal simultaneously with a number of players. Looking at the Israeli case and taking all the players—civilian and military—into account, one can identify a number of triads that play crucial roles in specific aspects of civil-military relations (see figure 2).

FIGURE 2
Taxonomy of Civil-Military Involvement in National Security Affairs

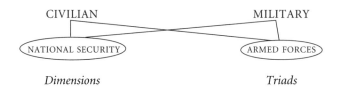

Dimensions	*Triads*
Strategic planning	Cabinet–Prime Minister–Defense Minister
Operational dimension	Prime Minister–Defense Minister–Chief of Staff
Force development	Defense Minister–Chief of Staff–Director-General

In the next chapter, I shall look more carefully at the concept of civilian control, analyzing it from a theoretical point of view and examining the experience of other countries. Chapter 3 describes the constitutional principles and legal aspects of Israeli civil-military relations. Chapter 4 examines the key issue of Israel's national command authority. Chapter 5 looks at the organizational structure of the defense establishment in Israel. Chapter 6 examines the intricate relations within each of the three key triads (shown in figure 2) involved in day-to-day civil-military relations. In chapter 7, the interaction between civilian and military involvement in national security affairs, as described in chapters 3, 4, 5, and 6, is summarized in terms of the areas of decision making, or the three key dimensions of interrelationship, shown in figure 2: the operational dimension, strategic planning, and force development. Three specific examples, each relevant to one of the three dimensions, will be analyzed the better to illustrate that specific dimension. In chapter 8 the focus returns to civilian control in Israel, and chapter 9 presents my conclusions and recommendations.

2 | Civilian Control

All agree that civilian control is an essential feature of any democratic state and a concept vital to understanding civil-military relations. There is far less agreement, however, as to what exactly civilian control is, what it entails, and even when it can be said to exist. Huntington's statement that "the role of the military in society has been frequently discussed in terms of 'civilian control' " is, no doubt, true, but, as he himself points out, "this concept has never been satisfactorily defined."[1]

A broad definition of civilian control along the lines of the model depicted in figure 1 could involve maximization of civilian involvement and minimization of military involvement. Such a definition, however, would run contrary to two key elements of the model: (1) the fact that in modern states military involvement in areas of society and in functions of state, including domestic affairs, is widespread; and (2) the need for professional autonomy. Going to the other extreme, a narrow definition of civilian control would entail the noninvolvement of the military in the area of political affairs. This definition is also unacceptable. There is a consensus among scholars in the field that civilian control means much more than the immunity of the electoral process and the political institution of the state from interference by the military. Most definitions relate, one way or another, to the relative involvement of both echelons in all areas, including that of military affairs, and attempt to strike a proper balance between civilian and military involvement in each of the various areas, although there are widely divergent views as to where such balance actually lies.

Some authorities feel that the crucial aspect of civilian control lies in who exercises ultimate control. In a report on civil-military relations by a blue-ribbon American panel, the authors write that "the ultimate authority in matters military must be exercised by those responsible to the ultimate political power—the electorate. The concept automatically excludes the professional military from exercising such authority. . . . The principle of civilian control must be absolute and indivisible."[2] Ultimate control is a recurring theme in American civil-military relations. As early as June 17, 1776, the Virginia Declaration of Rights stated: "In all cases the military should be under strict subordination to and governed by civil power."[3] This view has never wavered. As Dupuy puts it, "Civilian control over the armed forces of the United States is the practice of the constitutional provision that the armed forces are commanded by the President—a civilian—and that they are organized, equipped, and supplied as directed by the Congress—a body of civilians. It means neither more nor less than that."[4]

Not everyone, however, is willing to accept this limited definition of civilian control, a definition that puts the entire emphasis on the exercise of ultimate formal authority by elected representatives of the people. Lovell has characterized this definition as civilian control "in the old sense" and points out that the three great civil-military issues of the post–World War II decade in the United States—the administration of the occupied territories, the development and control of atomic energy, and the reorganization of the military establishment—did not raise questions concerning the "locus of power" or "civilian control in the old sense"; instead the essential problem was how properly to combine military advice and opinions with political input, civilian advice, and popular opinion.[5] And even before World War II, Lasswell, in formulating his concept of the "garrison state," already recognized that problems of popular control of government and the maintenance of individual liberty are broader than the concept of "civil control in the old sense" suggests.[6] President Eisenhower's warning, in his farewell speech, of the growing influence of the military-industrial complex was not intended to imply that military officers and industrialists might conspire to take over the government of the United States or that the generals would refuse to obey the president. Rather, it was meant to suggest that the growing size and economic power of the defense establishment—that is, the growing involvement of the military in the area of domestic affairs—posed a potential threat to the ability of civilians genuinely and effectively to control it.[7]

The view that military overinvolvement—even if it does not threaten ultimate formal civilian authority—runs contrary to civilian control is not limited to the area of domestic affairs. It also applies, perhaps even more strongly, to the area of national security. Nowhere is this demonstrated better than in the case of the American Joint Chiefs of Staff (JCS) during World War II. As a consequence of President Roosevelt's unique style of administration (which, inter alia, excluded not only the secretary of state but also the secretaries of war and navy from participating actively in any decision making regarding the war), military involvement in strategic and policy decisions reached unprecedented heights. Many decisions, including those related to diplomacy and economics—areas usually reserved for civilian involvement—were left to the military.[8] Many believed this threatened civilian control, even though what was at stake was the proper balance between civilian and military involvement in the area of national security, not the underlying principle that, in the end, civilians control the military. Because of this fear, Congress rejected the Joint Chiefs' proposals for the postwar organization of the Defense Department, which sought to preserve their situation, instead favoring the National Security Council, a strong secretary of defense, and firm civilian control.[9]

Many authorities in the field support the position that civilian control turns on who in fact (not in theory) establishes national security policy and determines the allocation of finite resources to fulfill security needs. Mahoney, for example, cautions against the situation that exists today, whereby "we have allowed our military leaders to become much more than planners of military strategy and tactics and commanders of combat units in the field. Beyond soldiering, we have allowed them to assume roles that require the qualities of the statesman, diplomat, business executive and lobbyist." He goes so far as to say that "democracy is threatened by assigning military leaders nontraditional roles to play." In the same vein, Segal and Schwartz point out that the advent of the atomic age and the power of modern weaponry have transformed the role of the military, both "broadening the function of the armed forces into the realm of politics even in periods of peace and necessitating more extensive civilian political control of the military, or at least more extensive articulation of military and governmental structures." They speak of the "need by society to contain military autonomy under detailed civilian control."[10]

The logical conclusion from this view is that one has no choice but to adopt a flexible definition of civilian control. According to this approach, while civilian control does refer to the appropriate balance between civilian and military involvement in all areas, this point is not fixed; rather, it varies from place to place and time to time. The recognition that civilian control is not a scientific constant but a social variable, that it is the subject not of a formal definition but of empirical study, and that it is not a standard by which countries are to be judged but a sliding scale on which societies adjust themselves according to their priorities and self-perceptions is an important step toward a better understanding of civil-military relations. It is strongly supported, for instance, by the undisputed fact that in almost all states civilian control during war differs radically from that in peacetime. This observation is confirmed by both experience and literature and was emphasized by almost all the Israelis interviewed for this book. In short, "civilian control by its very nature is subjective, dependent in large measure on personalities and circumstances."[11]

It follows that a proper understanding of civilian control necessitates a careful empirical examination of the experiences of different countries and of the various mechanisms employed in order to effect and maintain civilian control. It should be noted that civilian control—at least in its general or commonly accepted sense—is quite widespread, the prevalence of coups d'état and military takeovers in Third World countries notwithstanding. This holds true not only for all the major military and economic powers (including Japan, Canada, and those in Western Europe) but also for other major countries such as India (the second largest nation in the world), Mexico, and, of course, Israel. None of the major powers and almost no European state is dominated by a military regime. Indeed, the trend in the last few years (especially in Latin America) has shown a definite decrease in military regimes and a strengthening of democratic government and civilian control. Moreover, one should not make the mistake of equating democracy or individual liberty with civilian control. True, there can be no democratic government without civilian control of the military, but many totalitarian systems of government are also characterized by a high degree of civilian control—in some instances even much more so than in the Western democracies.[12]

Although civilian control is widespread today and may even be increasing, every nation has at times faced a crisis in civil-military relations and a threat to civilian control. Post–World War II France is the classic example, but even Britain and the United States—the only two countries that have had uninterrupted traditions of civilian control for hundreds of years—have faced, in this century, serious challenges to this fundamental principle.[13] Mechanisms developed by different societies are geared to deal with potential threats. Before examining the methods and procedures for establishing civilian control, therefore, it is necessary to identify the potential trouble spots in maintaining civil supremacy over the military. The various issues regarding civilian control fall into four general categories commensurate with the four areas of civil-military relations defined by the theoretical model (see figure 1). The challenges facing civilian control can thus be studied by looking into the threat of overinvolvement by the military in the areas of (1) political affairs, (2) the armed forces, (3) national security, and (4) domestic affairs.

As noted above, by any definition of civilian control, military involvement in the political affairs of a state is absolutely off limits to the military. It thus follows that such involvement poses the classic, and by far most severe, threat to civilian control. The most serious action is a total takeover of the government by the armed forces, such as in a coup d'état, commonly known as the "man-on-horseback" or the "man-on-the-white-horse" syndrome, a variation of which is the benign, objective military takeover. Such takeovers occur when the civilian government's inability to govern has thrown the country into a crisis and/or the armed forces view themselves as the guardians of civilian authority and political stability or of the constitution.[14] In such a situation, the military usually does not actually assume the reins of government; instead it replaces the existing civilian regime or administration with another—or at least exerts substantial military influence on the composition of a revamped government. The logic and motivation behind such actions has been aptly described by Perlmutter: "The client of the professional soldier is clearly the state and, hence, the nation. Praetorian symptoms may occur in the professional soldier, but only when leaders of the military establishment 'discover' that there is a 'contradiction' between the 'state' to which they had pledged loyalty, and the 'regime' that has taken over."[15]

This century has yielded many examples of such praetorian tendencies, even in developed nations. One would be Pétain's claim that the Third Republic had betrayed France, thereby justifying his takeover of the government and the establishment of the Vichy regime. Less than a generation later, a similar scene arose when the French army forced General de Gaulle on the French parliament. Unlike Pétain, de Gaulle—though having only scorn and condemnation for the Fourth Republic—was unwilling to be part of an unconstitutional takeover of power. Nevertheless, no one can doubt the crucial role played by the French army and the French generals in convincing the parliament to accept de Gaulle's demands.[16]

Huntington gives an illuminating description of the deterioration in civil-military relations and the breakdown of civilian control in both Germany during the Weimar Republic and Japan as a result of increasing involvement by the general staffs and the high command in the composition of the civilian government and the appointment of senior political officials. He concludes, "By the end of the [First World W]ar the General Staff was running the German government," and quotes a leading German general who observed in 1924, "We owe our ruin to the supremacy of our military authorities over civilian authorities. . . . In fact, German militarism simply committed suicide."[17]

A stark example of an outstanding military leader who while commanding the armed forces of a major democracy manifested the very praetorian symptom described by Perlmutter is none other than General Douglas MacArthur. Defending his behavior in Korea—which led to his dismissal by President Truman for insubordination—MacArthur denounced what he called the "new and heretofore unknown and dangerous concept that the men of our armed forces owe primary allegiance and loyalty to those who temporarily exercise the authority of the executive branch of government rather than to the country and its constitution which they are sworn to defend."[18]

If military involvement in the area of political affairs poses the most severe threat to civilian control, the most common challenge stems from overinvolvement by the military in the armed forces, an area in which the greatest potential exists for clashes between the military and civilian authorities. On the one hand, this area is the domain of professional soldiers. If they are not to be trusted to command, control, and conduct military operations in the field and to run the day-to-day affairs of the armed forces, what is left of their professional autonomy? On the other hand, even a narrow definition of civilian control upholds the principle that ultimate authority in all areas of society—including purely military matters—must be exercised by civilians. Indeed, as Edmonds points out, the complex characteristics of modern warfare have made the area of combat operations, "once a responsibility that devolved largely onto the armed services, one that political leadership has increasingly assumed the authority to control."[19]

The military has resisted this trend in the past and continues to do so, usually in one of three ways. First, it may undermine the aims, programs, and directives of the civilian authorities either by not implementing their decisions or by circumventing them. Second, military officers may act on their own initiatives beyond their orders and the scope of their authority. Third, and most dangerously, military commanders may refuse to obey orders originating within the civilian echelon, usually accompanying such refusal with the threat of resignation—either individually by a chief of staff or an area commander or collectively by the entire general staff or high command. Although senior military officers have every right to resign their commands, invoking such threats simply to resist orders poses a clear challenge to the principle of civilian supremacy. In such instances, it is not the resignation but the threat that is genuine.

Examples of generals resisting orders or acting either without appropriate orders or contrary to them are legion. A recitation of them all is, of course, beyond the scope of this book; I will therefore mention only a few to illustrate these three scenarios. During the American Civil War, for instance, Lincoln was beset with problems concerning generals who would not fight. These generals—the most famous and most recalcitrant of whom was General George McClellan, commander of the Army of the Potomac—never refused outright the orders of their commander in chief; they merely found countless reasons why they could not be carried out. Things reached such a stage that at one point—on May 6, 1861—Lincoln took over actual command of the troops at Fort Wayne, personally reconnoitering the Virginia coast, and ordered a successful landing against the Norfolk naval base! In 1817 General Andrew Jackson invaded Florida without authorization. His action enjoyed massive public support, and after many days of debate, Congress rejected any attempt to censure him or condemn his action. One hundred thirty-three years later, MacArthur ordered American troops into the northeastern provinces of North Korea, in direct contradiction to explicit orders received from Washington. Not only did Truman not reprimand him, but he went so far as to publicly, albeit belatedly and with considerable embarrassment, endorse MacArthur's strategy. Nor was MacArthur the last American general to exceed the bounds set by civilian authorities. As late as 1977, General John D. Lavelle, commander of the U.S. Seventh Air Force in Vietnam, stretched the rules of engagement governing the bombing of

North Vietnam to the point where the "protective reaction strike" became a preemptive strike.[20]

Both the United States and Great Britain have witnessed in this century instances where senior military commanders have refused or threatened to refuse to accept a military decision taken by the supreme civilian authority, and in one case at least such refusal came close to mutiny. During World War II, General Marshall in the United States and Field Marshal Alanbrooke in the United Kingdom torpedoed many pet military schemes put forth or strongly supported by Roosevelt and Churchill, respectively; their ability to do so rested to no small degree on the implicit—and at times even explicit—threat of resignation.[21] Churchill also faced insubordination from Field Marshal Montgomery. Dissatisfied with the balance of men and vehicles to be shipped with the invading forces to the Normandy coast, Churchill decided to take up the matter with Montgomery's staff. Montgomery informed him categorically that he would not allow it, adding that "the final decision has been given. In any case I could never allow you to harass my staff at this time and possibly shake their confidence in me. . . . If you think [my decision] is wrong, that can only mean you have lost confidence in me." Churchill did not pursue the matter any further.[22] There is no doubt that Montgomery—the victor of El Alamein—had his immense popularity in mind when he decided to risk a confrontation with the prime minister.

The most severe challenge of this sort to civilian control was what has become known as the Curragh incident or even the Curragh mutiny. In 1914, the Third Home Rule Bill, which granted a united Ireland its own parliament with control over internal affairs, was about to become law. The central question was how the recalcitrant north could be made to accept its provisions. Secretary of State for War Seely informed the commander in chief in Ireland, Sir Arthur Paget, that the cabinet was ready to use military force and that while those officers domiciled in Ulster (and thus facing a difficult and painful personal conflict) might "disappear," any others who failed to take action would be dismissed from the service. On March 21 Paget met with his officers to inform them of the government's instructions. Within forty-eight hours, he had to signal the War Office that he "regret[ted] to report that the commander of the 3rd Cavalry Brigade and seventy-five officers of 3rd Cavalry Brigade prefer to accept dismissal if ordered north." After a series of urgent meetings in London, the government backed down, and the cabinet issued a written document confirming that the government had "no intention whatever of taking advantage of the right to crush political opposition to the policy or principles of the Home Rule Bill" and "that the Army will not be used under any circumstances to enforce the present Home Rule Bill on Ulster."[23]

Had a mutiny occurred? Sweetman argues in the negative, claiming that in the final analysis no order had actually been disobeyed and quoting Gough as telling the adjutant general that "if the General Officer Commanding in Chief had ordered my brigade to go to Belfast, I should have gone without question."[24] Moreover, a preference for resigning rather than undertaking a given mission does not necessarily constitute mutiny. On the other hand, while it may not have been a mutiny, it did represent a clear case of undue interference in political affairs—the most serious threat of all to civilian control—albeit in the least sensitive area of the democratic decision-making process. The Home Rule Bill became law but was never implemented, ostensibly because of the outbreak of World War I and widespread public support for Ulster, but had it not been for these factors, the will of the legitimate civilian institutions of state, reflecting the will of the people, might very well have been thwarted by the decision and action of military officers.

The challenge to civilian control in the area of national security is much more subtle and relates mainly to imbalances in relative involvement. While professional soldiers cherish their control over military operations and, to a lesser degree, military organization, they generally do not question the right of the civilian authorities to determine foreign and defense policy. MacArthur's gripe with Truman was that the president was ignoring a firmly established U.S. military tradition, established by Lincoln and Grant in 1864, that once a field commander has been assigned a mission "there must be no interference with his method of carrying it out" (a tradition that MacArthur did not recognize had been made obsolete by the Cold War and the nuclear age), but even he did not question the principle that the setting of political objectives is the prerogative of the civilian leadership.[25] The issue here is not who ultimately decides but rather the relative input of the armed forces and the civilian bureaucracy. Overinvolvement by the military in this area is almost always the result of underinvolvement by the civilian sector, that is, when civilians, in effect, abdicate their responsibility for strategic planning and policy analysis and become a rubber stamp for the suggestions and proposals of the military. As will be shown later, the most severe challenge—indeed the only serious one—to civilian control in Israel lies in this area and for this reason.

As mentioned earlier, a classic case of de facto military domination of the policy-planning process in national security affairs occurred in the United States during the latter stages of World War II. As the war continued, the military found itself "confronting a power vacuum created by the lack of a high-level agency, particularly some sort of civil-military board, to establish governmental policy on the conduct of the war." Civilian control had been concentrated almost exclusively in the hands of the president. Roosevelt did indeed exercise this power in the early war years, but as time went by, he found himself at the head of a vast structure of military command—a structure that was becoming more and more impossible to control. "The relative independence of the theater commanders, the central position and influence of the planning staffs, the wide power and public respect enjoyed by his chief of staff—all these factors placed real limits on the commander in chief's independence of action."[26]

Huntington emphasizes the element of abdication of responsibility by the civilian echelon, pointing out that "when war came, the American military did not reach out for power. . . . Instead power was unavoidably thrust upon them." He quotes Secretary of State Hull's statement "I have washed my hands of it" and considers these words "symbolic of the civilian abdication." Huntington then goes on to describe in detail how by 1945 the War Department staff was consciously enmeshed in foreign policy and the military staffs dealt more and more openly with political questions. "Considerably more than half the papers [prepared by the operations division of the general staff] for the Potsdam Conference were devoted to matters other than military operations." That same year Admiral Leahy admitted quite frankly that "the Joint Chiefs of Staff at the present time are under no civilian control whatsoever," and, what is more, they were all in favor of perpetuating the situation.[27] It was only with the enactment of the National Security Act of 1947 and the establishment of a strong office of the secretary of defense and an effective National Security Council that this dangerous tide was reversed.

Strange as it may seem, civilian control faces the least severe threat in the area of domestic affairs. Military involvement in domestic affairs finds expression in two ways: in support of the civil power, i.e., as an instrument of the civilian authority, and as a result of role expansion by the armed forces. Paradoxically, the problem in the first instance is not over- but underinvolvement: the armed forces may actively resist becoming involved in internal political disputes because this would threaten their zealously guarded role as the embodiment of the national consensus. The ultimate expression of this predilection is outright refusal by the high command of the army to act against their fellow citizens—a situation that can put civilian control in jeopardy. This is what really happened at the Curragh.

Role expansion of the military in various domestic endeavors can create tension in civil-military relations, and some scholars have seen a challenge to civilian control in the expanding role of active and retired military officers in government and in the entrance of ex-generals into politics. As Huntington observes, more military heroes have run for and become chief executives in the United States than in any other country. In the past two hundred years, ten out of forty presidents have been generals; during the same period, only one British prime minister—the duke of Wellington—was also a general. Perhaps because of this, sensitivity regarding this issue is most pronounced in the United States. (It should be noted that a "two-career" life cycle is an institutionalized and accepted fact of life in the IDF.) Be that as it may, there is almost no evidence to suggest that the involvement of military heroes—as civilians—in politics constitutes a threat to civilian control. Indeed, it is worth recalling, in this context, that it was none other than Dwight Eisenhower—the only professional soldier to become president in this century—who first sounded the alarm about the dangers inherent in the military-industrial complex.[28]

Underlying many of the different threats to civilian control is the substantial political clout developed by certain leading military figures, reflecting their immense prestige and popularity. Groth calls attention to the fact that in certain instances a free press and an enlightened public opinion—the two basic bulwarks against all forms of tyranny or despotism—can become the very means by which the military can neutralize civilian control. It is precisely in the democracies that successful and glamorous military personalities usually receive the most generous amounts of media exposure, the resultant high level of popular acclaim "making it extremely difficult, if not impossible, for [civilian] political superiors to exercise rigid control over them or, ultimately, even get rid of them."[29]

Parliamentary supervision, partisan politics, and, most of all, periodic free elections all make it even more difficult for a civilian government to deal effectively with a charismatic military leader who enjoys great personal authority and popular support. Huntington writes that "the fundamental element in [the] tremendous expansion of military control [by the German general staff in the latter years of World War I] was the unprecedented popularity of the victor of Tannenberg [Hindenburg] with the German people. He was a national idol whom the Germans trusted implicitly to bring them success."[30] Many other examples of such figures come readily to mind: George Washington, George McClellan, George Marshall, and Douglas MacArthur in the United States, Montgomery and Alanbrooke in Britain, Weygand and Pétain in France, and, in Israel, Dayan, Rabin, Eitan, and Sharon.

What is it that allows certain states to overcome these challenges to civilian control while others succumb to them? Why is it that Washington, McClellan, and MacArthur did not undermine civilian control in the United States, whereas Hindenburg and Ludendorff in effect took control of the German government? What is the secret behind effective and balanced civilian control?

Four key factors appear to account for most of the variance in civilian control between one state and another and between one period and another. These are: (1) the civilian echelon's determination to uphold its authority, to maintain its privileges and prerogatives, and under no circumstances to abdicate its responsibilities; (2) the military's unwavering ideological commitment to democratic government coupled with a deep and unshakable belief in the principle of civilian supremacy; (3) the political leadership's respect for the professional autonomy of the military and a sense of confidence and trust in the high command of the armed forces; and (4) a clear constitutional framework and precise legal guidelines specifying the functions, authority, and responsibilities of both civilian and military echelons.

Most scholars would agree that in many instances the erosion of civilian control is due first and foremost to an abdication by the civilian authority.[31] This is certainly the case in democratic states and developed countries. An examination of various crises in civil-military relations— especially in the democracies and in modern times—clearly indicates that civilian control was maintained through resolute and decisive action by the civilian leadership. The MacArthur incident is a good example. Many people believe that MacArthur was fired because he disobeyed orders or because he acted in the field without authorization. The ostensible reason for Truman's decision summarily and quite unceremoniously to relieve MacArthur of all his commands was a series of press interviews and public statements by the general that had not been submitted for the required clearance from Washington. Yet while these statements may have constituted the straw that broke the camel's back and undoubtedly reflected a fundamental disagreement between MacArthur and his commander in chief over the nature and scope of the Korean War, the fact remains that Truman took this major political risk simply to make it clear that no military commander, however popular and charismatic, could publicly challenge the foreign and defense policies or military decisions of his civilian superiors.[32]

One hundred years earlier, President Lincoln took the same stand when he asked General Fremont to modify a proclamation that was out of line with Lincoln's policy. When Fremont refused to do so without a direct order from Lincoln, the president issued such an order, although the action caused him great political embarrassment, and six weeks later the general was relieved of command. At the height of the Persian Gulf crisis in late 1990, Secretary of Defense Cheney summarily dismissed the chief of staff of the United States Air Force for issuing an unauthorized press interview that contained statements contrary to administration policy. And de Gaulle's courageous stand against the attempt by strong elements in the French army to dictate policy on Algeria is another example. As Mahoney points out, there is little hope for effective civilian control if "civilian officials find it difficult, if not impossible, to dismiss a general." He concludes by saying that "the answer [to civilian control] is to be found in an aroused and informed electorate and stronger, more tough-minded civilians . . . who have a deep-rooted understanding and appreciation of the principle of civilian supremacy."[33]

The civilian leadership's appreciation of the crucial importance of civilian control and their readiness to act on its behalf are, however, not enough. Professional soldiers and the senior officer corps must be as committed as their civilian masters to establishing and maintaining civilian supremacy under all circumstances. It is true that in developed and mature societies it is quite difficult, if not impossible, for the military to challenge legitimate civilian authority effectively (the French generals' abortive rebellion attempt in Algeria in 1961 is a good illustration). Still, no one should ever underestimate the immense power, resources, and influence of the armed forces or the potential appeal of a military hero in times of war or national crisis. It is at crucial moments such as these that the loyalty of the military chiefs comes into play.

This loyalty should not be taken lightly. At times it can pose a grave dilemma for the conscientious professional soldier and lead to much soul searching. This happens, for example, when a highly experienced and very popular military leader is convinced that a government is embarking on a disastrous course that could endanger the cohesion, morale, and integrity of the armed forces, if not the very future of the country, and is further aware that he is strongly supported in this position by the entire military establishment as well as by public opinion. His willingness under these circumstances to accept the verdict of his political superiors and carry out their orders or to leave the service calls not only for iron discipline and strength of character but also for a steadfast commitment to the principle of civilian supremacy. MacArthur is, of course, a case in point. The general may have believed that he could convince or even force Truman—for whom he had little respect—to go along with ideas and plans for achieving victory in Korea, but on receiving the order relieving him of his command, he merely turned to his wife and said: "At last we're going home."[34] It is clear that MacArthur never considered any other alternative.

A similar though more striking example comes from the Civil War. Civil-military disputes hampered the Union war effort for several years; General McClellan, commander of the Army of the Potomac, the major eastern Union army, was at the center of many. Like MacArthur after him, McClellan had a fundamental disagreement with the president on the conduct of the war. Lincoln regarded McClellan as a general "who would not fight," while McClellan had only contempt for both Lincoln, whom he referred to privately as a "gorilla," and the Republican Congress. Finally, in November 1862, Lincoln relieved the general of his command. There was nothing standing between the Army of the Potomac and Washington and no one to prevent McClellan from marching on the capital. The officer corps was highly politicized and strongly Democratic, as was McClellan himself. His soldiers loved, admired, and respected him as they did no other general in the army—indeed, when McClellan took leave of his army, the soldiers gave him an almost hysterical farewell, and in his own words, "many were in favor of my refusing to obey the order and of marching upon Washington to take possession of the government." Washington itself was rife with wild rumors regarding the general's intentions. European observers found it incomprehensible that this devoted army did not go to the Capitol and, at the least, compel the president to reinstate its favorite general. But McClellan himself always swore he was loyal to the Union and, when put to the test, proved his loyalty. He was contemptuous of Lincoln the man and ran against him for president in 1864, but he never seriously considered challenging the ultimate authority of Lincoln the president.[35]

But no military officer's unwavering commitment to civilian control had a more major impact on his country than that of General George Washington. By the end of the Revolutionary War, Washington's reputation with both the army and the civilian population was so great that he would have faced little opposition had he decided to step into the power vacuum created by a weak and discredited Continental Congress to assure power for himself. Many admirers even suggested that he become king. But George Washington had a very specific set of beliefs regarding the duties of a soldier in a democracy, and on December 23, 1783, on his own initiative, he resigned his commission before the Continental Congress in Annapolis.[36]

Not only did Washington set an example for generations to come of military submission to civilian government, but he was also instrumental in defusing a potential military revolt at the end of the war. Although in full sympathy with the grievances of his men, who were discharged without having received any pay for years or the pension promised them, Washington adamantly quashed any suggestion of mutiny among the officers. At the end he quelled the rebellion by the sheer force of his own noble character, when after having failed to convince his men to set aside their plan, he put on a pair of eyeglasses, remarking, "Gentlemen, you will permit me to put on my spectacles, for I have not only grown gray but almost blind in the service of my country." Thomas Jefferson acknowledged the crucial contribution of General Washington's unyielding commitment to civilian supremacy when he said, "The moderation and virtue of a single character probably prevented this Revolution from being closed, as most others have been, by a subversion of that liberty it was intended to establish."[37]

Professionalism—for many the very basis of civilian control and of healthy civil-military relations—is inextricably related to professional autonomy. If a vigorous commitment to civilian supremacy by the soldier is one side of the coin, then a strong respect for the professional autonomy of the military by the civilian is the other side. A balanced civil-military relationship must incorporate both elements. Hendrickson makes this point quite clear when he emphasizes the importance of mutual deference, adding, "They merely establish a presumption in favor of deferring to the judgment of the military in those matters that concern its professional function. The military, for its part, has a corresponding duty to defer to its civilian superiors when questions of high policy or administrative efficiency arise. . . . The principles, of course, may be abused . . .

[and] may be invoked in circumstances where they are not applicable. But [they themselves] are sound, and civil-military relations will become deranged if they are systematically disregarded."[38] Even in the rare instances when the civilian authority needs to intervene even in purely military matters, the burden of proof that a position adopted by the military is untenable lies with the civilians.

Groth points out that acceptance of mutual deference and respect for professional autonomy are major factors differentiating between totalitarian and democratic states. "In decisions involving clearly military issues, the leaders of the Western democracies depended very heavily on their statutory military advisors and, in general, tended to accept the advice that they were given." Western politicians "lobbied" their military chiefs, but, on the whole, they did not "micromanage" the military or even countermand military orders or operations in progress—this in vivid contrast to the behavior of Hitler and Stalin. Even the mighty Churchill and Roosevelt rarely got their way on issues on which their chiefs of staff were united against them. The number of times during the entire Second World War that Churchill or Roosevelt overruled the unanimous advice of their chiefs or imposed a major military decision on them can be counted on the fingers of one hand. John Grigg writes that the British chiefs of staff "would humor Churchill, put up with his unsocial hours of work, defer to him on minor matters, and often pretend to defer to him on major issues. But as a rule they got their way on anything that they considered really important. . . . If [the three chiefs] stood together, they could be daunting even to Churchill."[39] And it should be remembered that it was neither the civilian leaders nor the chiefs of staff who made the final decision on whether to give the go-ahead for the invasion of Europe: it was the commander in the field, Dwight Eisenhower, who decided to postpone D day from the fifth to the sixth of June.

Respect for the professional autonomy of the soldier also manifests itself in the special status enjoyed by the military chiefs—a status that sets them apart from civilian counterparts occupying positions equally high in the governmental hierarchy. This special status, according to Broadbent, introduces an element of uneasiness into the relationship between defense ministers and chiefs of staff. It also accounts for the jealously guarded right of direct access to the prime minister enjoyed by the three chiefs of staff in Britain and for the fact that the chief of staff of the IDF is subordinate to both the defense minister and the authority of the government. Many chiefs of staff see themselves—and are regarded publicly—"as the symbol of the Service and, as such, a preserver of its heritage and a custodian of its future." Lord Harding summed up the task of chief of staff as "doing the best he can in the interests of the Army vis-à-vis the politician. You must stand up to them but always remember they have the last word."[40]

In an attempt to find the proper balance between the professional autonomy of the military and the ultimate authority of the civilian, one can define five possible roles for the military in politico-military affairs: (1) *advisory*—making available to the civilians their professional expertise; (2) *representative*—advocating the interests of the military in intragovernmental councils; (3) *executive*—implementing governmental decisions; (4) *advocacy*—explaining and defending, in public, the policies of the government (although at times this role may lead to attempts to convince the public of the wisdom of military policies at variance with those of the government); and (5) *substantive*—attempting to overturn the military or national security policy of the government by engaging in overt political activity. All agree that the first three roles are commensurate with the principles of civilian supremacy, while the fifth role presents a direct challenge to civilian control. The advocacy role is in the gray area. The trick is not to undermine the military's representative role but constraining it enough that it does not lead to an exaggerated advocacy role (as was the case with MacArthur).[41]

There is general agreement that the power of appointment is the limit of professional autonomy; it is and must remain an unchallenged civilian prerogative. Groth emphasizes that during World War II "civilian leaders enjoyed the uncontested power of appointment to the highest places in the military hierarchy. The choice of Eisenhower as supreme commander of American forces, Europe, by President Franklin Roosevelt was an example of elevating a relatively junior officer to a high position on the bureaucratic ladder." One could add Roosevelt's appointment of Marshall as Army chief of staff and Bush's appointment of General Colin Powell as chairman of the JCS; in both cases, the chief executives passed over more senior generals.[42]

The final factor determining civilian control relates to questions of legitimacy and legality. The word *legitimacy* is derived from the Latin *legitimus*, meaning "according to law," but it has acquired a broader meaning, referring to those customs that enjoy public approbation and support. Still, legality remains an important element of legitimacy. Law, especially fundamental constitutional law, enjoys a high degree of legitimacy among modern developed societies. Firmly anchoring the principle of civilian supremacy in the constitution of the state adds a sense of inevitability to civilian control. Legal clarity, including precise guidelines as to the functions, authority, and responsibility of civilian and military authorities, is an important check against encroachment by the military into civilian areas and a major guarantee of civilian control—especially in times of national crisis and social instability.

In the United States, the principle of civilian control over the military goes back to June 16, 1775, when George Washington accepted the appointment by the Continental Congress to become commander in chief of the United Colonies.[43] Since then, the United States has taken great pains to provide an adequate legal basis for civilian control. The Constitution established the authority of the president and the Congress in all military matters. In a more recent example, the Goldwater-Nichols bill of 1986 introduced major reforms in the organization of the Defense Department. A major element of the bill was the strengthening of the position and the role of the chairman of the JCS. Yet Congress went to great lengths to ensure (through the language of the bill) that the chairman remain subject to civilian control. Duties thus include "assisting the President and the Secretary of Defense in providing for the strategic direction of the armed forces" and "preparing strategic plans which conform with resource levels projected by the Secretary of Defense." The chairman is further expected "to advise the Secretary of Defense" and to submit "alternative program recommendations and budget proposals, within projected resource levels and guidance provided by the Secretary." This legal clarity appears to have paid off. Consider this quote from General Colin Powell, the chairman of the JCS during the Gulf War, who, in referring to the secretary of defense, said, "There is no competition. I work for him. He is my boss. I am his adviser. Period."[44]

3 | The Israeli System: Constitutional Principles

The civil-military system in Israel—as in other countries—is embedded within the overall system of government. This chapter deals essentially with constitutional principles of government, i.e., those principles that are relevant to civil-military relations.

In his illuminating essay "Military Organization and Policy Making in Israel," Aharon Yariv identifies four factors that are largely responsible for the particular nature of civil-military relations and civilian control in Israel:

> The historical background—that is, the prestate sociopolitical development of the Jewish community in Palestine, as well as the politically controlled growth of its major military arm in the underground: the Haganah.
>
> The centrality of defense to Israel's national existence, stemming from the country's peculiar geopolitical situation, and the traditional secrecy surrounding defense matters.
>
> The heavy and lasting imprint of Ben-Gurion, the chief architect of the state and of Zahal, the IDF.
>
> Israel's continuous need to maintain a capability for total mobilization as a nation in arms.[1]

It is vital to recall that Israel has experienced six wars (not including the Gulf War in 1991) during its forty-five years of existence. As I noted in chapter 2, in almost all states the nature of civilian control in wartime is radically different from its nature in peacetime.[2] Israel's wars have been of different durations—varying from six days to almost three years—but the major ones have been quite brief. However, the nonwar years—which account for most of Israel's history—have not been years of peace; on the contrary, for the most part they have been years of tension and violence. With the exception, perhaps, of the eight-year period from 1957 to 1965, Israel has been engaged in a bloody struggle against terrorism, and from its inception the country has always faced the threat of war. It is thus impossible to differentiate between peacetime and wartime civil-military relations in Israel, inasmuch as the country finds itself in a virtually permanent condition of no peace and no war. On the other hand, Israel has made great efforts to function as a normal country, irrespective of its security situation, and this holds true for the area of civil-military relations as well. Thus one has to view civil-military relations in Israel as reflecting a unique combination of wartime and peacetime conditions, although the fact that the IDF is, in essence, a fighting army has had a major impact on the development of civil-military relations.

Israel has no formal written constitution, but it has a definite constitutional system of government.[3] The material constitution is based primarily on a series of *Basic Laws* that deal with the central institutions of the state, constitutional conventions, and precedent-making decisions of a constitutional nature by the Supreme Court. These laws usually present only general constitutional principles of a fundamental nature, leaving the details for ordinary legislation. The system is thus evolutionary, reflecting changes in the objective internal and external environments as well as in the value system of the society at large. It is a highly flexible system, one that can be adapted relatively easily to changing conditions and to new needs or demands. To a large degree, the basic constitutional framework reflects mandatory rule and British traditions, as well as the accumulated experience of the democratically organized Zionist movement—the national liberation movement of the Jewish People.

Israel maintains a parliamentary system of government. There is a separation of powers, though not in the strict, almost absolute sense that one finds in the United States. Thus *The Basic Law: The Knesset* deals with the legislative branch; *The Basic Law: The Government* deals with the executive branch; and *The Basic Law: The Judicature* deals with the judicial branch. A number of additional *Basic Laws* relate to other vital areas or institutions of the state. Among these is the most important piece of legislation for the purposes of this book—*The Basic Law: The Army.*

The two key institutions in Israeli civil-military relations are the government and the military—both of which form part of Israel's material constitution. Though collective bodies, both are headed, run, and influenced by particular individuals. Immediately identifiable are three key actors in governmental-military interaction: the prime minister heads the government; the chief of staff heads the military; and the defense minister is the interface between the government and the military. Each minister has statutory authority and a constitutionally defined role. Not only is each in charge of a specific ministry and given sphere of action, but almost every law stipulates the specific minister in charge of its implementation—a statutory authority that, as will be shown later on, may have an important bearing on the defense minister's potential role and authority.

The Government

Among other things, *The Basic Law: The Government* states that

> The Government is the executive authority of the State. . . . The Government holds office by virtue of the confidence of the Knesset. The Government is collectively responsible to the Knesset. The Government consists of the Prime Minister and other ministers. . . . The Government may act through Ministerial Committees—which may be permanent, temporary or for particular matters. . . . The Government is competent to perform in the name of the State, subject to any law, any act the performance of which is not incumbent by law upon another authority. . . . A power vested in the Government under any Law may be delegated by it to one of the ministers . . . insofar as no contrary intention appears from the Law conferring the power or imposing the duty.[4]

A number of observations and clarifications are in order. The Hebrew word *memshala* is translated literally here as "government." However, from the point of view of British terminology and usage, a more accurate translation would be "cabinet." In Britain, the cabinet is a small body of senior ministers who act collectively on behalf of and in the name of the Crown and bear collective responsibility for running the affairs of the realm. The government is merely a category of individuals, i.e., all members of parliament with some executive responsibility (usually number-ing close to a hundred people and including junior ministers, ministers of state, parliamentary undersecretaries, and others). Since the government in Israel parallels the British cabinet—and was, indeed, shaped along its lines—henceforward I shall use, in the Israeli context, the words "govern-ment" and "cabinet" interchangeably and with the same meaning.[5]

The powers of the government, under *The Basic Law*, are far-reaching. They are derived not only from the definition of the government as the executive authority of the state but even more so from the residual power clause. This clause refers to section 29 of *The Basic Law*, which, as quoted above, authorizes the government to act on behalf of the state whenever the power to act is not conferred by law on any other body. The Supreme Court has interpreted this clause as giving the government sole and full authority in any and every area and over any and every function that is not dealt with otherwise by law.[6] So, for example, the government is authorized not only to conclude treaties but also to ratify them, even though no written law grants this power.[7] The same holds true for war powers in Israel. The very first law enacted by the Provisional State Coun-cil in May 1948 authorized the provisional government "to establish armed forces on land, on sea, and in the air which shall have authority to do all lawful and necessary acts for the defense of the State." Thus although no legislation expressly states who has the power to declare war, it is clear that this power, as well as the power to undertake military action of any nature or scope, is firmly in the hands of the government.[8]

The government's power to conduct the affairs of state is not limited or restricted even by the Knesset. True, the government holds office only by virtue of the confidence of the Knesset and is collectively responsible to the Knesset. Nevertheless, the accepted legal view holds that once it is affirmed by the Knesset and as long as it retains the Knesset's confidence, the government does not act as the Knesset's agent but rather as a free agent with independent authority. The Knesset cannot decide the gov-ernment's course of action in any given matter, and its decisions—whether in committee or in the plenum—though carrying great weight from a public, political, and moral point of view, are not legally binding on the government.[9] They are thus comparable to "sense of Congress" resolutions in the United States. The Knesset can, of course, bring the government down through a vote of no confidence. But even then the government would exercise full executive authority until a new govern-ment was established and received a vote of confidence from the Knesset—something that, given Israeli experience, can take weeks if not months and may even require new elections. The only way the Knesset can actually force the government's hand is through legislation, since every authority of the state—including the government—is bound by the law. The Knesset has frequently adopted this approach and has inserted clauses in many laws requiring prior approval, or approval within a given time, of the Knesset or one of its committees for governmental action.[10] Thus, for example, section 26 of *The Defense Service Law* provides that the defense minister's authority to command an emergency mobilization is subject to ratification within fourteen days by the Knesset's Foreign Affairs and Defense Committee.[11]

Before 1976, the government's authority over the armed forces was based on the residual powers clause and on constitutional convention—i.e., accepted custom. In 1976, *The Basic Law: The Army* was enacted. Section 2(a) of this crucial piece of legislation states that "the army is subject to the authority of the government"; section 3(b) states that "the chief of the general staff is subject to the authority of the government and subordinate to the minister of defense"; and section 3(c) stipulates that "the chief of the general staff shall be appointed by the government on the recommendation of the minister of defense."[12] The ultimate authority of the government over the armed forces is thus, today, firmly rooted in constitutional law.

The Basic Law: The Government enables the government to work through ministerial committees. Until 1991, there was no statutory requirement for the creation of any ministerial committee, and Israeli legislation mentioned no ministerial committees. The establishment of such committees was thus completely optional, left to the choice of each new government. Nevertheless, during most of Israel's history, there has been a ministerial defense committee (MDC), although its size, membership, importance, terms of reference, scope of activity, powers, and authority have all varied radically from government to government or, more accurately, from prime minister to prime minister. Under Israel's first prime minister and founding father, Ben-Gurion, the committee had minimal influence on national security decision making, which was the province either of Ben-Gurion, who doubled as prime minister and defense minister—at times in conjunction with the foreign minister and a small number of trusted aides—or of the cabinet as a whole. It was only with the ascendancy of Levi Eshkol to the prime ministership in June 1963, and especially after the 1965 elections, that the committee became a serious player, and even then it continued to lack a sense of permanence. The haphazardness of the MDC is dramatically illustrated by the fact that Prime Minister Begin did not form an MDC for a period of almost six months after the June 1981 elections and did not convene it even once during the Lebanon War—from June 1982 until almost the end of that year. The first Shamir government, established after Begin's retirement from politics in 1983 and in office for a little over a year, failed to establish an MDC at all![13]

The MDC emerged as the key decision-making body in the area of national security with the formation of the National Unity Government in 1984. As part of the political arrangements aimed at guaranteeing parity between the Likud and Labor, the *Kabinet* was established to function, in effect, as a government within a government. The *Kabinet* was constituted as the MDC and, according to the coalition agreement, all major political issues—covering the entire gamut of foreign affairs and defense—were to be dealt with by this committee.[14] It should be noted that once a ministerial committee is formed and operates, its decisions are as binding as if they were the government's. This is the legal and constitutional meaning of *The Basic Law*'s authorization for the government to "act through ministerial committees." The government rules of order normally permit a member of a ministerial committee to stay implementation of a committee decision pending action on an appeal to the cabinet plenum.[15] The cabinet can waive this rule, however, and it has done so in many instances with regard to deliberations and decisions of the MDC.

It was only in 1991 that the role and authority of the MDC were given a firm constitutional basis and the MDC itself was finally made a statutory body. According to legislation enacted in early 1991, a ministerial committee on national security would automatically come into being with the inauguration of a new government. The committee would be headed by the prime minister and would include the vice prime minister and the ministers for defense, foreign affairs, and finance. The government would be empowered, at the suggestion of the prime minister, to add members to the committee as long as its membership did not exceed half that of the cabinet.[16]

The Military

Given the importance of national security and defense to Israel's very existence, one would expect extensive legislation regarding the armed forces; yet the opposite is true—there is a paucity of legislation in this all-important area. The first piece of legislation enacted by the Provisional State Council that established the basic framework for governing the newly born state—*The Law and Administration Ordinance 1948*—included a brief reference to the armed forces. Section 18 of this act, under the heading of "The Armed Forces," states the following: "The Provisional Government may establish armed forces on land, on sea, and in the air that shall have authority to do all lawful and necessary acts for the defense of the State." Using this authority, on May 26, 1948, the Provisional Government issued the Israel Defense Forces Ordinance—the law that in effect, established the IDF. This act was issued initially as an executive order and signed by David Ben-Gurion but was enacted, one month later, with retroactive effect, by the Provisional State Council, thus giving it legislative authority.[17]

The Israel Defense Forces Ordinance states, inter alia, the following:

1. There is hereby established a Defense Army of Israel [IDF], consisting of land forces, a navy, and an air force. . . .

4. It is forbidden to establish or maintain any armed forces outside the Defense Army of Israel [IDF]. . . .

7. The minister of defense is charged with the implementation of this ordinance.[18]

This piece of legislation is characterized, more than anything else, by its extreme brevity. There is no mention of a national command authority, no mention of civilian control, no mention of command echelons within the army, and no reference whatsoever to the organization of the armed forces. One can perhaps understand why in May 1948 the Israeli leadership—locked in a life-and-death struggle for the very existence of the newly born state—had no time and little inclination to give detailed answers to these questions or to determine the permanent constitutional framework for civil-military relations. What is almost incomprehensible, however, is that it took almost thirty years to deal with these issues—and even then it did so in a highly limited and almost casual fashion.

What did the ordinance accomplish? Primarily, it established the twin principles of unification and exclusivity that have characterized the military in Israel to date: the IDF is a unified armed force, including within its framework land, sea, and air forces (section 1); and it is the only armed force within the state (section 4). Furthermore, by naming the minister of defense as the civilian authority over the armed forces, the ordinance also laid the foundation for the authority of the government over the military—something already inferable from the fact that it was the government that initially issued the order establishing the IDF (by virtue of the authority vested in it by *The Law and Administration Ordinance*).

Between 1948 and 1976—when *The Basic Law: The Army* was enacted—there were only two major pieces of legislation dealing with the military: *The Defense Service Law* of 1949 and *The Military Jurisdiction Law* of 1955.[19] The former has little significance for civil-military relations, save that it strengthened the position of the defense minister as the civilian immediately responsible for the army, not only placing the minister of defense in charge of its implementation but stipulating that certain actions, such as emergency mobilization, can be authorized only by the minister.[20] The Military Jurisdiction Law of 1955, on the other hand, deals with military hierarchy, discipline, and orders; as such, it is more relevant to civil-military relations.

Section 1 of this act, as passed in 1955, recognizes the existence of a "chief of the general staff of the army"—"the CGS." The law does not define the role or position of the CGS but grants him a variety of powers and authority in many areas, first and foremost among these being the authority to issue general orders binding on the entire army. The law recognizes two types of binding military orders: an individual order issued by a superior to a subordinate and general orders of the army. Section 1 of the act defined "army orders" as "instructions of the high command that the CGS has been empowered by the minister of defense to issue, orders of the general staff."[21] Instructions of the high command deal with the entire organization and structure of the armed forces, inasmuch as these are not addressed by either legislation or governmental decree.

The legislation of 1955 thus created a unique situation whereby the military, through the chief of staff, determines its own organization and rules of performance. The rank system of the IDF, for example, is covered by army orders, so, in effect, the IDF determines its own ranks, and the chief of staff grants himself whatever rank he deems fit![22] True, the CGS is empowered to issue the instructions of the high command by the minister of defense, but it seems clear from the wording of the law that this empowerment is of a general nature: once given permission by the minister, the chief of staff issues the instructions at his own discretion.

There is little, if any, precedent in Western nations for such a state of affairs, and it was directly contrary to the famous dictum of David Ben-

Gurion that "the army is not to determine by itself even its own structure, procedure, and policies." In 1958, a public mobilization drill was held without proper public preparation. As a result of the political fallout, Ben-Gurion (then prime minister and defense minister) demanded that the senior officers involved be disciplined. When it turned out that the regulations for such a drill were part of the high command instructions, issued formally under his authority, Ben-Gurion reacted with complete surprise, responding angrily: "Where is it written—show me that book!"[23] It would take close to twenty-five years for this serious flaw in the principle of civilian control to be partially corrected.

The Yom Kippur War in 1973 led to much soul-searching in Israel, and for the first time acute concern arose over the lack of clear legal guidelines regarding the military, the absence of a formal constitutional definition of civilian control, and ambiguity in the national command authority and the relationship among the different state authorities vested with power in security matters. The Agranat Commission of Inquiry, established by the cabinet to investigate the failings of that war, severely criticized this state of affairs, concluding that "there was no clear definition of the distribution of power responsibilities and obligations in security matters."[24] In the wake of the Agranat Commission's report, *The Basic Law: The Army* was enacted with the express aim of correcting these serious deficiencies.

The Basic Law: The Army states the following:

1. The Defense Army of Israel [IDF] is the army of the state.
2. (a) The army is subject to the authority of the government.
(b) The minister in charge of the army on behalf of the government is the minister of defense.
3. (a) The supreme command level in the army is the chief of the general staff.
(b) The chief of the general staff is subject to the authority of the government and subordinate to the minister of defense.
(c) The chief of the general staff shall be appointed by the government on the recommendation of the minister of defense. . . .
5. The power to issue instructions and orders binding on the army should be prescribed by or by virtue of law.[25]

This legislation went a long way toward correcting some of the more glaring deficiencies in the formal status of civil-military relations, although—as will be shown later—it still left much to be desired. It did, however, firmly establish the constitutional principle of civilian control over the military. As a result of this, and especially in view of section 5 of the law, serious doubt was cast on the legality of the high command instructions and general staff orders issued by the CGS. It was recognized that the existing situation, whereby all army orders were issued by the military echelon on the basis of a general delegation of power by a civilian authority, was untenable and contrary to the principle of civilian control. Thus an amendment to the Military Justice Law was passed in 1979 (*Military Justice Law* [amendment no. 12] 5739–1979).[26]

The amendment redefined "army orders" as referring to "instructions of the high command and orders of the general staff" and introduced a clause clearly defining these orders and the authority to issue them. This clause, known as section 2A, reads:

> (a) Instructions of the high command are general instructions issued by the chief of the general staff with the approval of the minister of defense, laying down principles for the organization and administration of the army, for order and discipline therein, and for ensuring the proper functioning thereof.
> (b) Orders of the general staff are general orders issued by the chief of the general staff laying down particulars as to the matters mentioned in subsection (a).[27]

The amendment further stipulated that when a discrepancy exists between an instruction of the high command and an order of the general staff, the instructions of the high command shall prevail. The final section of the amendment validated retroactively all army orders issued in the IDF "before the coming into force of this law." This legislation represented a definite improvement on the previous setup. All army orders issued before 1979 now enjoyed legislative sanction, and all further high command instructions were no longer to be issued on the basis of a general empowerment by the minister of defense, instead being subject to specific prior approval by the minister. Furthermore, all general orders of the army now had to conform to the high command instructions—instructions that must receive prior approval by a civilian authority. However, even after the 1979 amendment, it is still a military echelon—the chief of the general staff—who actually issues the high command instructions. That "principles for the organization and administration of the army" are laid down by the military itself—albeit with civilian approval—remains a serious formal flaw in Israeli civil-military relations.[28]

The Key Actors

The Prime Minister

The prime minister is the head of government and the chief executive of the state. As in Britain, the Israeli prime minister is in theory primus inter pares—first among equals; however, the first forty-five years of Israel's existence witnessed marked changes in the role of the prime minister. From an informal standpoint, one can safely say that no other prime minister in Israel has achieved the degree of authority and power exercised by David Ben-Gurion, and it is highly unlikely that any future one could do so. Ben-Gurion, virtually a legendary figure for many Israelis, practiced almost personal rule for many years and throughout his tenure combined the prime ministership with the Defense Ministry. On the other hand, from the formal or constitutional standpoint, i.e., as defined by law, the position of the prime minister has been strengthened over the years, putting recent and future prime ministers in a position clearly superior to that of the other ministers.[29]

The role of the prime minister is defined by *The Basic Law: The Government.* Section 5(a) of the law states: "The Government consists of the prime minister and other ministers"—hence the definition of the prime minister as first among equals. The legislation, as enacted in 1968, singled out the prime minister in two respects only. The first, mainly of a symbolic nature, requires that the prime minister—unlike the other ministers—be a member of the Knesset. The second is of a more practical nature—namely, that while the resignation of a minister or any group of ministers does not affect the government as a whole, the resignation of the prime minister (or his death) is equivalent to the resignation of the entire government, necessitating either the formation of a new government or new elections.[30] While the prime minister can thus bring about the fall of the government, however, he, unlike his British counterpart, cannot call for new elections. The ability to bring down the government and cause a political crisis is a potent weapon, and many a prime minister has brought around recalcitrant ministers or backbencher M.K.'s with a threat to resign—or, as is said in Israel, "to go to the president."[31] Its power, however, is limited, lying only in its potential use, for—like all threats—once used, it loses all its effectiveness.

A radical change in the prime minister's status came about with the Rubinstein-Shachal amendment in 1981. First, it added the following clause to section 4 of *The Basic Law: The Government*—the section dealing with the principle of collective responsibility of the government before the Knesset: "A minister is responsible to the prime minister for the functions with which the minister is charged." Second, it added section 21A, which states that "the prime minister may, after notifying the government of his intention to do so, remove a minister from office."[32]

This amendment clearly establishes the formal predominance of the prime minister. The government remains collectively the executive arm of the state, and important decisions must be taken by the cabinet—where each minister, including the prime minister, has an equal vote. Yet the fact that the law couples the collective responsibility of the government to the Knesset with the individual responsibility of each minister to the prime minister and grants the prime minister unlimited authority to terminate any minister's membership in the cabinet confirms the position of the prime minister as more than the equal of his fellow ministers. True, the prime minister has little means by which to supervise the ministers and, because of party and coalition considerations, may find it quite difficult to fire a minister; nevertheless, ministers' formal responsibility to the prime minister is of great symbolic and constitutional importance, and the authority to fire recalcitrant ministers has already proven to be a highly potent and effective weapon in the hands of the prime minister.[33]

Until February 1991 the prime minister as such was not mentioned in any legislation dealing with defense matters or with the IDF. *The Basic Law: The Army* only mentions the prime minister indirectly, by establishing the ultimate authority of the government with the prime minister as its head. The prime minister is given no direct role in defense matters. (At the time *The Basic Law: The Army* was enacted, there were many who called for such mention, especially with regard to the appointment of the chief of staff; however, political sensitivities and personal tension between the then–prime minister [Rabin] and defense minister [Peres] prevented it.)[34] Despite this, constitutional conventions as developed over the years have assigned a definite and powerful role to the prime minister.

In February 1991 the Knesset passed an amendment to *The Basic Law: The Government*, establishing a statutory ministerial committee of national security. The law stipulates explicitly that the committee is to be headed by the prime minister. This new legislation represented a departure in Israeli constitutional law: it was the first time the legislature intervened in the functioning of the executive branch and determined the existence, as well as the composition, of a governmental body, in this case, one intended to deal with national security. Whatever the long-range effects of this innovative legislation on Israeli civil-military relations, it can be seen as giving a formal-legislative-constitutional stamp of approval to the dominant role played by the prime minister in all defense matters.

Another major change in the position of the prime minister, though not in his role, came about in 1992 with the enactment of the law for direct election of the prime minister. According to this novel constitutional arrangement, the prime minister will be elected by popular vote in the general election, although executive authority remains in the collective hands of the cabinet. The Knesset can remove the prime minister by a majority vote of its members, but such a vote would result automatically in new elections, both for the Knesset and the prime minister. The prime minister will also be able, with the approval of the president, to dissolve the Knesset and call for new elections. The law will only come into effect in 1996, but there is no question that it will enhance the authority of the prime minister.

The Defense Minister

As discussed above, *The Israel Defense Forces Ordinance* of May 26, 1948, which established the IDF, placed the minister of defense in charge of its implementation, and he is so designated in all subsequent legislation dealing with the IDF. Some of this legislation, such as *The Defense Service Law*, grants him wide discretionary powers and far-reaching authority. Much of this authority has been delegated to senior military officers, but they exercise it in the name of the minister.[35]

Perlmutter writes that Ben-Gurion's legacy to civil-military relations was, among other things, the institutionalization of the minister of defense as "chief of war" and the chief of staff as its chief tactician. This may be so from an informal point of view but Israel law makes no clear expression to this effect (it is also worth recalling that Ben-Gurion was both prime minister and defense minister). In fact, considerable ambiguity still surrounds the exact role and specific authority of the defense minister. The Agranat Commission of Inquiry pointed this out when it determined that "one thing is clear at least from the constitutional aspect: it was never laid down that the defense minister was a kind of 'super-chief of staff,' authorized to instruct the chief of staff within his sphere of responsibility in operational matters, or that he was, in some way, supreme commander of the IDF by virtue of being minister of defense."[36]

This finding by the commission—which formed the basis for its decision to place the blame for the omissions and failures of the Yom Kippur War squarely on the shoulders of the military echelon, while exonerating the political one—was subject to bitter criticism. Some took issue with the commission's legal premise, while others contended that even if the commission's conclusion were correct from the strictly formal-constitutional aspect, it was very far from being an accurate description of the reality that had prevailed since early statehood. On September 20, 1972, the advocate-general of the IDF stated that since the IDF was established by the government, it is subject to the authority that established it and "since the distribution of tasks among the ministers rendered the [Defense] Minister responsible for defence, he represents the Cabinet vis-à-vis the IDF, and the army is therefore subject to his orders." He also interpreted section 7 of the Israel *Defense Forces Ordinance*, which placed the minister of defense in charge of implementing the ordinance, as meaning that the chief of staff, as head of the army, is subject to the minister.[37]

Perhaps the most telling testimony to the actual relationship between the defense minister and the IDF appears in a May 1975 memorandum to the prime minister from David Elazar, chief of staff during the Yom Kippur War and the main victim of the Agranat Commission:

> The Commission, in this matter, contented itself with a legal analysis and did not establish what the reality was since the establishment of the IDF. Such examination would have confirmed that the Chief of Staff and all IDF factors acted on the basis of subservience of the Chief of Staff to the Minister of Defense in all spheres of the responsibility and activity of the IDF, without excluding operational matters. In practice, the Minister of Defense intervened in operational and other matters. There was never any doubt that these matters were in its sphere of responsibility, so that there was never any question as to his authority.[38]

The controversy resulting from the Agranat Commission's report made clear the need to define, once and for all, the role of the defense minister, as well as those of other key government actors. As the Agranat Commission put it, "The lack of a definition of the powers existing in the present situation in the area of defense, which is an area of vital importance, makes effective action difficult, blurs the focus of legal responsibility, and even creates lack of clarity and confusion amongst the general

public." The enactment of *The Basic Law: The Army* was designed to eliminate this confusion. Sadly, however, though it established the principle of
civilian control, the law failed to clarify the specific roles and authority of
the key actors.[39]

An interesting question that has arisen regarding the defense minister's
role is whether that officer represents the military in the cabinet or the
government vis-à-vis the military. Peres, who served both as prime minister and defense minister, is of the opinion that each defense minister
decides for himself the answer to this all-important question.[40] Prime
Minister Begin, on the other hand, was adamant in support of the second
position. In a heated exchange that took place during a cabinet meeting
in May 1979 between Begin and Defense Minister Weizman, Weizman
maintained that he and the chief of staff were responsible for defense,
while Begin retorted that the cabinet was responsible for defense, that the
defense minister's role was to represent the government to the army, not
the army to the cabinet, and that Weizman did not understand the constitution.[41] Weizman subsequently resigned from the cabinet. Three years
later, during what was probably the most turbulent and heated cabinet
session dealing with the war in Lebanon, Prime Minister Begin reiterated
his unequivocal position—this time admonishing Ariel Sharon, then
defense minister. In an ominous tone, Begin reminded Sharon that he had
already pointed out this essential constitutional principle to a former
defense minister and that Sharon was not responsible for the IDF or for
defense and security any more than any other cabinet minister was.[42]

Begin's convictions and legal expertise notwithstanding, one can argue
with his reading of Israel's constitution. His contention that the minister
of defense does not bear any responsibility for the IDF beyond that of all
other cabinet ministers is questionable even from a strictly formal point
of view. True, ultimate responsibility for the military is vested in the government and, by virtue of the principle of collective responsibility, it is
shared equally by all the ministers; at the same time, however, the defense
minister is charged, by law, with the implementation of all defense legislation, and it is he who is individually "in charge of the army on behalf of
the Government."[43] Regarding the question of whom the defense minister represents, however, Mr. Begin's conception of Israel's constitutional
system appears to be correct.

The language of *The Basic Law: The Army*, in its entirety, makes it amply
clear that the defense minister is part of the civilian and not the military
echelon and that he signifies the personal incarnation of the government's

will vis-à-vis the IDF. However, the informal point of view appears to be quite different. To use an incisive American concept, the IDF is the bureaucratic constituency of any defense minister, and many a defense minister finds it necessary to represent the IDF and advocate its positions in the councils of state. Peres claims that in the final analysis a good defense minister must be both the IDF's ambassador to the government and the government's ambassador to the IDF.[44] In conclusion, as Perlmutter astutely observes, "the lessons of 1954, and to some extent of 1967, have shown that the absence of a powerful defense minister supported by his government and people who can command the confidence of the high command impedes the development of harmonious relationship."[45]

The Chief of the General Staff

The position of the CGS was first mentioned in *The Military Jurisdiction Law* of 1955, and prior to the enactment of *The Basic Law: The Army* in 1976, the command authority of the CGS was based mainly on the provisions of this law. In the case of the CGS, however, constitutional convention and custom were more important than formal legislation in forming and defining his role, inasmuch as the legislation itself was far from comprehensive. Section 1 of the law defines the CGS as the "chief of the general staff of the army" (the "army" itself is defined as "the IDF"), but nowhere in the law is there a definition of the CGS's role; nor, for that matter, is there any definition of the term "the general staff of the army." The law does not state that the CGS is the senior commander in the army or that he holds the highest rank in the army; it does not even make it clear that the CGS must be a soldier in the IDF.[46]

   The command authority of the CGS, on the basis of the Military Jurisdiction Law, is rooted in his authority to issue both general orders binding on the entire army and individual orders to any and every soldier in the IDF—orders that cannot be contravened by any other authority within the IDF.[47] From the very early days of the state, the CGS has held the highest rank in the IDF (until 1968 that of major general and after 1968 that of lieutenant general) and is the only soldier of the regular army to hold such a rank. Only former chiefs of staff on reserve duty (every CGS leaves the regular army at the end of his tour of duty) would hold a rank equal to the CGS, and the CGS's command authority over them is based on army usage—the custom and convention developed over the years.

Additional laws, as well as various regulations, invest the chief of staff with numerous powers in many spheres of military life and even beyond.[48] According to the updated version of the *Emergency Defense Regulations* of 1945—promulgated by the British Mandatory Authority and still in effect today—the CGS enjoys wide-ranging authority to intervene in civilian affairs and in the day-to-day life of the country.[49] But it was *The Basic Law: The Army* that gave formal legal expression to the CGS's constitutional role by stating that "the supreme command level in the army is the chief of the general staff" and "the chief of the general staff is subject to the authority of the government and subordinate to the minister of defense."[50] The command authority of the CGS is thus both clear and absolute.

By prefacing the CGS's subordination to the defense minister with the stipulation that he is individually "subject to the authority of the Government," the law grants the CGS a status enjoyed by few other public officials. A director general of any ministry is responsible to his minister and has no direct recourse to the cabinet. The same holds true for the heads of Israel's civilian intelligence services: they are directly and personally responsible to the prime minister but have no standing with the government as a whole. Even deputy ministers are only authorized to act on behalf of the minister who appointed them and in those areas designated by the minister. Only a cabinet minister, by virtue of the collective responsibility of the government and in view of the fact that the government consists of its ministers, has direct recourse to the cabinet. The law thus gives the CGS a status of quasi-minister.[51]

Many chiefs of staff, as well as others, have subscribed to this interpretation of the law. The claim has even been made that having the status of quasi-minister, the CGS is, in effect, a quasi–political figure. Thus former CGS Gur claimed that "authority in the military-tactical sphere is clearly that of the Chief of Staff; in the political sphere—it is equally clearly that it is that of the Defense Minister—the main problem in the relation between the Chief of Staff and the Defense Minister is their cooperation in the strategic-political sphere."[52] Even a senior political figure such as Shimon Peres says that the CGS is "three-quarters military and one-quarter political" and that he should be permitted to present to the cabinet not only military but also political ideas.[53] Indeed, during the deliberations over the interim agreement with Egypt in 1975, Prime Minister Rabin and Defense Minister Peres enabled CGS Gur to present to the cabinet a radically different strategic approach regarding the nature and scope of the withdrawal. Interestingly enough, Gur told the cabinet that the plan was his own, and—with the exception of his deputy—did not enjoy the support of the general staff. Although the cabinet rejected his suggestion, Gur emphasizes that his ideas were not of a tactical-military-operational nature but represented a novel political-strategic approach to the peace process.[54]

An anecdote reported by Gur illustrates the unique status enjoyed by the CGS in the cabinet. A few months after appointing Gur CGS in April 1974, Prime Minister Rabin appointed Ariel Sharon as his military adviser. Defense Minister Peres followed suit and also appointed a military adviser. Sensing Gur's discomfort, a senior cabinet minister took him aside and said: "Don't pay attention to these appointments. As far as the government is concerned, only one person speaks on behalf of the IDF, and he is the CGS—and decisions in the cabinet usually reflect the position of the IDF, as presented by the CGS." Former CGS Moshe Levy stated that he met freely with various cabinet ministers to present IDF positions and thinking, albeit with the knowledge of the defense minister.[55]

Parliamentary Control

Israel's first permanent constitutional legislation—*The Basic Law: The Knesset*—defines the parliament not only as the legislature, but as "the representative body of the State." The Knesset is thus the supreme authority of the state: in the absence of a written constitution and inasmuch as the separation of powers is not firmly rooted in that binding instrument, the Knesset is sovereign. As the sole representative of the people, it is the embodiment and repository of the nation's sovereignty.[56]

In reality, however, the Knesset has limited influence on executive activities and even less on civil-military relations. *The Basic Law: The Army* does not mention the Knesset, and the Knesset has no war powers. The government is authorized to declare war, wage war, and conduct and terminate military operations with no need for formal Knesset approval, although, according to legislation passed in 1992 and scheduled to go into effect in 1996, the government must inform the Foreign Affairs and Defense Committee of the Knesset as soon as possible of a decision to go to war, and the prime minister is obligated in such cases to deliver a statement as soon as possible to the Knesset.[57] Until then, the government can follow the lead of the Begin government, which never submitted to the Knesset its decision in June 1982 to enter the Lebanon War. (The Knesset did approve the war two days after its start, but only indirectly, as a result of a motion of no-confidence presented by the communist faction—a motion that was roundly defeated, with the opposition Labor Party supporting the government.)

The Knesset's major source of authority and avenue of involvement—as for most parliamentary bodies—is through legislation. However, as I've already shown, the Knesset's inclination to deal with military matters through legislation is minimal, limited to what is absolutely necessary. The constitutional act setting forth civil-military relations—*The Basic Law: The Army*—is highly circumscribed, comprising six short sections and only eighty-one words. The ordinance establishing the IDF in May 1948 was issued by the provisional government, under the signature of Ben-Gurion, and was only ratified retroactively by the Provisional State Council. The principles for the organization and administration of the IDF are outlined in the instructions of the high command, which are issued by the CGS with the approval of the defense minister and are not brought before the Knesset or even before the Foreign Affairs and Defense Committee. Although about thirty statutes and laws deal with defense matters—many empowering the defense minister to issue various regulations—there are only two major pieces of legislation: *The Military Jurisdiction Law* and *The Defense Service Law*.[58]

In view of the fact that Knesset decisions not anchored in specific legislation are not binding on the government, the Knesset has introduced a clause in many laws that conditions governmental action or the issuance of government regulations on the approval of the Knesset or one of its committees. This is especially common with fiscal and economic legislation. In the field of defense, however, the Knesset traditionally has been very reluctant to use this mechanism. With the exception of the extension of Emergency Regulations—approval of which is essentially automatic—there is only one significant instance where Knesset approval is necessary for executive action in the defense area, and that is the case of emergency mobilization. Section 34 of *The Defense Service Law 5746–1986 (Consolidated Version)* empowers the defense minister "to call, by order, upon any person . . . to report for regular service or reserve service" and adds that "an order [so issued] shall be brought as soon as possible to the notice of the Knesset Committee on Security and Foreign Affairs. . . . The order shall expire fourteen days after date of issue except if, and as, confirmed by the committee or by the Knesset before said time."[59] At first glance, this power seems to be quite far-reaching. The IDF is a reserve army—the vast majority of its battle order are reservists—and it is thus almost impossible for the IDF to conduct warfare or any substantial military operations without extensive mobilization of the reserves. Therefore in theory the Knesset, by refusing to confirm the defense minister's call-up of reservists, can easily bring any war to a halt within fourteen days. However, given Israel's unique security situation, such a scenario is completely hypothetical and almost totally inconceivable.

A second source of authority and influence for the Knesset is the traditional source of power of all parliament—namely, the power of the purse. In Israel, as in any parliamentary democracy, the budget—including that for defense—must be approved by the Knesset, and the government may not undertake any expenditure outside the limits of the approved budget. The draft state budget, as presented to the Knesset by the government, includes the total appropriation for each ministry as well as an itemized list of all expenditures within each ministry. In the plenum, the Knesset debates the overall budget, as well as that of each ministry. If approved by the Knesset in the first reading, the budget is sent to the Finance Committee, where it is prepared for the second and third readings.[60]

The committee holds hearings on the proposed budget of each ministry, after which it votes on all the line items included in that budget. At this stage, hundreds of amendments are presented, usually by members of the opposition. At the conclusion of its deliberations, the committee brings the budget and the various amendments back to the plenum for the second and third (final) readings. In a marathon session, the Knesset votes on all the amendments and all the line items of the various budgets proposed by the committee. The version of the state budget that emerges from the second reading is then put to a final vote (the third reading), after which it becomes law. (It should be noted that, unlike the U.S. Congress, the Knesset does not differentiate between the authorization and appropriation phases of the budgetary process; legislation authorizing an expenditure by the government simultaneously appropriates funds for that expenditure.)

The law, however, stipulates a special procedure for dealing with the defense budget. For reasons of security, the itemized defense budget is not presented to the full Knesset, nor is it discussed in the plenum. Parliamentary control over the defense budget is achieved through the creation of a special body consisting of the Finance Committee and the Foreign Affairs and Defense Committee. The two committees sitting in joint session serve as a "mini-Knesset, acting with regard to the defense budget on behalf and in the capacity of the Knesset itself."[61] The first, second, and third readings of the defense budget are all held in this forum. A joint subcommittee, acting in the same capacity as the Finance Committee with regard to the general state budget, conducts discussions on the details and specifics of the defense budget, preparing it for the second and third readings before the joint session of the two full committees. Initially, the chair of the Finance Committee headed both the joint body and the Defense Budget Subcommittee. However, in 1974, in the wake of the Yom Kippur War and the severe public criticism regarding the lack of proper parliamentary supervision of the defense establishment, the subcommittee received its own chair, usually a member of the opposition.[62] The draft budget submitted by the Defense Ministry to the joint committee for discussion and approval and to the subcommittee for more intensive deliberations is characterized by great detail and includes—as is the case for all other ministries—detailed item listings of all expenditures.

Theoretically, then, the Knesset has full control over the defense budget and can introduce changes in line items—such as decreasing the appropriations for one item and increasing them for another. The Knesset, however, is as reluctant to exert control over the defense budget as it is to impose restraints on executive action in the field of defense. The subcommittee holds many meetings and extensive discussions on a wide range of topics; it hears many senior officers and officials and visits a considerable number of military installations; but, in the end, it invariably approves the proposed budget with little if any change. Unlike the second reading of the regular budget in the Knesset plenum, the joint forum does not vote item by item, instead voting only on specific amendments, if submitted (these are quite rare), and then on the budget as a whole. It is as though there were a gentleman's agreement by which the defense establishment satisfies the curiosity of the legislators while they, in turn, rubber-stamp the budget.

The notion that the defense budget enjoys a certain sanctity and should not be seriously tampered with and that the legislature is not properly equipped to question the wisdom and judgment of the generals is expressed succinctly by the former longtime chairman of the Finance Committee, Israel Kargman: "Of course, we must rely on the general staff [when it tells us, for example, of the need for more missiles rather than planes]. Even if someone on the committee thinks otherwise, how can we, who know nothing about it, decide on our own?"[63] Interestingly enough, the subcommittee devotes much attention to so-called civilian topics, such as quantity and quality of food in army kitchens, general service conditions, pocket money for conscripts, transportation (free bus tickets for female soldiers), and even which newspapers should be distributed to the soldiers—topics that may be important to their constituents but have minimal, if any, effect on the defense posture of the country.[64]

In the late seventies and during the eighties, there was a growing tendency for the committee to scrutinize the various appropriations more carefully and to attempt to influence actual defense and procurement policy via the budget. This has yet to have much effect, although there was one attempt, in 1976, to alter the defense budget substantially. A rebellion by three coalition members in the Joint Committee resulted in the approval, by one vote, of an amendment to add over a hundred million dollars to the defense budget—something that had never happened before. However, after a dramatic personal appearance by the prime minister and the finance minister—both of whom demanded that the decision be rescinded—the committee held a new vote, which upheld, also by only one vote, the government's original budget proposal.[65]

The Knesset's final source of authority and influence is through its public-political and supervisory functions—motions to the agenda, debates and resolutions in the plenum, and the workings of the ten standing committees.[66] Because of security and secrecy considerations that severely limit public debate of defense issues, the prime arena for the fulfillment of these functions in the defense area is the Foreign Affairs and Defense Committee (FADC). The FADC is one of the ten permanent Knesset committees, and its mandate is "foreign affairs, the armed forces, and the security of the state."[67] If parliamentary control and supervision are truly "an integral and indispensable part of the overall civilian control of the army," then the acid test in the Israeli context is the degree of influence wielded by the FADC.

There is widespread agreement that over the years the effectiveness of parliamentary control has slowly but perceptibly improved, a change manifested in a gradual increase in the prestige, power, influence, and involvement of the FADC.[68] The FADC of the nineties is a far cry from the docile committee of Ben-Gurion's days. Lissak writes that Ben-Gurion's legacy was limited involvement by the cabinet and the Knesset in running the defense establishment. Yitzhak Navon, Ben-Gurion's political secretary and close adviser, characterized Ben-Gurion's conception of the committee's role as that of a consumer of information and provider of public support for government policies, describing the relationship between Ben-Gurion and the committee as one where "the views of its members were listened to, but they had little if any effect on Ben-Gurion." Interestingly enough, when Navon was chairman of the FADC twenty-five years later (1974–1977), he did not veer very far from his mentor's perception of the committee's limited role. Explaining why the FADC should not view itself as a civil arm controlling the military, he said: "The IDF draws its own conclusions and continually examines the problems it faces. It improves all the time, and does not need advice from anybody outside."[69]

Signs of change were already manifest during the Seventh Knesset (1969–1973). In 1970 a permanent full-time secretary was appointed. The practice of regular meetings and briefings with the political and professional leadership of the defense establishment was institutionalized: the prime minister, defense minister, foreign minister, and chief of staff had monthly appearances before the committee, and the head of military intelligence, as well as the heads of the Mossad and the General Security Service (Shabak), appeared periodically. During the Eighth Knesset (1974–1977), a special subcommittee was formed to follow up on the Agranat Commission's recommendations regarding the IDF—probably the first occasion when the FADC actually attempted to supervise implementation by the IDF of specific actions and policies.

When the El Al plane was hijacked at Entebbe in July 1976, Prime Minister Rabin, in an unprecedented move, consulted with the full committee before a cabinet decision, probably hoping to consolidate public support for an extremely difficult decision. Rabin had promised the committee that he would consult with it before deciding to accede to the terrorists' demands for a prisoner exchange. The terrorists' ultimatum was set to expire on Thursday, July 1, at 1 P.M.; at 10 A.M. Rabin appeared before an emergency meeting of the FADC. He reported that the cabinet was in session and he was planning to recommend that Israel accept the ultimatum and enter into negotiations with the terrorist organization holding the Israeli hostages of Entebbe; he was now ready to hear whatever the committee members had to say before he returned to the cabinet meeting.[70]

On the other hand, the FADC was not let in on the decision—taken on Saturday—to launch the Entebbe rescue operation. Immediately after the cabinet's decision to approve the raid, Rabin summoned the leaders of the opposition in the FADC (Begin and Rimalt), as well as the committee chairman (Navon), to inform them of the pending military operation. This use of the FADC as a mechanism of exchange between the government and the opposition in time of national crisis has become institutionalized in Israeli life. It was first employed by Ben-Gurion on the eve of the Sinai Operation in 1956 and repeated by Eshkol in 1967, by Begin at the onset of the Lebanon War in 1982, and by Shamir during the Gulf War in 1991.

The effectiveness of parliamentary control and the influence of the FADC received a big boost in 1977 with the change of government and Moshe Arens's assumption of the chairmanship of the committee.[71] Aware that the size of the committee (over twenty members) discouraged serious, in-depth examination of issues and prevented senior government and military officials from disclosing top secret information for fear of leaks, Arens instituted a system of small permanent subcommittees to deal with the more important defense issues. He also enlisted former senior military officers as well as experts from academia to serve as advisers to the various subcommittees. It was the beginning of a veritable revolution in the workings of the FADC—a revolution that continues to this day.

In the Ninth Knesset (1977–1981), the new four-member subcommittee dealing with the intelligence and secret services met regularly with the heads of all of Israel's intelligence and secret services, received briefings that included top secret and highly classified intelligence data, and visited the most clandestine installations. This subcommittee was formed despite strong objections by the heads of the various services. Their reservations notwithstanding, once overruled by Prime Minister Begin, the heads of all the services, including the head of military intelligence, complied fully with the directive of the civilian authority and cooperated fully with the subcommittee.[72] During the Eleventh Knesset (1984–1988), the subcommittee, under the chairmanship of Abba Eban, became the focus of national attention when it conducted a full-fledged secret investigation of the Pollard affair. (Jonathan Pollard was a civilian working for U.S. Naval Intelligence in Washington who was arrested by the FBI for spying for Israel. He was subsequently convicted of espionage and sentenced to life imprisonment, which led to serious tension between the United States and Israel.) It is not an exaggeration to say that the political future of a number of Israel's national leaders depended, in no small degree, on the subcommittee's verdict.

Other subcommittees include the Subcommittee on Research and

Development and the Defense Industries, the Subcommittee on Procurement, and the Subcommittee on IDF Preparedness. These usually number under ten members and rarely suffer from leaks. Small in size and specific in focus, the subcommittees are less prone to leaks and thus encourage a high degree of openness in the military. In 1981, the air force gave a top secret briefing to one such subcommittee on the operational concept for attacking and destroying the Syrian air defense system—a concept quite similar to the one that was subsequently implemented in the successful Israeli attack on the Syrian SAM missile sites in Lebanon in June 1982.[73]

Important as these changes in the functioning of the FADC may have been, the committee still remained essentially passive, receiving information—albeit in much greater detail and of a more classified nature—from the military and responding to it. In the Eleventh Knesset, however, the FADC appointed a Subcommittee on Israel's Defense Doctrine and Its Implementation, which initiated its own independent study of Israel's defense doctrine and the future battlefield and of the interface between the two. The subcommittee, headed by Dan Meridor (who later became minister of justice), held extensive hearings, inviting not only members of the defense establishment but outside experts as well, including individuals known to have radical opinions and to be highly critical of the IDF. After months of deliberation, the Meridor committee submitted a secret thirty-two-page report that took exception to many of the positions held by the IDF and put forth its own version of what Israel's defense doctrine should be. Although the IDF was critical of the subcommittee's efforts in the beginning, eventually it implemented many of its recommendations.[74] The Meridor committee's report brought the FADC a significant step closer to the workings of the U.S. Congress and is the culmination of a process initiated ten years earlier—a process that markedly increased the role of the FADC, thus the Knesset, in civilian control of the armed forces.

The Role of the Courts

The judiciary, unlike parliament, is not normally considered an integral part of overall civilian control of the army. By its very nature and definition, the judiciary exists to adjudicate disputes between parties, not to direct or oversee policy. Indeed, the very independence of the courts and the high level of confidence they enjoy is closely related to their divorce from any involvement in public policy. Mahoney emphasizes the limited role of the United States Supreme Court in overseeing the outcome of the military and the decisions of the president as commander in chief. This philosophy is expressed in the dissenting opinion of Justice Jackson in *Karematsu v. United States*: "The chief restraint upon those who command the physical forces of the country, in the future as in the past, must be their responsibility to the political judgment of their contemporaries and to the moral judgment of history."[75] Nevertheless, the past years have witnessed an ever-growing tendency for the judiciary to intervene in the area of public policy and an ever-greater willingness for it to review and, if necessary, overrule executive decisions.

In Israel, the Supreme Court is known not only for its independence but also for its strong inclination to engage in judicial legislation. When all other avenues of civilian control have failed, there is always recourse to the Supreme Court, and in the past decade the Court has shed its traditional reluctance to intervene in military affairs. The most recent example occurred just before the Gulf War. The army had decided, for budgetary reasons, to distribute gas masks only to the Jewish residents of the territories, claiming that the Arab population did not face any serious danger from Iraqi Scud missile attacks. This decision had been upheld by both the cabinet and the Knesset, but it was overturned by the Supreme Court, which ordered the IDF to distribute gas masks without delay to Arab residents in the Administered Territories. Immediately after the Supreme Court decision the CGS and the defense minister both announced that the IDF would naturally abide by it.

The ability of the Supreme Court to intervene in almost any area of Israeli life stems from the fact that it functions not only as a final court of appeals—both civilian and criminal—but also as the high court of justice. In this capacity, it has almost unlimited powers. *The Basic Law: The Judicature* spells out the authority of the high court of justice (HCJ) as follows:

> 15. . . .
>
> (c) The Supreme Court shall sit also as a high court of justice. When so sitting, it shall hear matters in which it deems it necessary to grant relief for the sake of justice and which are not within the jurisdiction of another court.
>
> (d) Without prejudice to the generality of the provisions of subsection (c), the Supreme Court sitting as a high court of justice, shall be competent . . .

(2) to order state and local authorities and the officials and bodies thereof, and other persons carrying out public functions under law, to do or refrain from doing any act in the lawful exercise of their functions.[76]

The defense minister, the CGS, and any other officer of the IDF are clearly "persons carrying out public functions under law" and thus come under the jurisdiction of the HCJ by virtue of section 15(d)(2). Furthermore, under section 15(c), the HCJ has unlimited jurisdiction whenever it deems its intervention necessary for the "sake of justice."

As early as 1948, the Supreme Court made it clear that it enjoyed jurisdiction over the IDF. In one of its earliest decisions, the Court unanimously rejected the argument that military courts are not subject to the jurisdiction of the civil judiciary, leaving no doubt as to its readiness to intervene in the workings of military courts and, even more so, those of all other military authorities.[77] Since then, no one has ever challenged the authority of the Supreme Court over the IDF. Because of Israel's security situation, the IDF was granted far-reaching powers under the Emergency Regulations of 1945 with regard to areas within Israel having a large Arab population. The Supreme Court took it upon itself to guarantee that these powers not be abused and as early as 1948 suspended an arrest order issued by the IDF, on the reasoning that it did not meet all the necessary formal requirements.[78]

The need for such judicial supervision increased greatly after 1967, when the IDF became directly responsible for one and a half million Palestinian Arabs in the territories. According to international law, the military governor of these areas is the de facto sovereign, and his decrees have the power of law. But the military governor is also an officer of the IDF, which means that, aside from being subject to the authority of the CGS (who is, of course, subject to the authority of the defense minister and the government), he is also subject to judicial review and the authority of the Supreme Court.

A landmark decision was handed down in 1979 in the famous Eilon Moreh case.[79] The IDF had confiscated privately owned land near Nablus from its Arab owners, supposedly for military needs. The government had approved the confiscation on the recommendation of the CGS and against the opinion and advice of the defense minister. The land was used to establish the Jewish settlement of Eilon Moreh. The Arab owners of the land appealed to the Supreme Court, claiming that the confiscation was based on political rather than military grounds. The Supreme Court agreed, ruling that the confiscation order was null and void and ordering the IDF to remove the Jewish settlers from the land. Although this decision was a major political blow for the Begin government and the prospect of forcibly evicting the settlers from the area a political nightmare, the decision was fully implemented.

Another important decision came in 1988, when the Supreme Court issued a permanent order nisi compelling the IDF to hold a formal hearing before using the authority granted it under the *Emergency Defense Regulations* to destroy homes of suspected terrorists.[80] And in what is perhaps the most far-reaching attempt to intervene in the actual functioning of the IDF, the Supreme Court created a new precedent in 1989, when it overruled the advocate-general's decision to take only disciplinary action against Colonel Yehuda Meir, a brigade commander in the West Bank, for issuing an order to beat Arab civilians. The Court ordered instead that Colonel Meir face a court-martial and that more severe charges be brought against him.[81]

The growing involvement of the Supreme Court in the affairs of the IDF is not limited to the territories. In a break with previous precedent, the Court agreed to hear an appeal against the directive of the defense minister postponing indefinitely the military service of yeshiva students. Although the Court upheld the defense minister's directive—ruling that inasmuch as the minister was merely following the accepted practice of all previous defense ministers, his action should not be viewed as being extremely unreasonable—it held that such a decision must be reviewed from time to time in light of changing circumstances and could very well be voided by the Court at some future date.[82] In another landmark decision, the Court overruled the decision of the military censor to ban a newspaper article severely criticizing the performance of the head of the Mossad.[83]

At the same time, the Supreme Court has been careful not to overstep its bounds and has always emphasized the special nature of the military and its needs—both in general as an institution based on a recognized hierarchy and absolute discipline and specifically by virtue of Israel's unique security situation. In particular, the Court took pains to emphasize that issues relating to the organization, structure, deployment, equipment, and operations of the IDF, as well as those related to appointments and promotions within the IDF, are not, except in the most extraordinary circumstances, subject to judicial review.[84]

It is worthwhile to conclude with one last illustration—although not from the court docket—of the powerful influence of the Supreme Court on the IDF.[85] In 1978 Chief Justice Meir Shamgar concluded a study of the entire system of military justice and of the military courts and recommended sweeping changes in the system, including:

> The creation of a nine-person committee for the appointment of military judges, which until then had been within the sole authority of the CGS. The committee would include four civilians (the chief justice, an associate justice of the Supreme Court, the president of the Israel Bar Association, and the minister of justice), four senior IDF officers (headed by the chief of staff), and the minister of defense as chair.
>
> The appointment of military judges for a five-year term of office, during which they would be immune from replacement. According to existing practice, the CGS could dismiss a military judge at any time.
>
> A limited right of appeal from the military court of appeals to the Supreme Court—a right hitherto nonexistent.

The IDF bitterly opposed Shamgar's plan and fought hard and long against its adoption and implementation, succeeding in delaying acceptance of the recommendations for over ten years. Shamgar, however, kept the issue alive, especially in the Knesset. Finally, in 1988, then–defense minister Yitzhak Rabin decided to implement the recommendations. CGS Shomron strenuously objected and requested permission to bring the issue before the entire cabinet. Rabin agreed, and after a long debate, his decision to adopt the recommendations was upheld by a cabinet vote of twelve to nine.

4 | The National Command Authority: Who Commands the IDF?

The Basic Law: The Army was enacted in response to the Agranat Commission's severe criticism of constitutional ambiguities and faults in the Israeli system. Its avowed purpose was to give clear constitutional expression to the principle of civilian control and to specify the precise relations among the key actors in the defense hierarchy. Unfortunately, however, the legislation failed to achieve its declared aim. During the deliberations over *The Basic Law: The Army*, Aharon Yariv, then minister of information and building on his long experience as head of military intelligence, lobbied in favor of a comprehensive bill that would outline the relations among the key actors in clear and precise terms.[1] His efforts, as well as those of others, were unsuccessful; the majority in the government favored a brief and essentially declarative law, which evaded the more complex issues.[2] As in so many other instances, the politicians' propensity for flexibility and constructive ambiguity had the upper hand. *The Basic Law: The Army* thus leaves many crucial questions unanswered and fails to define the national command authority clearly. Interestingly enough, defining who commands the IDF only became a concern when the defense minister wanted to order the release of an enlisted man from the regular army without his receiving the customary end-of-service grant. In the end, clarifying the national command authority was left to the legal advisers of the IDF and the Ministry of Defense; not surprisingly, they could not agree on a solution.[3]

The Hebrew word for authority, *marut*, conveys a sense of absolute subjection. There is no question that, from the formal point of view, the IDF is absolutely and totally subject to civilian authority, and there seems to be little question regarding the supreme authority of the government. Both the IDF and the CGS are, by law, subject to the authority of the government, and it is the government who is authorized both to appoint and dismiss the CGS. Few, if any, would thus argue with the conclusion that the cabinet, collectively, is the commander in chief of the IDF, exercising authority parallel to that of the president of the United States and the prime minister of Great Britain.[4] With the exception of former CGS Chaim Bar-Lev, all those interviewed agreed with the conclusion of the IDF's legal opinion: the authority of the government over the chief of staff is equal to that of the CGS over subordinate officers and is applicable, without exception, in the strategic, tactical, and operational spheres.[5]

The question, however, is how this constitutional formula can be applied effectively to the practical necessities of everyday life. It is inconceivable that a body of twenty or so ministers should act as commander in chief of a modern armed force and run the day-to-day affairs of the IDF or the day-to-day operations of a war. There has to be a single individual to whom the CGS can turn, at any given moment, for guidance. Israeli legislators were aware of this conundrum, and thus the section that states "the army is subject to the authority of the government" also stipulates that "the minister in charge of the army on behalf of the government is the minister of defense."[6] At first reading, this solution seems straightforward and rather elegant. Nonetheless, it leaves two issues open to interpretation: the relationship between the defense minister and the government, on the one hand, and that between the defense minister and the chief of staff on the other.

The situation is even more complex, however, for there is another individual who can be viewed as representing the government vis-à-vis the IDF, and that individual is the prime minister. The prime minister is not mentioned at all in *The Basic Law: The Army* and thus seemingly has no direct role with regard to the IDF nor any direct standing with the CGS. However, constitutional convention clearly subordinates the CGS to the prime minister as well as to the defense minister. In a cabinet meeting held during the Lebanon War, Defense Minister Sharon noted in passing that CGS Eitan had participated in a Phantom fighter plane reconnaissance mission over enemy territory. Prime Minister Begin interrupted Sharon's briefing and, turning toward Eitan, said: "As prime minister, I am ordering you not to fly anymore, under any circumstances, over enemy territory."[7] No one present questioned Begin's right to issue such an order to the CGS on a purely operational issue; nor was there any doubt that Eitan would obey.

This constitutional convention is supported by the fact that by virtue of his heading the government, the prime minister—more than anyone else—represents the will of the cabinet, thus invoking the cabinet's collective authority. It is further supported by the 1981 amendment to *The Basic Law: The Government*, by which each minister, including, of course, the defense minister, "is responsible to the prime minister for the functions with which the minister is charged" and especially by legislation enacted in February 1991 that created a statutory Ministerial Committee on National Security headed by the prime minister.[8] With the introduction of the prime minister into the equation comes the necessity to consider the relationship between the prime minister and the defense minister, especially vis-à-vis the IDF and the CGS.

There exists no formal definition of the government's sphere of responsibility on the one hand and that of the prime minister and/or defense minister on the other. Nothing in the cabinet's rules of order, or in the instructions of the high command, or even in any government decision spells out clear and obligatory guidelines regarding which issues and decisions must be brought before the cabinet or the MDC and which can handled at the prime ministerial or defense minister's level. There are, of course, informal arrangements—some oral, others written—and these will be discussed in chapter 6, but from a formal constitutional and statutory viewpoint, there is a total vacuum.

The power to declare or wage war and to initiate, conduct, or terminate military operations is—as of now—not expressly provided for in constitutional law. It would therefore seem that by virtue of its residual authority under section 29 of *The Basic Law: The Government*, such power is vested in the government.[9] This conclusion, too, is deeply rooted in constitutional conventions. Former CGS Moshe Levy states that if ordered by the defense minister or the prime minister to initiate general hostilities, he would have refused, for if decisions of far less importance are brought before the government, it would be inconceivable to go to war without an explicit cabinet decision.[10] In so doing he would probably have been on safe ground, for such an order, even if issued jointly by the prime minister and the defense minister, would probably be considered blatantly illegal. Decisions to undertake military operations have almost always been taken at the governmental level. The decision to bomb PLO headquarters in Tunis in 1985 was taken by the MDC, as was the decision to abduct the Hizballah leader Sheikh Obeid from south Lebanon in 1989. The decision to attack the Iraqi nuclear reactor in Baghdad in June 1981 was discussed intensively in the MDC and brought for final approval before the entire cabinet. Prime Minister Rabin ruled that the decision on the Entebbe rescue raid in July 1976 should be brought to the entire cabinet and not just the MDC. The reasoning behind his decision was based on the scope of the operation, the great distance from Israel, the grave risks involved, and the far-reaching internal political consequences of failure.[11] The IDF's proposal to set a trap to lure Russian pilots over Egypt into combat during the War of Attrition—an exchange in which four Russian fighter planes were shot down—was brought before the entire cabinet by then–Prime Minister Golda Meir and Defense Minister Dayan. (The plan was approved only after much discussion and in the face of considerable opposition.)[12]

In March 1992, as part of the legislation providing for the direct election of the prime minister by popular vote, the Knesset in effect rewrote *The Basic Law: The Government*. Section 51 of the new law reads as follows: "(a) The state shall wage war only by virtue of a decision by the government. (b) Nothing in this section should be construed as preventing military operations necessary for the defense of the state and for public security. (c) Notification of a decision by the government to go to war, in accordance with subsection (a), shall be given to the Foreign Affairs and Defense Committee of the Knesset as soon as possible; the prime minister shall also deliver a statement, as soon as possible, before the Knesset; notification of military operations, as stated in subsection (b), shall be given to the Foreign Affairs and Defense Committee of the Knesset, as soon as possible."[13] As noted earlier, however, the new law will come into effect only after the elections for the Fourteenth Knesset, scheduled for 1996. In any case, it still leaves enough leeway under section 51(b) for extensive military operations without a formal government decision to go to war.

After the government decides to undertake a military operation, the defense minister is responsible for its conduct, although he remains subject, to some degree, to government instructions and decisions. This area has been a major source of tension in Israeli civil-military relations. During the Lebanon War, for instance, extensive actions were taken without prior governmental authorization. Defense Minister Sharon, with Prime

Minister Begin's approval, ordered the IDF to enter West Beirut after the murder of President-Elect Bashir Gemayel; the action was brought to the cabinet for approval only eighteen hours later. Similarly, Sharon ordered the IDF to advance along the Beirut-Damascus road in the Bahamdoun area after the cease-fire of June 11, 1982—this time not only without prior governmental authorization or knowledge but also without the approval or knowledge of Acting Prime Minister Simcha Ehrlich (Begin was visiting the United States).[14]

Instances where a defense minister took a very broad view of the bounds of his authority are not limited to the experience of Ariel Sharon. In December 1955 Ben-Gurion, who was prime minister and defense minister and, at this specific moment, also acting foreign minister (Foreign Minister Moshe Sharett was out of the country), ordered, on his own, a large-scale retaliatory raid against the Syrians. The raid, known as Operation Kinneret, was successful but resulted in relatively heavy Israeli casualties. Afterward, Ben-Gurion faced severe criticism from members of the cabinet and acceded, against his better judgment, to the demands of the cabinet majority that major military operations beyond Israel's borders be brought for approval to the entire cabinet.[15] Even so, less than a year later Ben-Gurion engaged in preparations and international negotiations for the Sinai war without the government's knowledge, although he did seek, and received, cabinet approval before the actual initiation of hostilities.

In February 1986, after two Israeli soldiers were abducted from the security zone in Lebanon, Rabin, at the time defense minister in the National Unity Government, ordered a massive search operation beyond the security zone involving thousands of soldiers and dozens of tanks and armored vehicles—an operation that lasted for close to a week—without government authorization.[16] On another occasion, Rabin drew serious public criticism when, on May 3, 1988, he approved a large-scale IDF incursion into Lebanon and an attack against a major Hizballah stronghold at Maidoun. The operation—which lasted for close to two days, resulted in sixty dead and many wounded terrorists, as well as a number of Israeli soldiers killed in action, and brought IDF troops very close to the Syrian forward positions—was undertaken without the authorization or knowledge of either the cabinet or the MDC.[17] Vice Prime Minister and Foreign Minister Peres learned of the action, as did the other ministers, from the radio. Prime Minister Shamir was informed of the operation before it was launched but declared publicly afterward that he had been "unaware of its scope."[18]

Rabin claimed that he was acting within overall government guidelines and policy on the war against the terrorists and that the operation was routine and thus did not require the approval of the MDC.[19] When CGS Shomron was asked whether the operation had been discussed in the MDC, he replied: "I don't know. As far as I am concerned, the minister of defense represents the government. The political process and the discussions of the defense minister with the prime minister and the foreign minister are none of my business."[20] However, a number of key ministers sharply disagreed with this position, citing the duration of the operation, its wide scope, and especially the danger of it leading to a clash with the Syrian army as ample and compelling reasons for the defense minister to have sought prior cabinet or, at least, MDC approval—especially since, in the past, operations of a much more limited nature invariably had been brought before the MDC for approval.[21] In the wake of the public criticism, Minister Shachal placed before the cabinet a comprehensive proposal outlining which operations could be approved by the defense minister and prime minister, which should be brought before the MDC, and which would require full cabinet approval. Prime Minister Shamir, supporting Rabin, referred these proposals to the MDC and, as could be expected, nothing ever came of them.[22]

While there may be disagreement as to the defense minister's authority to act on his own in the absence of a government decision to the contrary, there is general agreement that once the government decides on an issue, its decision is binding on everyone, including the defense minister. It follows that, since the entire basis for the defense minister's authority over the IDF, according to *The Basic Law: The Army*, is by virtue of his being in charge of the army "on behalf of the government," he clearly has no authority when acting against the government, and any order he makes in contradiction of a government decision or policy is null and void. This position has been confirmed by the Supreme Court. In the Eilon Moreh case, Justice Moshe Landau ruled that, in light of sections 2 and 3 of *The Basic Law: The Army*, "as long as the government has not spoken on a particular subject, the chief of staff is obliged to fulfill the instructions of the defense minister. But once a matter is brought before the government, a government's decision on that matter is binding on the chief of staff, and the defense minister as one member of the government, together with his fellow ministers, bears joint responsibility for its decisions, even for the majority decisions resolved against his own dissenting opinion."[23]

The leaders of Israel's defense establishment are universally aware of this aspect of Israel's constitution. Rabin states unequivocally that if a CGS is aware that an order of the defense minister is contrary to the government's decision, "he should definitely not implement it," adding that in such a case the defense minister would "at least" need the support of the prime minister.[24] Real life, however, is slightly more complex. Obviously, if an order is against the better judgment of the CGS and he does not want to implement it, then he will surely refuse to do so and still be on safe ground. This is exactly what happened at Maalot. In May 1974 a group of terrorists crossing into Israel from Lebanon in the early hours of dawn took over a school building where about one hundred high school students on an outing were spending the night. The terrorists took the children and their teachers hostage and, in return for their release, demanded the release of some twenty terrorists being held in Israeli prisons. The cabinet, meeting in emergency session that morning, decided to negotiate with the terrorists and sent Defense Minister Dayan and newly appointed CGS Gur to the site, empowering them to take military action if and when they deemed it necessary. At noon Dayan told Gur that in his opinion the terrorists were becoming nervous and that therefore Gur should immediately attempt to release the hostages by force. Gur refused, claiming that the government had decided to negotiate and that there was no urgency to attack. Furious, Dayan told Gur, "Do as you wish," and left the command post. Gur immediately phoned Prime Minister Meir, who supported his position.[25]

When the defense minister and the CGS are of the same mind, however, it is easy for the CGS not to question the defense minister's instructions. Dan Shomron's response to the Rabin-approved attack at Maidoun, quoted above, is a classic example. Another good example is the Lebanon War, where Defense Minister Sharon and CGS Eitan cooperated in acting contrary, if not to the letter, at least to the spirit of certain government resolutions. Eitan himself admits that although whenever Begin questioned him about matters on which Sharon had not fully reported, he would always answer fully, he did not volunteer information on his own, even when he had reason to believe that the defense minister's report might not have been complete or fully accurate.[26] Issar Harel tells of instances in 1954 when Defense Minister Lavon clearly, and with CGS Dayan's knowledge, misled Prime Minister Sharett. When Harel upbraided Dayan and demanded to know why he did not tell Sharett the truth, Dayan replied that it was the defense minister who was responsible to the government and the prime minister, and if he wished to mislead them, it was none of Dayan's business.[27] The similarity—the almost identical note and tone—between Dayan's response in 1954 and Shomron's some thirty-four years later is remarkable; in Shomron's case, at least, the constitutionality of his position was highly questionable.[28]

There are a number of instances where the defense minister is granted direct power under a specific law. One example would be his authority to order emergency mobilization under section 26 of *The Defense Service Law (Consolidated Version)* of 1959. But what is the law when the government sees fit to order an emergency mobilization and the defense minister disagrees? There is no clear-cut answer, nor any definite legal precedent. According to one view, the opinion of the defense minister will prevail; the only recourse open to the government or the prime minister would then be either to transfer the defense minister's authority to another minister, under section 30 of *The Basic Law: The Government*—an action conditional on Knesset approval—or for the prime minister to fire the defense minister, under section 21A of the law—an action that goes into effect only after forty-eight hours. Another view, however, holds that a minister cannot exercise his authority in opposition to a government decision, even when this authority is conferred on him directly by law. This view would seem to be more in line with the principle of collective responsibility of the government and has received some support in Supreme Court judgments, as well as in practice.[29] On the morning of the Yom Kippur War, for example, the chief of staff demanded that then–Defense Minister Moshe Dayan order emergency mobilization of the entire IDF reserve force. Dayan suggested mobilizing only two divisions. The issue was brought before Prime Minister Meir, and she ruled in the CGS's favor. Fortunately for Israel, Dayan accepted Golda Meir's ruling and issued the necessary orders.

The specific authority of the defense minister over the chief of staff is the most complicated issue of all, and one about which there are many differing opinions—among both legal experts and defense ministers and chiefs of staff themselves. The ambiguity turns on the fact that the CGS is, at the same time, "subject to the authority of the government" and "subordinate to the minister of defense" (section 3b) and how to correlate this provision with the one stipulating that the CGS is "the supreme command level in the army" (section 3a). The IDF's legal opinion puts forth three possible positions.

The first is that of complete subordination of the CGS to the defense minister. According to this view, the defense minister is authorized to instruct the CGS on any issue, whether it is strategic, tactical, operational, or administrative. Proponents claim that this position is the clear intention of the law subordinating the CGS to the defense minister and that it can also be deduced from the provision stipulating that the defense minister is in charge of the IDF on behalf of the government, which is seen as signifying that, in the absence of a governmental decision to the contrary, the authority of the minister is equal to that of the government. Many consider such a wide interpretation necessary to give full force to the defense minister's explicit ministerial responsibility for the army. This point is emphasized, for instance, by Defense Minister Moshe Arens.[30]

The main criticism leveled against this view is that it turns the defense minister into a superior chief of staff and the chief of staff himself into a conduit for forwarding orders from the minister to the various units of the IDF—a situation that contradicts the spirit of section 3a, which defines the CGS as the supreme command level in the army. In answer to this criticism, two facts should be noted. First, considerable evidence suggests that over the years defense ministers have indeed acted as superior chiefs of staff—as indicated, for example, in Elazar's memorandum to Prime Minister Meir, quoted above (p. 40). Another prime example goes back to the very early days of the state: in an attempt to break the siege on Jerusalem during Israel's War of Independence, Ben-Gurion compelled Haganah commanders, against their unanimous and vociferous advice, to attempt the capture of the Jordanian stronghold of Latrun, which controlled the road to Jerusalem—an attempt that was repeated three times, only to fail.[31] Second, however, no one in Israel questions the right of the CGS to originate orders, both in his capacity as chief of the general staff and as overall commander of Israel's ground, air, and naval forces. This is not always the case in countries adopting broad views of the civilian authority's level of influence. In the United States, for example, the chairman of the JCS is indeed merely a conduit for transmitting the orders of the president and the secretary of defense to the commander in chief of the unified commands. Furthermore, under the American system the CJCS is prohibited from initiating orders on his own.[32]

The second position is that of strategic subordination. According to this view, the CGS is subordinate to the minister in the political-strategic area but not in the operational-command area. Thus the minister of defense can, for example, order the CGS to mount a military operation to rescue hostages held by terrorists, but the chief of staff is responsible for finalizing the plans and commanding the operation, subject to no authority save that of the cabinet itself. This approach takes its rationale from the different language used to define the relationship between the CGS and the government—"subject to the authority"—and that between the CGS and the minister—"subordinate"—the former reflecting a much higher degree of subservience than the latter.[33] This position is also seen as best reconciling the provision that the minister is "in charge of the army" (section 2a of *The Basic Law: The Military*) with the provision that the CGS is "the supreme command level in the army" (section 3a). The major criticism of this view is that the differentiation between the authority of the government and that of the minister is artificial and ignores the fact that the minister acts as an agent of the government and should thus enjoy the same authority as the principal. Furthermore, there is little legal sense in having the defense minister bear responsibility for the operational activities of the CGS if he cannot influence those actions (save by recommending the CGS's dismissal).

The third position, relative subordination, represents a compromise between the two just described. According to this view, the CGS is absolutely subordinate to the minister on all political-strategic issues, while on other issues (operational and command) he only needs the minister's approval. The minister cannot force his ideas on the CGS, but if he keeps rejecting different proposals presented to him by the CGS, in most cases he will eventually achieve his own ends. The proponents of this view claim that it creates a delicate but healthy balance between the CGS and the defense minister. Opponents claim that it can easily lead to a stalemate and that it undermines the principle of civilian control.

One question remains regarding the relationship between the defense minister and the CSG or the IDF: Can the defense minister issue orders directly to officers of the IDF, and are such orders binding under *The Military Jurisdiction Law*?[34] There are numerous examples of defense ministers issuing orders to commanders in the field. Moshe Dayan did not hesitate to give orders directly, not only to generals but to lower- and middle-ranking officers—in some instances even to lieutenants commanding outposts on the Suez Canal.[35] During the Lebanon War, Defense Minister Sharon acted similarly.[36] But the most famous example is Moshe Dayan's order, on the morning of June 9, 1967, to the officer in command of the northern command, General Elazar, to take the Golan Heights. Elazar, who had been pleading with the government for such authorization, did not hesitate and, without CGS Rabin's knowledge, began the assault.

Elazar knew, however, that Rabin supported the planned attack on the Golan, and thus he could take Rabin's approval for granted.

At the same time, there are a number of dramatic examples of senior officers refusing to execute orders unless conveyed to them by the CGS. During the Yom Kippur War, Moshe Dayan instructed the officer in command of the southern command, Major General Gonen, to attack a site where an Egyptian division was camped. Gonen, who questioned the military justification of the order, refused, telling Dayan, "You cannot give me orders. You are not the chief of staff." Indeed, on learning from Gonen that Dayan was trying to give him direct orders, CGS Elazar told Gonen, "Whatever the minister tells you is very interesting. However, orders you receive only from me."[37]

The best-known example, however, occurred in the aftermath of the Yom Kippur War. On October 31, 1973, a week after the cease-fire, Major General Tal was appointed commander of the southern command, while retaining his post as deputy chief of staff. Defense Minister Dayan wanted to respond aggressively to any cease-fire violation by the Egyptians, not caring—or perhaps even secretly hoping—that this would lead to a renewal of hostilities. General Tal, on the other hand, was adamantly opposed to doing anything that could endanger the cease-fire. The cabinet, meanwhile, opted for a political agreement and against a resumption of hostilities. Despite this, Dayan issued orders to either Tal or his subordinate both to open fire if provoked as well as to move forces forward. Tal refused to obey and may even have countermanded the orders. According to one version of the story, the general asked Dayan, "Has the government's policy changed since we were both present at the cabinet meeting that decided to keep the area quiet?" Dayan responded, "Leave the government to me." At that point, an angry Tal retorted, "If that's what you have to say, then my commander is the chief of staff—from him I take orders and not from you."[38] Major General Chofi, officer in command of the northern command at the time of the Yom Kippur War, states that had he received orders from the defense minister that he knew to be contrary to the CGS's policy, he would have refused to obey them; were the orders not contrary, he would have notified the CGS. Under no circumstances, would he have undertaken action without the knowledge and agreement of the CGS.[39]

Legal experts agree that, under normal circumstances, the defense minister may not issue orders directly to soldiers of the IDF and that no soldier or officer is bound to obey such orders unless they are transmitted by the CGS.[40] To support this, they cite *The Military Jurisdiction Law*, in which the defense minister does not come under the definition of "commander," and *The Basic Law: The Army*, where the CGS is termed "the supreme command level in the Army." Proponents of all three positions mentioned above accept this interpretation.

Could unusual or unique circumstances lead to a different interpretation? On this question, there is sharp disagreement. Section 32 of *The Basic Law: The Government* states that "a minister charged with the implementation of any law may, insofar as no contrary intention appears from the law, assume any power, other than a power of a judicial character, vested in a state employee under that law; he may do so in respect of a specific matter or for a specific period."[41] Zvi Hadar, former IDF adjutant general, is of the opinion that this authorizes the defense minister to assume the powers of the CGS, including the power to issue general orders in the army and individual orders to any soldier in the IDF.[42] Such assumption of power is not automatic, however: if it is for a specific period, it must be published in the official gazette; even if it is ad hoc, it must be for good causes, and, most probably, the CGS would have to be heard beforehand.[43]

The dissenting opinion holds that section 32 is inapplicable in this case for two reasons. First, *The Basic Law: The Army* states unequivocally that the CGS is the supreme command level in the IDF and makes no provision for the assumption of this power by the defense minister. Since this law is a specific act that spells out the constitutional basis for civil-military relations, it takes precedence over general legislation, including the provisions of *The Basic Law: The Government*. Second, even if section 32 were applicable in principle, it is clearly contrary to *The Basic Law: The Army*, which, because of its constitutional nature, must be read in conjunction with *The Military Jurisdiction Law*.

Although there have been many attempts to sweep the problem under the carpet, the system has remained acutely aware of the dangerous ambiguity that exists in this area.[44] In view of the conflicting opinion in the IDF's legal brief, the matter was referred to the attorney general, but he refrained from issuing any final verdict on the issue.[45] Unfortunately, a review of practice and customs over the past fifteen years (since the enactment of *The Basic Law: The Army*) is no more illuminating. Among the positions held by former defense ministers and chiefs of staff, disagreement reigns. Not surprisingly, civilians support the first view, while the generals tend to adopt a position somewhere between the second and third. The former emphasize the subordination of the CGS to the minister; the latter interpret the fact that the CGS has more than one master (the defense minister, the prime minister, and the government) and the constitutional definition of the chief of staff's role as clear signals regarding the limits of the defense minister's authority.

Moshe Levy, chief of staff in the early eighties, asserts that "the army is absolutely subordinate to the government, whose authority over the CGS is equal to that of the CGS over subordinate officers; this is not the case with regard to the defense minister." The defense minister is, in his eyes, an intermediary—after all, one cannot consult with the cabinet every day—and as such cannot and does not enjoy absolute authority. Levy admits that some of his purely operational decisions—such as moving a battalion from northern command to central command—were vetoed by Defense Minister Rabin. He thought it was improper for Rabin to have intervened but accepted his decisions. Levy insists that "the civilian echelon should determine the mission and, perhaps, approve the overall method, but beyond that it should not become involved." Yet he recognizes the right of the minister to stop implementation of organizational changes proposed by the CGS and even to dictate organizational and administrative matters, albeit after serious and in-depth discussions with the military.[46]

Rafael Eitan, who was chief of staff for five years, including during the Lebanon War, also asserts that the defense minister is not the commander in chief of the IDF but merely represents the government. The commander in chief, in his view, is the government and the prime minister. Chaim Yisraeli, head of the defense minister's bureau since the days of Ben-Gurion and an eyewitness to Israeli civil-military relations for close to forty years, emphasizes the statutory professional responsibility of the CGS. Echoing the concept of professional autonomy, he points out that the CGS is responsible for the functioning of the IDF.[47]

Gur, chief of staff after the Yom Kippur War, has a rather original point of view. He rejects the distinction between the strategic and operational spheres. Modern war is total, and operational considerations have political overtones, just as political considerations have operational consequences. In World War II, it was the commander in the field—Eisenhower—who chose the day on which to launch Operation Overlord; in the Yom Kippur War, the decision on when the IDF should cross the Suez Canal was taken by the cabinet, not by the general staff. The proper distinction to be made is between political-strategic and professional considerations. Thus the civilian authority, including the defense minister, can issue any order motivated by a political-strategic concern, but it cannot and must not decide professional issues. Ben-Gurion ordered the attack on Latrun not because he rejected the professional assessment of his military advisers but despite that assessment. He overruled his military advisers not because he felt the attack would succeed but because he was convinced that there were compelling strategic and political reasons for it to be undertaken even if it were to fail—and this is the prerogative of civilian authority. But while the defense minister can determine priorities, he cannot substitute his professional judgment for that of the CGS. To quote Gur, "the CGS is not the defense minister's operations officer." If Dayan or the prime minister had ordered him to attack at Maalot because the people of Israel could not tolerate Israeli children in the hands of the terrorists for even one more hour, Gur would have obeyed—although he would have deemed the decision a grave mistake. But when Dayan ordered the attack because he judged the terrorists to be nervous and edgy and thus an immediate threat to the children's lives, Gur refused to obey because that judgment could be made only by the CGS, not the minister. The defense minister—especially someone like Rabin or Dayan—may offer professional advice but, to use the famous phrase coined by Dayan in the Yom Kippur War, this is to be regarded merely as "ministerial advice"—something not binding on the military authorities.[48]

Bar-Lev, who succeeded Rabin as chief of staff after the Six Day War in 1967, strongly supports Gur's view. He points out that the defense minister exercises ministerial responsibility for the army but not professional responsibility. Thus while every officer in the IDF is absolutely subordinate to the professional authority of the CGS, the chief of staff is subordinate to the defense minister in principle but not on professional military questions nor on matters related directly and specifically to the army. Bar-Lev illustrates his position in an interesting anecdote. During the War of Attrition, Defense Minister Dayan would often visit the outposts along the Suez Canal. He would receive briefings from senior officers but refrained from talking with the soldiers manning the outposts. Bar-Lev told Dayan that his behavior had a negative effect on the morale of the troops and demanded that he devote some time to the ordinary soldiers. Bar-Lev also warned Dayan that if he would not heed this request, he would refuse to provide him with a helicopter or any other form of military transportation, thus preventing him from visiting the canal. Dayan relented. Bar-Lev goes even further than Gur by asserting, as already noted, that in purely professional matters the CGS is not subject even to the government, although of course he risks summary dismissal.[49]

The Gur–Bar-Lev formula is an eloquent exposition of the principle of professional autonomy. The problem is that according to their view the final delimiter of professional autonomy is the military. In most democracies, while there is widespread recognition of the principle of professional autonomy, the ultimate arbiter of what lies within that domain is the civilian authority. It comes therefore as no surprise that former defense ministers firmly reject the Gur–Bar-Lev formula. Arens, for example, questions the proposition—rooted, supposedly, in the findings and recommendations of the Agranat Commission—that the CGS bears responsibility for the success or failure of the IDF, arguing that since the minister and the government will ultimately be held responsible by the people for any failure of the IDF—strategic or operational—they must both enjoy absolute authority. And in fact the distinction made by the Agranat Commission between the military and political echelons was never accepted by Israeli public opinion.[50]

Ezer Weizman, who was defense minister in Begin's first government (1977–1981), rejects the notion of strategic subordination outright, favoring instead a position somewhere between complete subordination and relative subordination. In support of his stand that the minister is intimately involved in technical and operational matters as well as in strategic and political issues, he cites the fact that when proposing military operations or a military action to the defense minister, prime minister, or cabinet for approval, the CGS presents not only the strategic or political consequences of the planned operation but the operational details as well. The universal and unquestioned practice of presenting to all levels of civilian authority the operational, tactical, and technical aspects of military operations—in minute detail—is not merely in order to satisfy the minister's curiosity but reflects the authority of the minister in all spheres.[51]

Yitzhak Rabin—the only individual in Israel's history to fill all three key roles in the civil-military equation (CGS, defense minister, and prime minister)—is adamant in support of the first view. In his words: "there are no two ways about it—'subordination' means absolute subordination." Rabin goes out of his way to emphasize that when he was CGS, he practiced what he preached and accepted, without exception, the ultimate authority of the defense minister—whether Eshkol (who also doubled as prime minister) or Dayan. He illustrates this with the case of Ezer Weiz-man. Eshkol suggested to Rabin the appointment of Weizman, comman-der of the air force, as head of the general staff and operations division of the IDF—a position considered a stepping stone to that of chief of staff. Rabin strongly objected, believing that an air force officer should not become chief of staff. After three or four rather difficult conversations, Eshkol called Rabin and told him that he had decided and "that's that." Rabin saluted, accepted the verdict, and did not question the defense minister's right to dictate a senior appointment in the IDF.[52] It is note-worthy that Rabin is consistent, and during his tenure as defense minis-ter he acted, perhaps more than any other defense minister, as a superior chief of staff.[53]

The issue remains unresolved and has the potential for creating a major crisis in civil-military relations. One such crisis, which was narrowly avoided, was the Drori affair.[54] In early 1987, Defense Minister Rabin decided that the next CGS would be Dan Shomron. Major General Drori, who had been a major contender and the outgoing chief of staff's candi-date for the post, held a press conference in which he bitterly criticized Rabin on the appointment of Shomron and suggested that the defense minister had acted irresponsibly. On hearing Drori's comments, Rabin immediately demanded that CGS Moshe Levy summarily dismiss Drori from the army. Levy refused. He agreed with Rabin that Drori was clearly out of line—both in the contents of his statement and by virtue of the fact that he had not received prior permission for meeting with the press—but he felt deeply that in view of Drori's record of over twenty years of exem-plary service in the IDF and given that he was due to leave the army any-way in a few weeks, the punishment called for by Rabin was exaggerated and uncalled for. Each side dug in, and a serious crisis began to brew. The opponents consulted with their legal experts and, of course, received con-tradictory opinions. The Defense Ministry's legal adviser claimed that under section 14 of *The Interpretation Law*, since Rabin had approved Drori's appointment, he had the authority to terminate it; the IDF's advo-cate-general ruled that although the CGS needed the defense minister's approval, he alone had the sole authority to appoint and dismiss officers in the IDF. Eventually a compromise was reached—Drori apologized in writing for what he had said. Rabin claims that from the beginning he had been ready to accept a written apology, although he would have preferred Drori's dismissal. In reality, it would seem that both sides bent a little rather than face a showdown whose outcome was unpredictable.

One gray area remains: the relationship of the prime minister and the defense minister to the IDF and the CGS. Huntington claims that the presence of a single civilian authority is of crucial importance for effective, objective civilian control, arguing that the principle of "dual control" (between the president and the Congress) constitutes "a major hindrance to the development of [objective] civilian control in the United States."[55] Division of authority within the civilian echelon and the absence of a single master enables the military to play the various sides against each other and is a sure prescription for trouble in civil-military relations. Despite the division of power between the executive and the Congress, however, within the executive branch itself there is a clear chain of command. At the top of the pyramid is the president, who as commander in chief exercises ultimate and supreme authority over the armed forces; under him is the secretary of defense, who functions as a kind of deputy commander in chief.[56] This arrangement was evident and proved itself during the Gulf War. In Great Britain the prime minister, acting in the name of the Crown—though subject to the decisions of the cabinet—is the supreme civilian authority vis-à-vis the armed forces. In France, during wartime, the president of the republic assumes the role of commander in chief.[57]

Israel surely does not suffer from a division of power between the executive and legislative branches, but its executive branch is characterized by a fragmented and unclear chain of command—primarily because of the ambiguous division of authority between the prime minister and defense minister. During the first twenty years of Israel's existence, with the exception of one year (1954), one individual held both posts, so the problem only arose after the separation of the position of defense minister from that of prime minister in the wake of the Six Day War. The fusion of the two roles before 1967 prevented a normal and gradual development of a relationship between the two offices and caused a great deal of confusion as to what belonged to whom.[58] Peri comments extensively on the tug-of-war between the prime minister and defense minister for control over the IDF, seeing it as a focus of the rivalry between two sub-elites of the Israeli political establishment. He also tries to show that many a chief of staff has put this rivalry to good use, using it as a means of getting his own way.[59] Perhaps to avoid these consequences, when Rabin formed his government in 1992 after Labor's victory in the general elections of that year, he retained the defense portfolio for himself, reverting to a pattern abandoned in 1967.

There are two aspects to this issue. First, can the CGS appeal the decision of the defense minister to the prime minister? If so, can he do so always or only in certain circumstances? If the latter, what are those circumstances? Written law provides no answers to these questions. There does exist, however, a fairly well developed constitutional convention regarding this issue. Its essence is that the CGS is entitled to appeal any decision or to raise any issue with the prime minister, but he can do so only through the defense minister. The defense minister can theoretically refuse such a request, but in practice he will invariably approve it.[60] There is no reported instance of a defense minister refusing the CGS access to the prime minister. However, former CGS Gur tells of a letter he wrote to Prime Minister Begin, setting out his reservations as chief of staff concerning certain statements made by Begin at a general staff meeting. The letter was sent by means of Defense Minister Weizman, and Weizman held it up for three days. During a meeting at the prime minister's office, Gur turned to Begin and said, in Weizman's presence, "I wrote you a letter. The defense minister has held up its delivery for three days now. This is impossible. He has no right to do so." Weizman had no convincing answer, and Gur took out a copy of the letter and handed it to Begin. As a result of this incident, Begin arranged for the CGS to meet with him once a month for a tête-à-tête.[61]

The second aspect relates to what happens if and when the CGS receives contradictory orders from the prime minister and the defense minister. This question is entirely hypothetical—in all of Israel's history, no CGS has received a directive from the prime minister contradictory to that received from the defense minister or vice versa—but it is not meaningless or academic, for in the context of Israeli politics, anything can happen. Once again, written law is silent, but here constitutional convention also provides no guidance, since the issue has never arisen. I posed the question to the interviewees in this study, however, and it elicited a number of different responses.

Most of those interviewed made a clear distinction between contradictory orders that do not demand immediate action or necessitate an immediate decision and those in which delay is impossible and the CGS must decide one way or another. In the first case, almost everyone agreed that the CGS would demand that the cabinet or the MDC be convened in order to decide the issue and would refuse to take action in the absence of a government decision one way or another.[62] Another possibility would be for the CGS to inform the prime minister that he had received contradictory orders from the defense minister and that if the prime minister objects to those orders, he should dismiss the defense minister from the cabinet.[63]

The problem becomes more complex when, for some reason, there is no time or it is impossible to convene either the cabinet or the MDC and thus the CGS has to act without recourse to the ultimate authority of the government (if, for example, an unidentified aircraft entered Israeli airspace, and one party ordered the CGS to intercept and shoot the plane down if necessary, and the other ordered him not to open fire under any circumstances). In such a case, there are, essentially, two approaches. The prevalent opinion is that the prime minister has the upper hand, and his orders should prevail. The logic behind this view is that the prime minister, more than anyone else, speaks on behalf of the government, and the defense minister cannot act contrary to the government's wishes. According to this approach, a clash between the prime minister and defense minister is a clash between the defense minister and the government—the result of which cannot be in doubt.[64] Thus Shimon Peres, former prime minister and defense minister, says simply, "The prime minister is the boss." Weizman concurs, saying that in the final analysis, "the prime minister is the commander in chief because it is he who represents the government." He adds that if, as defense minister, he had ever been overruled unequivocally by the prime minister, it would never have entered his mind not to accept the prime minister's verdict. In the same vein, former defense minister Arens emphasizes that the defense minister "as a 'good soldier' must accept the ultimate authority of the prime minister." Eitan says that as CGS, he would have put the case before the prime minister, telling him that he was receiving contradictory orders, and would have done whatever the prime minister told him to do.[65]

The second approach does not argue with the supremacy of the prime minister but adds a certain nuance; namely, that in such a dramatic situation, the CGS would be guided, to a large degree, by his own inclinations and his own judgment. Thus Gur admits that he would apply his own judgment and "his own value system," and in the absence of a clear-cut government decision or at least pending such a decision, he probably would do what he considered right under the circumstances. Former CGS Moshe Levy says he would follow the orders of the prime minister, but only if he believed in them; if he felt that what the prime minister was suggesting would be a catastrophe and he had the backing of the defense minister, he probably would refuse to obey the prime minister's orders and would insist that the issue be brought before the government. Perhaps the most interesting response was Rabin's. His reaction to the question was almost visceral. Initially he refused even to entertain it, claiming that such a situation was totally inconceivable, could never happen, and "would represent a total breakdown of the civilian authority." The consequence of such an occurrence would be "that there simply was no government." Finally, he acknowledged that, if such an event ever did occur, "the chief of staff would have no choice but to act as he saw fit."[66]

5 | The Israeli System: Defense Organization

All states maintain not only a military organization—the armed forces—but also some form of civilian bureaucratic organization that deals directly with the armed forces and defense. As Broadbent observes, the threat the armed forces pose to the democratic character of the state requires an organization to control them and to decide on their use.[1] Moreover, to a large degree, armed services are a means for implementing national security policy. Thus the elected political leadership—i.e., the civilian government, which bears ultimate responsibility for national security—needs to establish some central bureaucratic mechanism to control and supervise the armed forces.

Edmonds sees the central organization of defense in different states as a core issue of civil-military relations:

> [The] issue is a fundamental one since it is within the structure of government that armed services and the political authorities come directly into contact. They have the combined, rather than the joint, responsibility to take decisions regarding the defense and security of the state. Armed services do not live in isolation, independent of governments, and while much responsibility in defense matters is delegated to them as professionals, decision making about the direction and control of security and defense is not one of them.

It is within the context of government that top political and service planners meet to decide on policy. In the words of Broadbent, "there must be arrangements and structures which permit a continuous and effective dialogue between the politician and the military." The structure of a state's central organizations of defense and processes of decision making reflects—and even determines to a large degree—the relative influence and involvement of civilian and military echelons in the armed forces and in the area of national security.[2]

Early studies of civil-military relations "were restricted to central defence decision making," and although in the last few years the discipline has broadened its outlook, this does not diminish "the relevance of where the apex of civil-military relations really lies, in the central organization of defence." Lovell writes that the central issue in the relationship between the military and society is not formal legal control but the problem of the organization of defense, budgeting procedures, priorities, etc. Sweetman notes that the organization of Britain's Ministry of Defence is an expression of the civilian authority's ability genuinely to oversee the military, including its activities, strategies, operations, and force building.[3]

Organizational frameworks for defense in the advanced industrial states undergo constant evaluation and change. The post–World War II era, especially, has been marked by a rapid increase in the attention paid to defense organizations and by the accelerated pace of change. Calls for wide-ranging reforms of defense organizations have been heard in most Western countries since the end of World War II and can still be heard loud and clear today. Edmonds goes so far as to say central organizations of defense "are a relatively new phenomenon in the experience of modern government," claiming that "none effectively existed before the Second World War."[4]

The civil-military dilemmas and organizational problems facing states with modern armies are quite similar. As a result, the changes experienced by defense organizations in the major Western countries over the past four decades conform to a common pattern. Although each defense organization has its own history, reflecting such aspects as past military experiences, ideological background, political experience, and tradition, careful study discloses three dominant goals that account for most of the changes over time. These are the trends toward unification, centralization, and integration. Although there have been and still are some reservations, especially in the United States, regarding the desirability of these goals, and although their advancement has met with opposition—in many instances, very stiff and stubborn opposition—that still lingers in some quarters, the supporters of unification, centralization, and integration have, by and large, had the upper hand. Bear in mind, however, that these goals represent evolutionary steps along a continuum, not absolutes.

Unification deals with the military side of defense organization. In its ultimate sense, it means the creation of a single, unified command and staff structure for all elements of the armed services. Before World War II, the armed forces of the major Western nations consisted of totally separate services—an army and a navy and, after World War I, an air force.[5] Each individual service has its own unique service tradition, going back—for the army and navy—for hundreds of years, and each tends to guard its independence zealously. All branches of the armed services were, of course, subject to civilian control, but there was no central coordination whatsoever at the military level, nor did a single military personality exercise command and control over all the individual services.

Modern warfare—the highly technological nature of modern weapons, the global reach of modern wars, and the combined nature of military operations—created an urgent need for interservice coordination at the highest military level.[6] Such coordination was first established in Britain only in 1924, with the formation of the Chiefs of Staff (COS) Committee. Constituted as a permanent subcommittee of the ministerial Committee of Imperial Defence (CID), it was chaired by a civilian—the prime minister or some other minister to whom the authority was delegated—and continued to function without an independent chairman until as late as 1956.[7] During World War II, General Lord Ismay, Churchill's personal chief of staff and military secretary to the War Cabinet, served as chair, but only as the personal representative of the prime minister.

American efforts at interservice coordination lagged behind those of the British. Although a joint board composed of four high-ranking officers from each of the two services was formed as early as 1903, its duties were minor, and it had little significance. Furthermore, unlike the British COS Committee, the joint board was not responsible to a single civilian authority; instead, each representative simply reported back to his civilian secretary. Only in July 1939 did President Roosevelt order the joint board to report directly to him as commander in chief of the army and navy, and it was only after the United States entered World War II, creating the need for a counterpart to the British COS Committee, that the

Joint Chiefs of Staff was formed. It, too, had no independent chairman, although for most of the war its sessions were chaired by Admiral Leahy in his capacity as personal military adviser and chief of staff to the president. The position of chairman of the JCS was not created until 1949.[8]

The end of the Second World War and the advent of the nuclear era gave a new urgency to the debate on the need for unification. At the unification end of the continuum is Canada which, in 1968, took the extreme step of abolishing its army, navy, and air force and replacing them with the Canadian Forces—composed of land, air, and maritime elements—in which all military personnel wear the same uniform. Not far behind is Israel, where the general staff of the IDF serves as the operational directorate for all elements of the armed forces, and the CGS is the nation's senior officer and the supreme military echelon of command for all the IDF. At the same time, however, the air force and navy maintain separate staffs and different uniforms.[9] At the other end of the continuum is the United States. England and Germany remain in the middle, with England closer to unification and Germany closer to the United States.

Centralization, the civilian counterpart of unification, relates to the concentration of civilian control of the armed forces in the hands of a single political and civilian bureaucratic authority (ministerial authority, that is, not the ultimate civilian authority of the state). Huntington makes the rather evident point that the modern officer corps prefers to be subordinate to only one other institution—the civilian or small group of civilians exercising effective final authority—as was the case with the German general staff and the Kaiser during World War I, the American Joint Chiefs of Staff and President Roosevelt during World War II, and the British service chiefs and the prime minister–cabinet–CID for the better part of this century. Developments during the twentieth century, however, have made this position more and more untenable. The increased demands on the time and energies of the executive branch as a result of stepped-up government involvement in the various areas of social endeavor (especially in political and domestic affairs) coupled with the growing size, complexity, and diversity of the armed forces, have made it all but impossible for the chief executive to exercise effective direct control over the military. To put civilian supervision and direction of the armed forces solely in the hands of a president, prime minister, ministerial committee, or cabinet is to make a farce out of civilian control. It is for this reason that most, if not all, states have found it necessary to insert another level of political authority between the officer corps and the sovereign, normally in the form of a department minister who is supported by a full-fledged departmental bureaucracy, i.e., a minister or secretary and a ministry of defense[10] The interesting point here is that although the initial steps toward unification preceded any form of centralization, by now the process of centralization has by far outpaced that of unification. Today, although the individual services still retain some vestiges of independence in the military sphere, centralization of defense organization in the civilian sphere has been more or less fully realized.

Integration, the most recent trend of the triad, refers to the merging of civilian and military staffs dealing with essentially the same tasks into one integrated civil-military staff. Its basic aim is to eliminate unnecessary duplication and overlapping administrative structures (Dupuy lists no less than nine competing general staffs in the Pentagon) that result in repetitiveness, inefficiency, and massive waste and are prohibitively costly.[11] More and more states are moving toward integration—the creation of a single integrated civil-military administrative structure that will deal comprehensively with a given defense function. These structures are usually responsible jointly to the senior military and civilian personalities in the department or ministry and, through them, to the political head of the defense establishment.

The country that has moved furthest down the road toward integration is Canada. Although the 1968 abolition of the individual services, discussed earlier, drew more attention outside Canada, the truly "revolutionary change came in 1972, when Canada integrated its military and civilian headquarters in Ottawa." The entire defense headquarters was completely restructured, and the separate military and civilian divisions for various functional tasks were reorganized into a single integrated civil-military staff, consisting of five major groups or divisions. Each group is headed either by a civilian civil servant or a military officer, while the second in command—known as an associate—is from the opposite echelon. The entire integrated staff is responsible jointly to the chief of defense staff and the deputy minister (who is comparable to the British PUS, the Israeli director-general, or the American deputy secretary), who are viewed as coequals and are, in turn, responsible to the minister of national defense.[12]

All this said, it is vital to remember that almost all states (with the odd exception of Israel) have established staff and planning facilities to deal with national security at the highest government level. Indeed, the very first steps toward central civilian control of defense were taken at this level. Already in 1903, the British had established the ministerial CID, from which evolved today's Defence and Overseas Policy Committee. Headed, like its forebear, by the prime minister, this body is the standing committee of the cabinet for discussing and deciding foreign policy and defense issues; it is serviced by the Overseas and Defence Section of the cabinet secretariat. In the United States, the *National Security Act* of 1947 established the National Security Council (NSC), headed by the president; its function was to advise the president with respect to the integration of domestic, foreign, and military policies relating to national security. The legislation also stipulated that the council shall have a permanent staff. In Germany, the Bundeskanzleramt (BKA) is directly responsible to the chancellor and acts as the administrative and political center of Germany's national security system. In France, the main staff facility dealing with national security is the Secrétariat Général de la Défense Nationale (SGDN), attached to the office of the prime minister. It is only through these bodies that the ultimate civilian authority is able to achieve some reasonable balance with the military and to guarantee an appropriate degree of civilian involvement in the area of national security.[13]

Unification

In Israel, the IDF manifests a relatively high degree of unification although it falls short of the Canadian example.[14] *The Israel Defense Forces Ordinance* of May 1948, which established the IDF, stated in its first clause that "there is hereby established a Defense Army of Israel [IDF], consisting of land forces, a navy, and an air force."[15] The act thus spoke clearly of a single service while at the same time emphasizing that this single armed service consists of three different forces. This duality has left its mark on the IDF, which has been characterized throughout its history by two conflicting trends: a strong desire on the part of the air and naval arms for more independence, and a constant pressure by the general staff and the CGS for complete interdependence and for preservation of a unified command and staff structure. Contradiction abounds, even in details: for example, unlike Britain and the United States, but in line with the Canadian example, the IDF has a single set of rank designations and insignia; unlike the Canadian forces, however, it maintains different uniforms. (When referring to differences between the air force and the ground forces, Israelis speak of the blues versus the greens.)

With the conclusion of the War of Independence in 1949, a serious struggle broke out within the senior military echelon regarding the structure and organization of the IDF. The commander of the air force, General Remez, lobbied strongly for an independent air force organized as a separate service with its own chief of staff, along the lines of the British RAF. The CGS, Yigael Yadin, favored the preservation of a single unified military force. Ben-Gurion decided in favor of Yadin's position; nevertheless, the air force and navy were given their own staffs, which included the traditional functions of operations, manpower, intelligence, and logistics.[16] The air force never gave up its desire for more independence, from time to time skirmishing with the general staff. As years passed, it received high priority and grew steadily in strength, power, and prestige. This became more and more apparent, and after its spectacular victory in the Six Day War, its demands for recognition of its special status within the IDF grew. As CGS Dan Shomron is reported to have said, the Israeli Air Force's relationship with the IDF resembled that of "a foreign army but a friendly one."[17]

General Benny Peled, commander of the air force from 1972 to 1977, for example, contended that the air force was subordinate to the CGS only, claiming that the various branches and departments of the general staff—such as the chief of operations—function with regard to the air force in a coordinating capacity with no command authority. According to this line of thought, the general staff is a staff structure for the ground forces, and the CGS functions both as the chief of staff of the ground forces and as head of all defense forces, similar to the British chief of the defense staff (CDS) and far more powerful than the American CJCS. True to this approach, General Peled also maintained that he enjoyed the right of direct access to the defense minister.[18]

Needless to say, Peled's ideas—shared, at least in part, by other air force commanders—were rejected outright by successive chiefs of staff. Although the air force, because of its size, stature, and importance as well as its high standing in the eyes of the Israeli public, does enjoy certain trappings of autonomy not always shared by the navy, the accepted view is that while the general staff is—or, at least, was—a general staff headquarters for the ground forces, it also serves as a joint defense staff for the entire armed forces. Yariv described one of the functions of the general staff as constituting "what the famous Soviet World War II Chief of Staff General Shaposnikoff called the 'Brain of the Army' and [dealing] with short and long range overall concepts at the strategic and higher tactical levels." This view is supported by the fact that the chiefs of the air force and the navy are integral members of the general staff and by the fact that the heads of the general staff departments are usually senior in rank to their colleagues in the air and naval staffs.[19] The creation in 1983 of a headquarters for the field corps (artillery, infantry, armor, engineer, signal, and so on), which is taking over from the general staff more and more of the staff functions for the ground forces, gives this view even further credence.

In recent years, the air force has come closer to accepting the prevailing view and sees itself more and more as an integral part of the IDF. The main reason for this change of heart is the appointment during 1980s of senior air force officers to key positions on the general staff previously reserved for officers of the ground forces (positions that include the Deputy CGS, the head of the planning branch [G5], heads of other departments within the planning branch, the head of the manpower branch [G1], the head of the strategic planning department, the financial adviser to the CGS, the chief education officer, and others).[20] Such a relatively high degree of integration at the various levels of the general staff structure reinforces its unified nature and accentuates its role as a joint defense staff.

Yariv sums up Israel's staff structure by saying that "we do not, therefore, have an integrated staff structure. What we do have is integration in dynamics, that is, in the staff work at the highest military level, with the General Staff playing a somewhat senior role to the staffs in air force and navy headquarters."[21] Former CGS Gur notes that the existence of even semi-independent air and naval forces is an important contribution to civilian control because it prevents the military from speaking in one voice and allows the civilian authority to receive diverse opinions and evaluations on many key issues. As a result, there is a better chance that the minister of defense and perhaps even the prime minister will make the real decisions.[22]

Unification in the Israeli context also manifests itself in the strong military component at the central service level—namely, the general staff and the CGS. Like its civilian counterpart, this was instituted by Ben-Gurion, but the central role and immense power of the general staff and of the CGS do not simply reflect Ben-Gurion's inclination toward centralization and unification.[23] The multipurpose general staff is also Israel's response to its grave and complex security concerns. Israel's security environment is characterized by a constant state of war with its neighbors; a long-term condition of no peace and no war punctuated from time to time by short and violent wars; a need for constant preparedness; rapid transition from peacetime procedures to operations on a full wartime basis, at times with no warning at all; manifold day-to-day security duties, including prevention of terrorism, securing borders, and maintaining security in the Administered Territories; and frequent conduct of individual military operations, such as retaliatory raids, forays across the border, air attacks, and rescue operations. This security environment necessitates a military structure that can simultaneously raise, equip, and train the army, meet day-to-day security needs, and be flexible enough to move, without warning or at very short notice, from normal peacetime conditions to all-out war. In addition, Israel faces severe manpower and budget constraints. Ben-Gurion fully recognized that Israel could afford only a small and compact regular army—including a limited number of highly trained and dedicated senior officers—and would have to rely heavily on a sophisticated reserve system. The only way that such a small regular army could meet the myriad needs of Israel's security was by combining functions and by having key military structures as well as principal senior officers fill double and even triple roles.

As has already been shown, the general staff serves a double staff function: it is the joint defense staff of the IDF, Shaposnikoff's "Brain of the Army"—the policy-making level—and the headquarters or general staff of the ground forces—the operational level. Similarly, the CGS serves as chief of the defense staff (comparable to the British CDS or the American CJCS) and as chief of staff of the ground forces. However, the general staff also serves a third function, as a theater headquarters for all military operations. According to IDF doctrine, Israel and her neighboring Arab states constitute a single theater of operations; even so, it is still much smaller—both in area and in force size—than the United States Central Command (CENTCOM) or European Command (EUCOM). Using American terminology, one could say that the Israeli theater of operations constitutes a unified command—the general staff serving as operational headquarters for the unified command, and the CGS acting both as commander in chief (CINC) of the unified command and as commander of all ground forces. The chiefs of the air force and the navy serve, respectively, as commanders of the air and naval components of the unified command, under the overall guidance and command of the CGS.

Air and sea battles are directed centrally by the air force and navy headquarters, respectively. On the ground, the theater of operations is divided into three fronts, or arenas, roughly corresponding to the three territorial commands: northern, central (east), and southern. Land-air battles are conducted through the headquarters of the three territorial commands, under the overall direction and command of the CGS. The territorial commands have no air elements; all air support—both fixed-wing and helicopters—is allocated by the air force commander, subject to the ultimate decision of the CGS. Thus, in his capacity as CINC unified command, the CGS can determine—on the basis of the air force commander's recommendation and of developments in the land-air battle—how many aircraft are to be devoted to air defense or to strategic bombing and how many to close air support for ground operations; then, in his capacity as commander of the land battle, he can allocate air support to the various territorial commands. The IDF works on the principle of close lines, moving ground units from one territorial command to another and redirecting aircraft from one arena to another in midflight.

One could say that the Israeli CGS combines in one person the roles held by Eisenhower and Marshall in World War II. Or, drawing a comparison from the Gulf War, one could say that the Israeli CGS wears four hats: that of General Schwarzkopf, CINC Central Command (CENT-COM); that of General Colin Powell (the CJCS); that of the chief of staff of the United States Army; and that of the commander of the United States Army service component of CENTCOM, under General Schwarzkopf (COMDR ARCENT). A number of other senior officers also hold double appointments: a regular appointment to a staff function in the general staff during peacetime and an emergency appointment to a combat function—usually in a reserve unit—during wartime.

Of the few significant changes in the IDF's structure and organization since 1949, the most major stemmed from direct civilian involvement—in effect, dictated by Defense Minister Arens. The change, initiated in 1983, was the establishment of a headquarters for the field corps (FCH) that serves mainly as a staff structure for the ground elements of the IDF and thus assists—and is gradually replacing—the general staff in carrying out its function as general staff for the ground forces.[24] Arens had become a strong supporter of the FCH during his tenure as chairman of the FADC (1977–1982).[25] During that period, a subcommittee held discussions on the advisability of instituting the FCH—which had been proposed by then–Defense Minister Weizman—and came out strongly in favor of doing so. However, neither the parliamentary committee nor Defense Minister Weizman himself succeeded in overcoming the strong opposition of the general staff and the CGS.

On his becoming defense minister in 1983, one of the first decisions awaiting Arens was the appointment of a new CGS from among a number of candidates. Seizing the opportunity, he made the establishment of the FCH a condition for Moshe Levy's appointment to the post. Levy agreed but extracted one important concession from Arens—namely, that the new structure be established as a headquarters not for the ground *forces* but for the field (or ground) *corps*. As a result of this apparently minuscule change, the FCH took over from the general staff many of its staff functions with regard to the ground forces but none of its command functions as a theater headquarters responsible for the overall direction of the land battle. Since 1983, while the FCH has increased its authority with regard to force development, doctrine, personnel, training, and research and development of the ground forces, it has remained completely powerless as far as command and control of military operations is concerned.

The motive behind Levy's change was straightforward: every CGS wishes, in addition to his role as CINC of the unified command, personally to direct and control the land-air battle through the officers in command (O/Cs) of the three territorial commands. Recent chiefs of staff have been willing to restructure their *staff* role along the lines of a CDS, but all adamantly refuse to content themselves with the *operational* role of CINC. The result is a certain imbalance in IDF structure; the chiefs and staffs of the air force and navy operate on both the policy-making and the operational levels, fulfilling both staff and command functions, whereas the FCH and its chief are restricted to policy making and to a staff role.

For all its advantages, the general staff's multipurpose nature has caused it to become top-heavy. Today, it numbers at least twenty members: the CGS; the deputy CGS, who also heads the general staff and operations branch (G3); the heads of the four other general staff branches: personnel (G1), intelligence (G2), logistics (G4), and planning (G5); the chiefs of the air force, navy, and FCH; the heads of the three territorial commands; the head of the Training Division; the director-general of the Defense Ministry; the head of research and development, who also serves as the scientific adviser to the minister; the financial adviser to the CGS, who doubles as head of the Defense Ministry's budget division; the coordinator of activities in the territories; the military aides to the prime minister and the defense minister; and the comptroller of the defense establishment. A twenty-member body will find it very difficult to function as an effective policy maker.

Centralization

Centralization is the hallmark of Israel's civilian defense establishment. As noted in chapter 3, from the very inception of the state, civilian direction and control of the armed forces was concentrated in the hands of a single civilian bureaucratic authority—the Ministry of Defense. *The Israel Defense Forces Ordinance* spoke of a single service comprising land, naval, and air forces, but it left no doubt that all elements of the armed forces—whether genuinely unified or not—were subordinate to the central authority of a single individual—the minister of defense.[26] As early as 1946, the Zionist Congress decided that Ben-Gurion, in addition to his post as chairman of the Zionist Executive, would be in charge of the defense portfolio and directly responsible for the entire defense effort of the Yishuv.[27]

Centralization in Israel has reached a degree unprecedented in the Western world. That for close to half of Israel's history, the defense portfolio and the prime ministership were combined contributed enormously to the process, but even more important is the fact that Israel's large defense industry is directly controlled almost entirely by the Ministry of Defense (MOD). In many countries, the industrial base of the military-industrial complex is privately owned. In Israel, however, almost all the defense industries are either government companies (like Israel Aircraft Industries and Israel Military Industries) or administrative units of the MOD (such as the Weapons Development Authority). The MOD thus not only serves as the central civilian authority for the military and its support systems but also controls the entire military-industrial complex.

Integration

Integration directly affects and may even partially determine the relative influence of the two civilian and military echelons. In the absence of integration, defense functions are divided between the military and civilian components, resulting inevitably in a struggle over power, authority, and spheres of responsibility. Complete integration, as practiced, for instance, in Canada, is aimed at striking a proper balance between the two echelons, under the overall direction of the civilian political authority. In this area, Israel falls far short of its achievements in unification and centralization; indeed, it still lags behind most of the Western countries. Moreover, its record is not consistent; far from showing steady movement toward integration, there have been many ups and downs along the way.

Ben-Gurion's legacy included a distinct division between the military component (the IDF) and the civilian component (the MOD) of the defense organization.[28] He believed strongly that the officer corps should concentrate on military operations and that every effort should be made to minimize contact between the military and other government agencies and nongovernmental actors.[29] Convinced that Israel's very existence depended on the high moral fiber of the officer corps, he did everything possible to free the military from activities that corrupt the moral character of its members. (In late 1990, with the exposure of a major bribe and graft scandal in the senior echelons of the air force, the Israeli public and the IDF received a stark reminder of how right and wise Ben-Gurion had been.) On October 18, 1953, Ben-Gurion presented to the cabinet guidelines on the division of functions between the IDF and the MOD. According to these guidelines, the IDF would deal with fighting and preparations for war—i.e., all matters relating to military operations, at all levels, from the strategic to the tactical—whereas the MOD would be responsible for the entire fiscal and support system, including procurement and production, construction, real estate, rehabilitation, and finance.[30] All elements were, of course, subordinate to the Minister of Defense.

Ben-Gurion's model was clear, and theoretically it remains in effect to this very day. Yitzhak Rabin uses almost an identical formula when defining the roles of the two components: the function of the IDF is to present what it needs within budgetary constraints, and the function of the MOD is to determine how the various needs will be met. The reality, however, is far from being so simple. Over the years, mainly as a result of the many wars Israel has had to fight, the IDF has slowly but surely encroached on the MOD's domain.

Ben-Gurion's great mistake was that he did not formalize the structure or clearly define it legally or normatively, leaving it open to ambiguities and different interpretations.[31] Like many great leaders, he relied on the strength of his personality to ensure that his aims were met, and indeed as long as he remained at the helm, no one dared question his authority. But no sooner did he leave than problems arose, and the so-called wars between the Jews broke out. One of the major sources of friction between the military and civilian echelons during Lavon's short tenure as defense minister (1954) was over the question of who should have the final word on a major weapons system: for instance, CGS Dayan wanted to buy

French AMX tanks, while Defense Minister Lavon preferred old Sherman tanks.[32] Lavon went so far as to put forward far-reaching proposals for enhancing the authority and control of the minister by buttressing the civilian sector of defense and establishing firm rules regarding the relationship between the IDF and the MOD; however, Prime Minister Sharett rejected them, as did Ben-Gurion later on.[33]

Former CGS Gur states that the IDF has never come to terms with the division between the what and the how. Not satisfied with stating what sort of equipment it needs, the IDF also wants to dictate the source and the specific supplier, because the IDF officers, as professional soldiers and as the ultimate users, know best which source is preferable and which supplier has the best product. In his view, this struggle is an inherent feature of the system.[34] And in fact the MOD does have a serious problem maintaining all the professional expertise needed for the vast procurement job it has to perform (especially with regard to sophisticated systems used by the air force and the navy). The MOD, being a regular government ministry and a relatively small organization, is subject to stringent limitations on the number of people it can employ and on the working conditions it can offer. The IDF, on the other hand, operates and maintains huge quantities of equipment and enjoys much greater flexibility; it follows that within its ranks are large numbers of experts, especially in the air force and navy. As a result, in many instances the MOD is left with no alternative but to involve military personnel in all the stages of the procurement process.[35]

The military has also insinuated itself into the area of defense exports, which, by all accounts, should be a purely civilian function.[36] The MOD has a specific directorate responsible for this area and formally exercises sole authority over all export activities. However, exports of Israeli-developed systems can reduce their cost to the IDF and thus affect how much the IDF will be able to acquire. In many instances, the very development of a certain product or system for the IDF is conditional on foreign investment or an export order. Clearly, the military has a direct interest in furthering exports. And since the best promotion for Israeli products is their use and endorsement by the IDF, many Israeli industries and even the MOD itself have solicited the assistance of IDF officers in marketing as well as maintaining equipment. The IDF is also heavily involved in the marketing of surplus military equipment—an area that has grown rapidly in recent years and has become an important source of funds for renewal of IDF equipment.

The increasing involvement of the military in both procurement and export—two clearly defined civilian areas—is a cause of serious friction. It is a classic example of permeable boundaries. The current director-general of the MOD, David Ivri, has spoken out forcefully on this issue: "There are times when the IDF tries to intervene in matters in which it has no business, such as procurement, or negotiations with foreign firms. I am not willing to accept this. We are dealing with [what should be] a clear-cut division of authority and responsibility with regard to procurement and development of future weapons systems."[37] Ivri claims that encroachment by the military on areas of civilian authority occurs mainly during wartime or during times of increased security tensions. During such periods—certainly not rare in Israel—the preferences of the military take precedence, and it enjoys greater weight and influence. In peacetime, the pendulum usually swings back, but it may take quite a long time.[38]

Chaim Yisraeli, head of the defense minister's bureau since the early days of the state, emphasizes the importance of the personalities involved, especially those of the CGS and the director-general (D-G).[39] In his view, during Ben-Gurion's tenure—when Peres was D-G and later deputy minister of defense—control of the budget was largely in the hands of the civilian echelon. This was also the case under Eshkol, who also appointed a strong D-G (Kashti) as well as a deputy minister who dealt specifically with such matters, and continued under Dayan, who appointed a former CGS (Zvi Zur) as assistant minister in the capacity of a deputy minister. A significant change occurred during the tenure of Peres as defense minister and Gur as CGS. Gur, a strong and imperialist-minded CGS, was not counterbalanced by a strong D-G, and as a result the civilian echelon lost much of its control—especially on budgetary matters—to the IDF.[40] This trend continued under Weizman and Sharon.[41]

Gur admits that Peres, as defense minister, attempted to enhance the authority of the MOD, proposing that all IDF suggestions in the area of procurement and R and D go through the bureaucratic machinery of the MOD before being presented to the minister. If accepted, this proposal would have turned the MOD into a strong organization, along the lines of the office of the secretary of defense in the United States. Gur refused to cooperate, however, claiming that such a procedure would turn the general staff into a fifth level in the defense hierarchy. He insisted that IDF proposals be presented directly to the defense minister for discussion, at which time, of course, the D-G or anyone else from the MOD could put forth their reservations or alternative suggestions.[42] As might be expected Gur won, and Peres gave up the idea.

The appointment of David Ivri as director-general in the latter part of the 1980s halted, even partially reversed, the trend toward military domination of the defense establishment and significantly strengthened the civilian component. Ivri, a former air force commander and deputy CGS, came to the MOD with a lot of prestige and a great deal of experience. He was determined to restore a proper balance to civil-military relations within the central defense organization and, in his own words, was "not ready for anyone to undermine my authority or to interfere in my sphere of responsibility."[43] Ivri enjoyed the confidence of two defense ministers under whom he served: Rabin and Arens. He also benefited from the weakening of the CGS as a result of the intifada and other factors. Ivri himself states that the authority and responsibilities of the MOD are respected more than before and that especially in the fields of procurement and export the civilian echelon is reestablishing control.[44]

So where does Israel currently stand in terms of integration? At this point, two functions are fully integrated, while two others are partially integrated.[45] The first function—and the one first integrated—is that of the budget. The financial adviser–head of the budget (FA-HB) heads a relatively large integrated unit that deals with all budgetary matters at the MOD level and advises the CGS and the general staff on all economic and financial questions. The FA-HB is invariably a senior IDF officer, and the unit is staffed primarily by military personnel, for the most part IDF career officers, although it also employs civilians. The deputy FA-HB is traditionally a civilian, and the head of one of the four divisions within the unit is a civilian. The FA-HB participates, on a permanent basis, both in meetings of the general staff and in the senior MOD forum, headed by the D-G. The appointment is subject to the approval of both the CGS and the D-G.

There is a consensus that the integration of these two functions in one unit, especially under the direction of a single individual, facilitates coordination and cooperation between the military and civilian components and thus has a positive effect on the entire system.[46] There is less agreement about the advisability of this crucial position being occupied by someone from the military; however, any attempt to have this unit headed by a civilian—as is the case in almost all other countries—even on a rotational basis, would no doubt provoke intense opposition from the CGS and the general staff. The IDF insists that only a senior officer can adequately understand and address the complexity of military problems and that the CGS needs the advice of a soldier who can provide the proper economic perspective.[47]

In reality, however, the military's domination of this important function is primarily a means by which the IDF preserves its preeminent position and maintains a high degree of influence and authority in areas that in most other countries are considered beyond the sphere of responsibility of the military. A former FA-HB admitted openly that the IDF has a vested interest in the present setup because under it "the army has a central, if not decisive, influence on the budget."[48] Ivri states clearly that, from his perspective, the fact that the FA-HB is a member of the IDF and is dependent on the CGS has a negative effect, adding that in many instances the FA-HB comes to him as a representative of the CGS.[49] To compensate for the military's influence, in the early 1970s the MOD created the position of Economic Adviser of the Defense Establishment. This position is occupied by a civilian, who reports to the D-G and is in charge of a small unit consisting of twelve economists.[50] While this innovation does give the D-G an independent staff facility for economic and financial issues, thus enabling him to challenge some of the evaluations and assessments of the military, it falls far short of being a genuine and effective counterbalance to the far larger, powerful unit of the FA-HB.

Research and development is the second completely integrated function, and its integration has a long history. The general staff and operations branch (G3) of the general staff used to include a weapons development division; at the same time, the relatively large Chief Scientist's Office operated within the MOD. By 1971, tension between these two units was beginning to pose a serious problem. As a result, the CGS at that time (Elazar) and the defense minister's assistant (Zur) suggested to Defense Minister Dayan that both units be integrated into a joint R-and-D unit, to be headed by a senior officer (a brigadier general) who would report both to the CGS and the D-G. Dayan agreed but retained a chief scientific adviser, who headed a small bureau.

On attaining the post of defense minister in 1981, Ariel Sharon set out on an ambitious program of large-scale integration between the civilian and military components of the defense establishment.[51] Had he succeeded, defense organization in Israel today would look quite different and be far more advanced. As part of his approach, Sharon proposed combining the R-and-D unit, the procurement directorate of the MOD, and major elements of the logistics branch of the general staff (G4) into one large integrated unit that would deal with all aspects of acquisition from R and D, through local production, to procurement. The plan faltered as a result of sharp disagreement over whether the unit would be headed by a civilian or an IDF officer. Then, when there was finally agreement that the position would rotate between a civilian and a soldier, the Civilian Employees Committee of the MOD demanded that the first head be a civilian, while the IDF insisted that the unit be headed initially by an IDF general.[52] Sharon gave up; instead, he amalgamated the existing R-and-D unit, the chief scientific adviser's bureau, and a number of specific development projects into an enlarged R-and-D unit to be headed by a civilian who would report jointly to the CGS and the D-G and would also function as scientific adviser to the minister.

The integrated R-and-D unit has proved to be a success. It employs both civilians and military personnel. One division, dealing with R and D, is headed by a brigadier general; a second division, dealing with infrastructure, is headed by a civilian; and a third division, dealing with contractual arrangements, is also headed by a civilian. The head of the unit is a member of both the general staff and the senior MOD forum. The current head of the R-and-D unit, Uzi Eilam, claims that it shortens the decision-making process, facilitates coordination, prevents unnecessary functions and disagreement, and improves communications between the different echelons. Conflicts of interest between the military and the civilian sectors certainly remain, and in many instances the head of the unit must tread a cautious path, but the existence of the integrated unit allows the system to identify conflicts at a much earlier stage and thus deal with them more effectively.[53] The degree of integration achieved here is even greater than in the case of the FA-HB. The FA-HB reports both to the CGS and the D-G, but he is responsible to each for different functions: to the D-G for budgetary functions and to the CGS for advisory functions. The head of R and D, on the other hand, heads a completely integrated unit for which he is responsible jointly to the D-G and the CGS. At the same time, he is also responsible directly to the minister in his capacity as chief scientific adviser.

The two areas in which there is partial integration reflect what is perhaps the central problem of defense organization in Israel: namely, the absence of staff facilities for the minister of defense. The minister of defense does have a small bureau with a number of aides and advisers, but he has no planning or evaluation facilities of any significance. In those areas with which the MOD deals—finance, procurement, R and D, administration, defense industries and infrastructure, defense exports, and economics—the minister can at least benefit from the services of its civilian bureaucracy, although this bureaucracy has its own agenda and its own vested interests. However, in the key areas of intelligence and strategic planning—with which the MOD, unlike other modern defense organizations, is not involved—the minister is at the complete mercy of the military, with no independent check or control over its findings and activities. Over the years, the system has tried to resolve this structural and organizational dilemma—so far with little success.

In Britain, Canada, the United States, and many other countries, the civilian component is intimately involved with intelligence. In Israel, however, the MOD is completely excluded from any control over or even involvement in the area of intelligence.[54] To compensate for this, the director of military intelligence (DMI) is, to a certain degree, subordinate not only to the CGS but also to the defense minister. There is thus widespread—though by no means unanimous—agreement within the system that the DMI fills two roles, serving as head of the intelligence branch (G2) of the general staff, which is roughly comparable to the United States Defense Intelligence Agency, and, as such, subordinate to the CGS and holding the responsibility for preparing the national intelligence estimates and, as such, subordinate to the defense minister.[55] There are even those who claim that inasmuch as the DMI is charged with responsibility for the national intelligence estimate, he is also subordinate, to some degree, to the prime minister.[56]

In practice, there is a special relationship between the DMI and the defense minister, and in fact he can and does report directly to the minister. Further, with the establishment of the second National Unity Government in 1988, Prime Minister Shamir initiated the practice of meeting alone with the DMI once a month, for an in-depth intelligence briefing. Defense Minister Rabin approved this arrangement.[57] Arens, who strongly supports the view that the DMI is subordinate not only to the CGS but also to the defense minister and the prime minister, states emphatically that while serving as defense minister he never once felt that the DMI had any doubt as to his right and duty to present independent assessments to the prime minister and to the cabinet irrespective of the positions of the CGS and the defense minister.[58]

Yet this arrangement has never been formalized or normatively institutionalized. Indeed, nowhere can there be found a binding formal written determination that the DMI is responsible for the national intelligence estimates. Rabin claims that as prime minister (during his first government—1974–1977) he codified and defined the role of the DMI as having responsibility for "the national intelligence estimates for war."[59] Rabin thus does not accept the common perception that the DMI is responsible for the overall national assessment. Former defense minister Moshe Levy contests the entire concept that the DMI is also subordinate also to the defense minister. In his view, the DMI's contacts with the defense minister and the prime minister should be via the CGS. The DMI is always free to give his independent view to the minister and to the cabinet, as is any other IDF officer, but this has nothing to do with wearing a double hat.[60]

The situation with regard to strategic planning is far more complex, and it is probably the most serious and dangerous flaw in Israeli civil-military relations. Until 1969 there was no formal strategic planning in Israel, although within the general staff and operations branch (G3) of the general staff, there was a planning and organization division.[61] That year Defense Minister Dayan decided to establish a civilian strategic planning unit within the MOD. The IDF applied all its lobbying power to thwart this design and brought strong pressure on Dayan to incorporate this function within the IDF general staff. Dayan gave in and agreed to appoint General Tamir assistant head of the general staff and operations branch in charge of planning. In 1973, immediately after the Yom Kippur War, the planning unit was transformed into a full-fledged branch of the general staff—the planning branch (G5). No sooner was it established than it began to acquire considerable power, primarily because its establishment coincided with the start of intensive negotiations between Israel and her neighbors in the wake of the war, a process that eventually culminated in the Israeli-Egyptian peace treaty. The CGS charged the planning branch, as part of its strategic planning function, with preparing Israel's proposals for possible political arrangements (such as the separation of forces agreements) or political settlements. In other words, in the absence of any civilian policy-planning facility (either in the MOD or in the prime minister's office), the IDF took over control of the entire strategic and political planning process.

Aware of this anomaly, in 1975 Defense Minister Peres convinced the IDF to turn the planning branch into a joint unit, serving both the IDF and the MOD. Although a small number of MOD functions were transferred to the new joint unit (the planning of settlements and of defense industries), it was hardly an integrated structure. It remained essentially a military unit whose head wore two hats and was subordinate to both the CGS and the defense minister. This arrangement, however, became a source of serious friction. Tamir himself was caught up in a tug-of-war between the defense minister and the CGS.

In 1979 Defense Minister Ezer Weizman decided to correct the situation, allowing the planning branch to revert to the IDF with its own commanding officer and appointing Tamir as his own adviser on national security affairs, with a small staff. Ariel Sharon, appointed defense minister in 1981 under Prime Minister Begin, expanded this staff into a full-fledged national security unit (NSU). For the first time, the defense minister had at his disposal a significant independent staff facility for strategic planning. At its peak, the NSU had a staff of over twenty officers, including a major general, a brigadier general, and seven colonels. Unfortunately, however, the NSU became enmeshed in the ugly politics of the period, a symbol of the ill-fated Lebanon War and Sharon's undemocratic management style. It also earned the enmity of the IDF, which claimed that the NSU was becoming an alternative general staff. As a result, one of the very first decisions taken by Moshe Arens when he became defense minister in 1983 was to abolish the NSU, reverting to the previous arrangement by which the head of the planning branch was also subordinate to the defense minister. Naturally, both Arens and his D-G claim that their decision was based on objective reasons: the NSU was too large, represented an unnecessary duplication of the general staff, and created friction in the system. Nevertheless, one cannot escape the feeling that the NSU's entanglement in the politics of the period played at least some role in its demise.

Opinions differ as to how this arrangement has worked. Some claim that the subordination of the planning branch to the defense minister is more wishful thinking than reality. Naturally, most of the output of the planning branch is at the disposal of the minister and contributes heavily to his thinking and actions, but the branch itself remains a purely military unit, functioning as an integral part of the general staff under the direction and control of the CGS.[62] Former CGS Moshe Levy went so far as to say that he had never heard of the planning branch being an integrated unit until I brought it up.[63] Arens and Rabin, on the other hand, both strongly support the view that the planning branch is an integrated structure, although Rabin admits that the integration of the planning branch suffers from a basic structural flaw, inasmuch as—unlike R and D and the FA-HB—it is not subordinated to the D-G, as should be the case to guarantee effective integration.[64] The planning branch is subordinated to the D-G in the area of strategic cooperation with the United States, but this is because the heads of the American Group—from both the State Department and the Pentagon—are civilians, and thus Israel also found it necessary to send a civilian, i.e., the D-G of the MOD.[65]

The most recent chapter of the tale of strategic planning in Israel began in 1990. A few months after reassuming the position of defense minister, Arens announced that he was establishing a small advisory planning staff in his office. The move—which caught everyone, including the CGS, by surprise—was universally interpreted as a clear attempt by Arens to create means for maintaining an independent check on the work of the IDF. Arens emphasized that he was not—at this time—reestablishing the NSU, but the new structure was seen by many as a mini-NSU.[66] In April 1991, however, with the appointment of a new CGS and a new head of the planning branch, Arens suspended his plan for creating an independent unit in the office of the defense minister; instead, he reached an agreement with the new CGS (Ehud Barak) that the planning branch would be recognized as an integrated unit serving both the IDF and the MOD and that its head would report to both the CGS and the D-G.[67] With the head of the planning branch now subordinate to the D-G, the civilian echelon will be much more involved in the area of strategic planning. Only time will tell whether the attempt will be successful this time around.

Two other functions in Israel are part of the military component: legal services and public relations. Every army has an advocate general's office, but usually its sole function is to administer military justice (military courts, prosecution, defense, and so on); all questions of a legal or constitutional nature are handled at the civilian level of defense organization. In the IDF, however, there is a legal advice and legislative section within the advocate general's office. As a result, if the defense minister wants to fire a senior officer, there are two contradictory legal opinions: one by the legal adviser of the MOD and the other by the legal advice and legislative section of the advocate general's office. The same thing occurs when guidelines are prepared for defining the relationship between the defense minister and the CGS. The very fact that such a document is issued by the advocate general's office and not by the legal adviser of the MOD is a glaring instance of military involvement in political affairs. The same can be said for a phenomenon that would be inconceivable in other democracies: namely, that a uniformed officer of the IDF (from the legal advice and legislative section) may appear before the law committee of the Knesset and present the opinion of the IDF on legislation dealing with the functioning of the cabinet (for example, the creation of a statutory ministerial Committee on National Security with a permanent staff).[68] It is difficult to understand why the IDF needs a section dealing with legislation. Certainly, legislation is not an integral part of military operations; at the most, it is a support system that should be handled solely by the MOD.

The story is repeated in the area of public relations. A public relations officer by definition maintains close contact with the local and foreign press, with opinion leaders, and with many other segments of society, all of which are part of the civilian sphere. As Peri so aptly points out, reporting defense policy information is thus a civil-political activity par excellence, and this function usually falls to—or is at least shared with—the civilian component.[69] In Israel, though, not only does the IDF maintain a spokesperson, but that individual's office is a large organization, employing dozens of officers and enlisted personnel. The defense minister does have a media adviser, but this individual deals almost solely with the personal public relations of the minister as a senior political personality. The MOD, too, has a spokesperson who deals only with specific MOD matters. Naturally the defense minister can issue guidelines on public relations policy, just as he can in other spheres of IDF activity, but the actual implementation of all public relations on defense matters is performed by the IDF office, which is an integral part of the military organization, headed by someone subordinate solely and directly to the CGS. Clearly, public relations is not an integrated function.

The problems in such anomalous arrangements are evident in the case of military censorship. Emergency Defense Regulations promulgated in 1945 by the British authorities in Palestine and still in effect today in Israel grant the government wide-ranging authority to apply media censorship on security grounds. With the establishment of the state, Ben-Gurion reached an agreement with the editors of Israel's daily newspapers by which the censorship was voluntary—the government would not enforce the law with regard to Israel's major daily newspapers, and, in return, the editors of those newspapers would forward to the censor any material relating to matters of defense, security, or foreign affairs. All decisions of the military censor are, of course, subject to judicial review by the Israeli Supreme Court. Censorship of the press is certainly an example of direct involvement in the area of domestic affairs and may even, in certain circumstances, touch on the political process itself; as such, the function would seem to fall within the purview of the civilian component of the defense organization. Yet the censor under this arrangement, who also enjoys all the powers of censorship under the law, is a senior IDF officer.

One last point must be made. Two additional areas in the defense organization do reflect a certain degree of integration: coordination of activities in the Administered Territories and civil defense. In both these areas—at present or in the past—the people in charge wear two hats and are directly and jointly responsible to civilian and military authority. However, both these functions are examples of military intervention in the area of domestic affairs and are thus beyond the scope of this book.

6 | Relationships Among the Key Actors

This chapter looks at the informal relationships among the key actors involved in the Israel civil-military system, primarily to see whether they are significantly different from the formal relationships examined in depth in the previous chapters. Informal relationships are, of course, important everywhere, but especially so in Israel because it is such a small country, characterized by informal, even intimate, social interactions.

Cabinet–Prime Minister–Defense Minister

Until 1967, no relationship could exist among cabinet, prime minister, and defense minister, inasmuch as the posts of prime minister and defense minister were combined. Furthermore, during most of this period Ben-Gurion was at the helm of government, so the input and involvement of the cabinet was even more limited. Ben-Gurion did not question the principle of the government's collective responsibility for defense affairs and in the early years of the state—especially as long as Moshe Sharett was foreign minister—did indeed lose a number of important votes in the cabinet on defense matters. Nevertheless, he did come close to one-man rule; for example, in 1956, he presented the Sinai Operation—a decision to go to war—to the cabinet as a fait accompli.[1]

Ben-Gurion was an advocate of constructive ambiguity. He did not want a constitution, opposed defining the country's borders in the Declaration of Independence, and in the same vein refrained from defining the boundaries between the prime ministership and the Defense Ministry. It was only in December 1953, when Ben-Gurion retired for one year—during which the two posts were separated—that he decided that the civilian intelligence agencies, the Mossad and the Shabak, were to be under the control of the prime minister. (Before this, Peres, as D-G of the Defense Ministry had been involved in intelligence affairs, suggesting that Ben-Gurion had no absolute objection to the Defense Ministry being involved in intelligence; perhaps his decision was motivated by a certain distrust of Lavon, who was to succeed him as defense minister.)[2] And it was only in 1967 that atomic energy, nuclear research, and the nuclear center at Dimona were officially named the sole responsibility and jurisdiction of the prime minister, although Peres, as deputy defense minister, had been extensively involved in this area.[3] This last decision was a major victory for civilian control, paralleling the decision in the United States, after World War II, to establish the independent Atomic Energy Commission.

The appointment of Moshe Dayan as defense minister on the eve of the Six Day War, for the first time separating this post from the prime ministership, was a watershed in Israeli civil-military relations. It immediately became apparent that there was an urgent need to establish some guidelines for the newly created relationship between the prime minister and defense minister. Former CGS Yigael Yadin, representing Prime Minister Eshkol, worked out an agreement with Dayan, which was approved by Eshkol. The agreement contained two paragraphs: the first stipulated those actions that the defense minister would not take without prior approval of the prime minister—commencement of general hostilities against any country, military action in wartime deviating from fixed guidelines, commencement of military action against a country not yet involved in hostilities, bombing of central towns in enemy territory, and retaliatory action in response to incidents. The second paragraph stipulated those defense personnel whom the prime minister, with the knowledge of the defense minister, could invite to give information: the CGS, the DMI, the D-G of the Defense Ministry, and the defense minister's assistant.[4] The agreement, which made no mention of the cabinet, was voluntary, not binding legally or constitutionally.

After the Six Day War and with the onset of the War of Attrition, it became clear that this informal agreement failed to deal properly with the three-way relationship. The military secretaries of the prime minister and defense minister (Yisrael Lior and Yehoshua Raviv), with the active participation of Minister Galili, drew up a more detailed document, which was then formalized in an exchange of letters between the two ministries and brought to the attention of the CGS.[5] The document, unofficially known as "the constitution," outlined those military operations that the defense minister was authorized to approve on his own (such as reacting to fire from across the border or pursuing an enemy plane that had penetrated Israeli airspace), those of which the prime minister needed to be informed, those actions that were conditional on receiving the prime minister's prior approval, and finally those operations that had to be submitted to the cabinet or the MDC. Military operations not mentioned at all were supposedly within the authority of the CGS.[6]

The so-called constitution, as informal and voluntary as its predecessor, was never formally approved by the cabinet and had little, if any, legal or constitutional validity. It failed to become a permanent or significant feature of Israeli civil-military relations, and as years passed, it receded into the background. Of all the key actors active on the scene during the 1980s, everyone had heard of the constitution, but no one could tell me exactly what it said; even more important, no one could tell me where the document could be found.

The nature of the relationship is essentially a function of the personalities involved and, in particular, of the personal relations between the prime minister and defense minister. Both former defense ministers Weizman and Arens state that no clear policies define which issues need be reported to the prime minister and which actions require his prior approval; defense ministers often play it by ear, guided by custom, precedent, and the inclination of the prime minister.[7] Shamir, for instance, took much less interest in military detail than did Rabin as prime minister. Weizman, as defense minister, would notify the prime minister's bureau of planned aerial reconnaissance flights but did not ask for specific approval. Naturally, if the prime minister expressed an objection or asked for a postponement, the flight would be canceled.[8] Peres, having served in both capacities, sums it up by saying that each prime minister and defense minister must decide what issues he is genuinely interested in and on those issues reach agreement with the other.[9]

This is probably the most accurate description of what actually goes on. Both the prime minister and the defense minister have strong vested interests in mutual cooperation. If they stand together, they are almost unbeatable; apart, each walks on thin ice and can find himself very quickly in deep trouble. Without the support of the prime minister, the defense minister could find it very difficult to retain the confidence of the cabinet. Conflict and disagreement with the defense minister, who is seen as representing the IDF and the defense establishment, is a sure way to erode the popularity of the prime minister and public confidence in him. Nowhere has the saying "politics makes strange bedfellows" been realized more fully than in the relationships between Israeli prime ministers and defense ministers in the past twenty-four years. Not only have the two rarely been close friends or even political allies, but in most cases they have been political rivals. Yet they have almost always maintained a common front on key defense issues.

Dayan and Golda Meir almost invariably coordinated their positions on defense policy. The CGS would present proposals for military action to Dayan, and if Dayan approved, he would usually say to the CGS, "Now go and present the plan to Golda." On October 12, 1973, Bar-Lev (acting commander of the southern front) and Elazar (the CGS) presented the plan for crossing the Suez Canal to Dayan, who gave his approval. Elazar said that he wanted to bring the proposal to Golda Meir, to which Dayan agreed. The meeting with Meir was arranged, only for Elazar to find out that Dayan did not plan to attend. Elazar notified Dayan's military secretary that if the defense minister would not attend the meeting and openly support the plan, he saw no point in holding the meeting. Dayan relented and agreed to attend.[10] Elazar did enjoy free access to Golda Meir, but on issues that were within the authority of the defense minister, she almost invariably backed Dayan.[11]

The Entebbe rescue operation was proposed to the government jointly by Prime Minister Rabin and Defense Minister Peres. Had Peres proposed it without Rabin's support, it would never have had a chance of passing the cabinet. Had Rabin supported the plan with Peres opposing it, the cabinet also likely would have withheld approval.[12]

Begin went out of his way to support his defense minister, whether Weizman or Sharon. In one case, Defense Minister Weizman was interested in advancing a certain project and needed the support of another agency. The head of that agency was adamantly opposed to the whole idea until Prime Minister Begin ruled in Weizman's favor and instructed him to cooperate.[13] All the initial resolutions regarding the Lebanon War were proposed to the cabinet jointly by Begin and Sharon. Sharon knew only too well that without Begin's support he could never muster a majority in the cabinet and therefore made great efforts to keep Begin in his corner. Begin, for his part, kept quiet about a rift with his defense minister, only acting when Sharon completely overstepped his bounds and, by continuous bombing in Beirut, threatened to torpedo a political agreement for the evacuation of the PLO from Lebanon and to damage American-Israeli relations seriously. Unwilling to take any chances, Begin pushed through the cabinet a specific resolution prohibiting the use of the air force without explicit prior approval by the prime minister.[14] There was no precedent for such a restriction during wartime.

Although Shamir and Rabin were leaders of rival parties, their cooperation as prime minister and defense minister is almost legend. Throughout the intifada years, Rabin was subject to severe and even violent criticism from the right, including leading members and large segments of the Likud, yet he never lost Shamir's consistent support. During the Gulf War and the period preceding it, Shamir and Defense Minister Arens also presented a united front. The cabinet's decision not to respond to the Iraqi Scud missile attacks on Israel's cities reflected the joint position held by both men. It is difficult to tell what would have happened had they held opposite positions.

Israeli civil-military relations have also known clashes between these two key actors. Conflicts between the prime minister and defense minister arise in three circumstances: when a disloyal defense minister withholds information from the prime minister or offers inaccurate information; when a prime minister undertakes major political initiatives without the knowledge of the defense minister; and when a genuine disagreement exists between the two. There are only two examples of the first case, and both men were ignominiously ousted from their posts within a relatively short time. In the first instance, Pinchas Lavon acted disloyally toward Prime Minister Sharett, withholding information from him and trying to run the show by himself. The second incident involved Ariel Sharon. Begin's military secretary, Ephraim Poran, reports that Sharon demanded to be allowed to converse with the prime minister in private, without Poran's participation, because Poran frequently contradicted Sharon's reports and information; Begin, of course refused.[15] For that matter, the Lebanon War itself is perhaps the prime example of a strong defense minister intent on implementing his own policies and willing to manipulate the prime minister toward that end.

There is only one example of prime minister acting without the knowledge of his defense minister, and, surprisingly, that was Begin himself when he sent Foreign Minister Dayan to meet Tohamey in Morocco with a proposal for an Israeli-Egyptian peace settlement based on almost total Israeli withdrawal from the Sinai. This initiative had far-reaching ramifications for Israel's defense posture, for her security, and, of course, for the future deployment of the IDF, yet Begin pursued it in total secrecy, confiding only in Dayan and leaving Defense Minister Ezer Weizman, the CGS, and the entire defense establishment completely in the dark. The event was unprecedented in Israel's history, and, though it has not been repeated, it is perhaps the best evidence of real civilian control in Israel. But is undertaking such an initiative without the knowledge of the military or at least of the civilian-political head of the defense establishment consistent with healthy civil-military relations? Weizman claims that he was not hurt by Begin's action and believes that Begin was within his rights (he was merely peeved that Dayan used one of "his planes," a Westwind jet from the Israel Aircraft Industries, without telling him the true purpose). He admits, however, that this may only be so because he later came to play a key role in the peace process.[16]

There are, of course, a number of examples of genuine disagreements with no clear resolution. Begin strongly advocated the appointment of General Saguy—the DMI during the Lebanon War—as military attaché in Washington. Arens refused, arguing that the Kahn Commission of Inquiry after the Sabra and Shatilla massacre had ruled out any senior post for Saguy. Eventually, Begin gave in.[17] When Shamir was prime minister, he gave Secretary of State Shultz a private commitment, without Defense Minister Arens's knowledge, precluding a certain Israeli action against the PLO that the defense minister was strongly advocating. Arens had no choice but to accept the fait accompli.[18] Begin and Weizman had many disagreements regarding policies in the territories. These differences were brought to the cabinet or to the MDC for a decision.[19] The sharpest example of a harsh and open conflict between a defense minister and a prime minister is the cancellation of the Lavie project (which is discussed at length in the next chapter). Both sides put all their prestige on the line. The issue was brought before the cabinet, and Defense Minister Rabin won against Prime Minister Shamir by one vote. This victory, however, was achieved largely because of the strong support of the finance minister, a member of the prime minister's party and of the IDF, and the CGS.

Cabinet involvement in defense decision making has grown steadily since Ben-Gurion left power, with the volatile nature of Israeli politics probably also contributing to the cabinet's greater role. An additional factor is the increase in media coverage of defense issues. In the past, the defense establishment would iron out its differences on its own and then present the cabinet with a single operational plan (usually supported jointly by the CGS, the defense minister, and the prime minister) on a take-it-or-leave-it basis. In recent years, by contrast, the cabinet or the MDC has been asked to decide between options. For example, the Israeli action against PLO headquarters in Tunis in 1986 was originally brought before the MDC in two different versions: one, supported by Defense Minister Rabin and the air force commander, called for an aerial bombing; an alternative was presented by the CGS and his deputy. The MDC decided by majority vote (which, not surprisingly, included the prime minister) to authorize the bombing.[20] A second example relates to the Israeli withdrawal from Lebanon in 1985 and the creation of the security zone in south Lebanon. Rabin enabled the O/C northern command to appear before the MDC and present his conception of the security zone, which differed from Rabin's. The MDC approved the defense minister's proposals.[21]

Finally, one should mention cabinet involvement in aspects of force development and resource allocation—i.e., decisions related to R and D and the procurement of weapons systems—although this is still in its embryonic stage. The decision on the cancellation of the Lavie project is an example of such involvement, if motivated, to a large degree, by the internal political debate. A bitter controversy within the IDF regarding the acquisition of submarines was also referred to the MDC.

Prime Minister–Defense Minister–Chief of Staff

The relationship among prime minister, defense minister, and CGS is the hub of Israeli civil-military relations. A serious breakdown in the working relations of these three actors or a basic lack of cooperation and trust within the trio could easily have disastrous consequences for Israel in general and for the civil-military system in particular. Such a situation has occurred only twice in Israel's history—during 1954 with Sharett, Lavon, and Dayan, and in 1981–1983 with Begin, Sharon, and Eitan. In both cases, the conflict led, in almost no time, to dire results that posed a grave threat to the very integrity of the system. These two events, almost thirty years apart, have evidently had a salutary effect on all other figures occupying these three posts; in any case, their relationship has for the most part been smooth, or at least correct.

Peri describes the relationship within this trio during much of Israel's history as one where two rival political sub-elites vie for power, with the CGS taking sides with one or the other, thus enhancing his own authority and freedom of action.[22] The facts, however, offer little evidence to support this theory. Apparently, chiefs of staff have realized that to act in this manner would destabilize the system—a consequence that would only make their lives more difficult. Thus CGS Elazar—though strongly identified with Golda Meir—refused to present his plan for the crossing of the Suez Canal to her without the presence and support of the defense minister. Former CGS Bar-Lev states categorically that he never presented recommendations or proposals for military action to Prime Minister Meir before having presented them to Dayan and received his approval. He admits to having been closer politically to Golda Meir but closer personally to Dayan. Former CGS Gur also emphatically denies that "he played ball" with Defense Minister Peres against Rabin. He claims that Rabin knew that his CGS was loyal to government policy and always gave his own independent opinions. In support of this statement, he cites the case of Entebbe, where he sided with Rabin and resisted attempts by Peres to approve a premature and improperly prepared rescue operation. Former CGS Eitan says that it is certainly very important and helpful to the CGS for him to be known to enjoy the strong support of the prime minister—as he did with Begin. But it is something that should be kept in the background and never used.[23]

As with the relationships discussed previously, the nature of this relationship is influenced to a very large degree by the personalities involved and by the personal relations among the three actors.[24] For instance, Weizman points out that as defense minister he enjoyed a much better relationship with CGS Eitan than he did with Gur. While his relations with Gur were strained, he and Eitan would "close matters privately over a glass of good brandy." True, Weizman inherited Gur and appointed Eitan, but in Weizman's view, the difference was primarily a matter of "personal chemistry."[25]

The importance of personalities is evident in the interesting phenomenon whereby the influence of a given CGS changes dramatically with a new defense minister. Rabin as CGS under Eshkol enjoyed immense power and authority.[26] Some even go so far as to claim that Rabin was the de facto defense minister or that Eshkol was Rabin's political adviser. Rabin says that this is pure legend and that Eshkol was involved in armed forces affairs to a greater degree than Ben-Gurion. Furthermore, he asserts that he had less influence under Eshkol than did Dayan as CGS under Ben-Gurion—a view that enjoys considerable support.[27] It seems more accurate to say that during the Eshkol-Rabin period the CGS acquired, for the first time, a more visible political role and became a politico-military personality. The outward manifestation of this development was the frequent participation of the CGS in cabinet and/or MDC meetings—something unheard of and unthinkable under Ben-Gurion.[28] Be that as it may, no sooner did Dayan become defense minister than Rabin was shunted aside to assume a more circumscribed and less influential role.[29] The same thing happened to Gur, who under the Rabin-Peres team was certainly one of the strongest and most influential chiefs of staff but under Begin-Weizman lost much of his clout.

There are, of course, alternative explanations for these changes in the standing of the CGS. Changing political conditions might be responsible. Or, as in both of the examples just given, a defense minister with little or no military background may be replaced by someone who had previously been a very senior IDF officer (Dayan was a former CGS, Weizman, a former air force commander and head of the operations branch).

The debate over whether the appointment of a former senior military officer as defense minister increases or undermines civilian control is an old one. In the Soviet Union, the defense minister is invariably a professional military officer; in the United States, on the other hand, the law stipulates that the secretary of defense must come from civilian life, and no former military officer may serve in the post for ten years after leaving the service. Peri claims that the appointment of former generals as defense ministers in Israel is an expression of the country's political-military partnership and an indication of weak civilian control mechanisms.[30] Weizman, on the other hand, feels that the greatest danger to civilian control in a democracy is the military's perception that it can exert inordinate influence on national security policy as a result of the political echelon's lack of familiarity with and lack of in-depth understanding of complex politico-military issues. This danger is averted by a defense minister with military experience, who knows only too well the inside workings of the IDF. This view is supported by others, such as Eitan, who states that because of Israel's security situation as a country in a constant state of war, there is a definite advantage to having a defense minister with extensive professional military knowledge.[31] In addition, a chief of staff will usually try to test a new defense minister to see how far he can go; a defense minister with many years of prior military experience in the IDF may cope better with such challenges. All in all, it seems that while there is no evidence whatsoever—with the possible exception of Sharon—that former IDF generals acting as defense ministers have compromised civilian control, there is also no evidence that they enhance civilian control above and beyond defense ministers who come from civilian life.

The nature of the working relations that develop among the members of the trio is influenced to a certain degree by the military secretaries of the prime minister and defense minister. The military secretaries are not involved in policy making and serve mainly as channels of communication. Information is a key commodity in the system, however, and its smooth and speedy flow is essential for a proper working relationship. As politicians, both the prime minister and the defense minister are involved in many other activities—primarily of a political and public nature—and therefore much of the business between them and the CGS is conducted between their respective military secretaries and the CGS bureau. Both military secretaries are, of course, senior IDF officers, and it is accepted practice for them to maintain direct and frequent contact with many senior IDF officers (such as the chiefs of the air force and navy, and the O/Cs of the territorial commands) for the purpose of obtaining information. In this way both the flow and the accuracy of the information is facilitated. Today, in fact, information no longer flows vertically, i.e., through channels up to the CGS, to the defense minister, and to the prime minister; rather, it flows horizontally, i.e., simultaneously to the CGS, the defense minister, and the prime minister, via the military secretaries.[32] It is not surprising that the military secretary can, if he so desires, prevent or smooth over many misunderstandings. He can also, of course, work in the opposite direction, although there are few if any such examples.

The major issue all defense ministers and chiefs of staff need to address is the informal definition of their working relationship. In effect, this is a question of the professional autonomy of the military, about which they, usually and not surprisingly, hold different views. Many a CGS advocates the proposition that within the IDF he should be free to do, more or less, as he sees fit; only when the IDF must interact with an outside factor—whether it be the enemy, the United States, or a part of Israeli civilian society—should the defense minister come into play. Very few defense ministers, if any, are willing to accept such a narrow definition of their role. This was the essence of the bitter conflict between Dayan as CGS and Defense Minister Lavon in 1954. Dayan held that the authority of the defense minister should be limited to decisions of war and peace and to financial control over the army. In his view, all professional and technical matters—down to which tank to acquire—were the exclusive province of the CGS, who was meant to be the sole link between the uniformed military and the political masters. Lavon held that the minister was empowered to oversee the army's activities in all spheres and to enjoy free and direct access to all echelons of the IDF; he saw the chief of staff as little more than an executive officer.[33]

Today, hardly anyone would advocate the extreme position of professional autonomy put forth by Dayan in 1954—least of all Dayan himself as defense minister in 1967. Already in 1952 Ben-Gurion had decided to cut the defense budget drastically and to fire thousands of IDF officers and personnel. When CGS Yadin claimed that he could not take responsibility for such cuts, Ben-Gurion's response was "I am responsible," and he accepted Yadin's resignation.[34] Virtually everyone now accepts that the defense minister has the right to dictate organizational changes in the IDF or to veto changes proposed by the CGS—both of which Arens and Rabin have done more than once.[35] In line with the rest of the Western world, the IDF, too, has come to terms with the defense minister's greater authority and involvement. There is, however, one prerogative that no CGS is willing to forgo, one issue on which the military is not ready to compromise: namely, that the CGS be heard and that his opinion be considered, i.e., that he should be part—at least in an advisory capacity—of the decision-making process. This crucial point was poignantly made by Janowitz over thirty years ago: "Fundamentally, this means that civilian supremacy is effective because the professional soldier believes that his political superiors are dedicated men who are prepared to weigh his professional advice with great care. At a minimum, military leaders want to be assured that they will have effective access to the seats of power."[36]

In Ben-Gurion's days, the participation of the IDF's high command in the national security decision-making process ended with Ben-Gurion—because the decision-making process itself ended with him. This began to change with Ben-Gurion's exit from national leadership. Indeed, Rabin speculates that the dramatic increase in the frequency of attendance by the CGS, and, in many instances, by the DMI as well, in cabinet and MDC meetings during Eshkol's administration stemmed from a change in the status not of the CGS but of the cabinet and the MDC.[37] These bodies, and especially the MDC, became genuine national security decision-making forums.

The IDF zealously guards its right to participate in whichever body is the de facto decision-making forum, as when O/C Northern Command David Elazar insisted in June 1967 that he be permitted to appear before the entire cabinet and present his case in favor of taking the Golan Heights (the opposite of Defense Minister Dayan's position)—a request that Eshkol eventually granted. The IDF dominates strategic planning in Israel and thus almost always has "effective access to the seats of power" and ample opportunity to present its views to the government. If and when this all-important access is called into question, there is apt to be trouble, and one can expect noise in the relationship. Former CGS Moshe Levy explains that the reason Weizman as defense minister failed to implement the field corps headquarters (FCH) while Arens succeeded was that Weizman tried to force it on the IDF from above without giving the army a fair chance to present its case: Weizman announced it to the press and appointed General Tal to the task before coordinating it with the CGS and the general staff; Arens worked with and through the CGS.[38]

In 1971, when the cabinet discussed Kissinger's proposal for the opening of the Suez Canal, Defense Minister Dayan strongly supported the idea, although both the IDF and Prime Minister Golda Meir had serious reservations, especially regarding the degree of Israel's withdrawal. Dayan attempted to prevent the general staff from presenting the cabinet with its position—which was at odds with his own—claiming that the issue was political and thus one in which the general staff had no say. Bar-Lev, as CGS, insisted on his right to give the cabinet the general staff's independent view, and Golda Meir eventually ruled in his favor.[39]

An even more extreme example is the case of CGS Gur and the negotiations on a separation of forces agreement in the Golan Heights in May 1974. Gur participated in the actual negotiations with Kissinger. One evening, Prime Minister Meir called Gur—who had been raising various suggestions during the negotiations that angered Defense Minister Dayan—and told him that Kissinger had returned from Damascus and his personal report to her indicated that the talks had failed. The following morning, the full negotiations team met, and Kissinger presented his proposals, which, according to Gur, were quite different from Golda Meir's version. Gur then sent a note to Meir, saying that "on the basis of what Kissinger said, I have some new suggestions." The prime minister, whose face did not hide her anger, asked for a recess and convened the Israeli delegation in private. Both she and Dayan strongly upbraided Gur for undermining Israel's position and for constantly raising unnecessary suggestions. Gur responded, "You don't have to invite me to the negotiations, but if you do, anytime I have something to suggest, I will suggest it to you. You don't have to accept my suggestions or ideas, but you cannot prevent me from suggesting them. I participate in cabinet meetings and know that the government wants to reach an agreement with the Syrians. If I am convinced that we can reach such an agreement without compromising our security, it is my duty to the government to say so." In the end, Gur presented his proposal, and Golda Meir accepted it.[40]

The CGS is by no means a secret partner in the government. He is not present during discussions on domestic affairs—economic, social, religious, legislative, or internal political—and even if he were present, he would never offer an opinion on such issues. In this sense, he does not have the same status as the attorney general, who acts as the legal adviser of the government and, as such, participates on a permanent basis in cabinet meetings and offers opinions on any issue. Nevertheless, although few question the propriety of the CGS's participation in the MDC, his presence in the cabinet is another story. The cabinet meets weekly, on Sunday mornings, and for the past few years (especially since the outbreak of the intifada) every such meeting is usually opened with a report on security and defense matters given by the CGS or some other senior IDF officer.[41] The number of senior IDF officers participating in cabinet meetings is constantly on the rise.

Peres severely criticizes the present situation. In his view, "the natural place for the CGS to be is the general staff, while for the defense minister and prime minister it is the cabinet." Israel's leading military correspondent, Zeev Schiff, and Chaim Yisraeli, head of the defense minister's bureau for over four decades, emphasize the danger of a breakdown of the boundaries between the military and civilian systems as a result of open, all-out discussion between cabinet ministers and IDF officers. They also feel that civilian control and proper civil-military relations can crumble when officers witness acrimonious debates between ministers. Weizman, too, objects to the exaggerated presence of the CGS at cabinet meetings. He believes that the defense minister, not the CGS, should report on defense matters, just as the police minister, not the inspector general of the police, reports on internal security. His opinion is that the CGS should be invited to attend cabinet meetings only in times of war or before major military operations (such as Entebbe).[42]

On the other hand, former CGSs Eitan and Levy not surprisingly strongly support the participation of the CGS in cabinet meetings. The rationale behind their view is that inasmuch as the government is the commander in chief of the IDF, it is only appropriate that those charged with responsibility for the army should hear the army directly from its supreme command level and not only via the defense minister. Eitan adds that participation of the CGS in cabinet meetings is beneficial for both the CGS, who can better comprehend the government as a result, and the ministers, who benefit from a firsthand and uncolored exposition of the military's views. Gazit makes the point that CGS participation in cabinet meetings acts as a check and control over the defense minister.[43]

The IDF in general, and the CGS in particular, insist that ample weight must be given to the military view not only on strategic issues or on questions of force development and resource allocation but first and foremost on operational issues. The IDF high command believes deeply that the government should not order it to undertake action that goes against its better professional and military judgment; to do so would be a cardinal infringement of professional autonomy. The government may, of course, refuse to approve or severely limit military action, even if strongly recommended by the general staff, for political or other reasons—as was the case during the waiting period prior before the Six Day War or with the refusal to approve a preemptive airstrike on October 6, 1973. But to compel the IDF to engage in military activities to which it is utterly opposed and that it deems not feasible or ill-advised is something that simply is not done.

This issue—probably one of the most explosive in this entire area—could create a grave crisis in Israeli civil-military relations. So far, with the exception of Latrun, there has been no such case in Israel's short history—although there have been close shaves. During the Entebbe affair, CGS Gur had serious reservations about the feasibility of a rescue operation, although many of his subordinates, as well as Defense Minister Peres, were forceful advocates of such an operation. Gur extracted a promise from Peres that he would not recommend to the government a rescue operation unless it was supported by Gur. Many plans were overruled, and only after fresh intelligence was received from Entebbe was Gur ready to support the rescue operation.[44]

During the Gulf War in 1991, CGS Dan Shomron and his deputy and CGS-designate, Ehud Barak, both strongly advised against an Israeli response to the Iraqi Scud missile attacks. There was serious concern among the IDF high command that in view of the government's composition, the cabinet might succumb to the pressure of its right-wing members and order an attack on Iraq despite the military's opposition. The CGS was reported to have remarked that never in Israel's history had the government ordered the IDF to act against its will and against its better judgment, and it was inconceivable that it should do so. There are also reports that both Shomron and Barak made this point rather strongly in private conversations with Prime Minister Shamir.[45] Perhaps Shamir had his own good reasons for not reacting or maybe he was swayed by the IDF's position; in any case, as already noted in the introduction, Israel sat out the war—belying statements made by its political leaders before January 1991.

In the difficult early days of the intifada, the IDF was under heavy pressure from certain ministers to use a far greater degree of force against the Palestinians in the territories. At one stage CGS Dan Shomron is reported to have threatened, at least implicitly, to resign if the army were forced to act against its moral code.[46]

One of the most severe—and until now little-known—civil-military confrontations in Israel's history broke out over this issue. In late 1975, supporters of the Greater Israel movement established an illegal and unauthorized settlement at Sabastia on the West Bank. The army ordered the squatters to leave. The Greater Israel movement mobilized thousands of supporters and, in defiance of government decisions, announced that the settlers refused to move and would resist any attempt by the army to remove them forcibly. Prime Minister Rabin saw in this action a direct challenge to the government's authority bordering on open rebellion and ordered CGS Gur to remove the settlers by force. Gur objected strenuously, claiming that it was impossible to accomplish such a mission without the use of live fire, which would endanger Jewish lives. Without specifically mentioning the use of live fire, Rabin reiterated his demand that Gur use as much force as necessary to remove the settlers. Gur flew to the scene and on returning repeated his deep conviction that the mission was totally unfeasible and would have disastrous results for the IDF and for Israel for years to come. He claimed that although the settlers were acting against the law, they were not trying to overthrow the government; therefore the use of massive force by the army was unjustified. Without saying so explicitly, Gur implied that if Rabin insisted on the use of force, he might resign rather than obey the order.[47] In the end, Rabin backed down, probably influenced not only by Gur's position but also by the lack of support from Defense Minister Peres and pressure from his own political backers. In an interview given fifteen years later, Rabin listed as his greatest mistake the fact that he did not act much more forcefully toward the defense establishment, which did not function properly during the Sebastia incident.[48]

Irrespective of the personal relationship between the defense minister and the CGS, it is always apt to involve a battle of wills. After examining the evidence, it seems safe to say that the defense minister generally keeps the upper hand. In order to achieve and maintain effective control over the defense establishment, however, the defense minister must meet four conditions: he must be convinced that he is right; he must be ready and willing to assume responsibility for the successes and failures of the IDF and be ready to accept the consequences; he must be determined to stand behind his decisions, even if one leads to the resignation of the CGS; and, finally, he must have the support of the prime minister.[49]

A short anecdote will demonstrate how powerful a defense minister can become. One Saturday morning, Defense Minister Dayan flew from Tel Aviv to Sharm-a-Sheikh for an inspection tour. The air force plane stopped over at an air base in the south to pick up the O/C southern command, who had decided to take along his wife for the day. Dayan slept through the landing and takeoff at the air base. When he woke up, he asked who the lady was. On being told, he ordered the pilot to return to the air base and put her off the plane. Even though Dayan had no legal right to issue such an order, the pilot unhesitatingly obeyed.[50] Had the O/C southern command contradicted the defense minister's order— which he had the good sense not to do—the pilot would probably have radioed the air force commander for instructions and, no doubt, would have been told to obey Dayan.

One last example should illustrate that when the four conditions are met, the defense minister will, indeed, have the upper hand. In early 1984, it became clear to the general staff that the IDF's position in Lebanon was becoming untenable and a further withdrawal was essential. The CGS, Moshe Levy, with the support of the general staff, pressed strongly for withdrawal and for a redeployment of the IDF southward, arguing that the continued presence of the IDF along the existing lines would have extensive negative effects on the morale, training, and preparedness of the army. Arens, fresh from civilian life, refused to accept the general staff's proposal, claiming that he, as defense minister, had a different strategic concept and a different set of priorities. Arens was convinced that he was right, was willing to accept responsibility, had the support of the prime minister, and was not ready to give in; the result was that the CGS backed down and accepted the ruling of his civilian superiors.[51] It was only a year later, after the establishment of the National Unity Government and the replacement of Arens by Rabin, that the IDF finally withdrew from Lebanon to the security zone.

As a last resort, the CGS can always appeal to the prime minister. Former CGS Eitan says that although he rarely found it necessary, he never hesitated to approach to the prime minister, even in opposition to the defense minister and without his approval. On the other hand, he said, he would never have gone to the cabinet without the prime minister's permission. (In one instance, Begin did enable Eitan to bring a disagreement between them to the cabinet; as could be expected, the cabinet supported Begin.) Eitan enjoyed direct access to Begin, often meeting with him privately but always notifying the defense minister beforehand. On many occasions, he spoke with the prime minister by telephone.[52]

On assuming the post of CGS, Gur was told by Defense Minister Dayan: "You will report everything to me, and I will report to Golda."[53] From a formal point of view, however, it seems that the CGS enjoys access to the prime minister, if only through the defense minister and with his approval.[54] In practice, certainly, the CGS seems to have no problem bringing issues before the prime minister, and it is difficult to conceive of a defense minister even attempting to prevent a CGS from having free contact with the prime minister.[55] Levy emphasizes the importance of the right of direct access and of the need to formalize this right in law. In his view, the CGS should have to notify the defense minister about meetings with the prime minister or any other minister, but such contacts—certainly with the prime minister—should not be dependent on the defense minister's approval.[56]

Under what circumstances, then, would the civilian authority seriously consider the dismissal of the CGS? The constitutional position (outlined in chapters 3 and 4) is clear: the defense minister cannot dismiss the CGS; the government can, at any time, on the recommendation of the defense minister. Dismissal of the CGS therefore requires the recommendation of the defense minister, the readiness of the prime minister to bring the issue before the government, and a majority in the cabinet. By constitutional convention, the CGS is appointed for three years, and afterward the government can extend his tour of duty for yearly periods. Most chiefs of staff have served for four years.

There is no precedent in Israel's history for the outright dismissal of a CGS. Two chiefs of staff have resigned: Yadin, in 1952, as a result of rift with Ben-Gurion over the defense budget; and David Elazar, in 1974, in the wake of the Agranat Commission report that found him responsible for the failures of the Yom Kippur War. There is one case where a defense minister was determined to dismiss the CGS for insubordination but was prevented from doing so by a combination of circumstances and the prime minister's opposition.

A few days before Sadat's historic visit to Jerusalem on November 21, 1977, a major Israeli daily newspaper headlined an interview with CGS Gur, in which Gur stated that Sadat's visit was a hoax and a pretext for war. The interview was given without the approval or knowledge of the defense minister or the prime minister. Gur admits that this constituted an act of insubordination but attributes it to the unprecedented phenomenon, outlined earlier, of a prime minister (Begin) undertaking a major political initiative with far-reaching consequences for Israel's security without any consultation or discussion with the IDF. Gur states: "This was my way of protesting the fact that there had been no proper discussion in the cabinet and that I was not given an opportunity to present to the cabinet the views of the general staff."[57]

On reading the interview, Defense Minister Weizman was furious and ordered Gur, who was on a secret visit to Iran, to return to Israel immediately. Gur went straight from the airport to Weizman's office, where the defense minister severely reprimanded him. Gur explained his reasons for giving the interview and suggested that Weizman not dismiss him, since no serious damage had been done, but stated that if Weizman decided to do so, he would salute and leave without a word. Gur left the meeting with the impression that the defense minister would be satisfied with a joint statement. Weizman, however, immediately telephoned Begin and demanded that Gur be dismissed forthwith, arguing that it was inconceivable that at such a historic moment a chief of staff should issue a statement that could easily sabotage the government's policy. Begin was skeptical and did not give his agreement. Weizman decided to drive to Jerusalem to urge Begin in person to approve Gur's immediate dismissal. On the way, there was an accident; Weizman suffered a multiple leg fracture and was hospitalized for a week. He claims that had he not been derailed because of the car accident, he would have convinced Begin; Begin himself told Gur a number of years later that Gur should thank him for not letting Weizman fire him.[58]

The fact that no CGS has ever been dismissed is not a fluke, but it reflects less the popularity of the CGS than a perception deeply held by civilian and military alike that such a dismissal would have a traumatic effect on the Israeli public's sense of security and could potentially undermine the deterrent image of the IDF. This perception acts as a strong brake and greatly enhances the power of the CGS, and it is almost unanimously supported by the interviewees.[59] Former defense minister Arens admits that he would recommend the dismissal of the CGS only if he were totally unsuitable for the job or blatantly insubordinate. He would never even consider dismissing the CGS for making unauthorized statements (as in the case of Gur) or for delaying the implementation of appointments or programs authorized by the defense minister. Former CGS Bar-Lev thinks the defense minister would have grounds for dismissing the CGS if the CGS were not up to the minimum standards of the job, if there had been a major military catastrophe, or if the working relationship between the two suffered a total breakdown. In Rabin's view, only a grave and blatant challenge to civilian authority would justify the dismissal of the CGS.[60]

Defense Minister–Chief of Staff–Director-General

There is no genuine three-way relationship among the defense minister, the CGS, and the director-general, for the simple reason that the CGS and the D-G work in different circles with very little overlap. The main point of contact between the two is the defense minister, but, even there, contact is usually within a much wider context.

The relationship is characterized by a basic asymmetry. The CGS is involved in all aspects of defense organization. The most important function of the MOD, the budget, is headed by a military officer who doubles as financial adviser to the CGS. R and D is an integrated function, and such functions as procurement and construction—although formerly under the sole jurisdiction of the D-G—are also closely coordinated with the IDF. The D-G, on the other hand, has little or no involvement in military affairs. He is a member of the general staff and is invited to attend its meetings, just as he is welcome to participate in almost all discussions at the ministerial level. In practice, however, military affairs are considered off-limits to the D-G. Ivri, the D-G under Arens and Rabin, states that not only does he have nothing to do with intelligence or operations, but, in principle, he does not intervene or even offer an opinion on matters that are the responsibility of the IDF, such as priorities among the various elements of the armed forces. This line of thought is echoed strongly by former defense minister Arens, who admits that he "sees no reason why the D-G should be involved in any way in purely military affairs." He emphasizes that in Israel there is no tradition for such involvement and that, indeed, there is "no justification for it."[61]

A good illustration of the total involvement and power of the CGS is provided by former CGS Gur. One day, the FA-HB reported to CGS Gur that, contrary to the estimates of the MOD's purchasing office in New York, three hundred million dollars of surplus American aid had not yet been used or committed. Gur demanded that a joint examination of the accounts be conducted in the New York office with the participation of the IDF. The D-G refused, arguing that this was a purely civilian matter. Gur threatened that if the IDF were not be allowed to participate in an in-depth examination, the general staff would refrain from presenting requests for the next years, essentially bringing procurement activity to a halt. Defense Minister Peres ruled in favor of the CGS, and a significant surplus was, indeed, found.[62]

The key to this relationship lies with the defense minister, and it is he who determines the relative influence of the CGS and the D-G. This is clearly illustrated in the example of Shimon Peres. Probably no D-G had as strong and far-reaching an influence on defense organization and on the overall defense posture of the country as Peres had in the fifties and early sixties, both as D-G and as deputy minister under Ben-Gurion; this was so primarily because he enjoyed Ben-Gurion's complete confidence. The establishment of Israel's defense industries (Israel Aircraft Industries, Israel Military Industries, Israel Shipyards, and so on) was a direct result of civilian initiative instigated by Peres. The decision to undertake extensive R and D aimed at missile development (air-to-air, sea-to-sea, and others) was advocated and strongly supported by Peres and taken by Ben-Gurion in the face of strong opposition by the IDF.

In 1952 Peres advocated the transfer to civilian hands of many of the projects and services run by the IDF, thereby decreasing expenditure on maintenance and manpower and transferring those sums to R and D and weapon acquisitions. CGS Yadin vehemently opposed these suggestions, but Peres found support in the person of Yadin's deputy, Makleff. Aided by Makleff, he succeeded in convincing Ben-Gurion to adopt his position and impose his proposals on the IDF, a development that contributed to Yadin's resignation and replacement by Makleff. Peres intervened in many other issues directly related to the IDF, such as salaries, vacations, fringe benefits, and so on, claiming that all these issues had a direct bearing on the budget. He demanded that just as the CGS had access to everyone in the system, so was the D-G entitled to access for the purpose of acquiring information (not to give orders) to all levels of the system, including IDF officers. This approach put him on a collision course with CGS Chaim Laskov, who argued that the IDF reported only to the defense minister and all contacts between the IDF and the D-G or the deputy minister could only occur via the CGS. Ben-Gurion again sided with Peres.[63]

There are other instances of defense ministers supporting the D-G against the CGS, but such cases are not the rule. One constant source of friction is the perennial debate between local R and D and production versus weapons acquisition from foreign sources—or, in IDF parlance, buying off the shelf (usually an American one). The MOD is in charge of the defense industries, most of which are government corporations, and is sensitive to domestic concerns such as unemployment and the advancement of the development areas. It thus has a vested interest in increasing IDF orders for domestically produced equipment—whether weapons systems or uniforms. It is also interested in having more money devoted to R and D, most of which is spent locally. The IDF high command, on the other hand, is more concerned with short-range goals and immediate needs and is strongly influenced by budgetary constraints. For this reason, it shows a definite preference for buying American equipment and products, which are more readily available and usually cheaper and can be bought by American military aid. The IDF is judged by its daily performance and must be prepared every day for an outbreak of general hostilities; it is no wonder that it attaches more importance to acquiring state-of-art weapons systems from the United States than to funding Israeli R and D.

This tug-of-war is built in to the system, and its outcome depends on the defense minister. In the early 1970s, for instance, there was a serious debate regarding a new fire-control system for the armored corps. The MOD favored developing such systems in Israel, while the IDF preferred buying them or developing them at Hughes in the United States. CGS Bar-Lev and his deputy Elazar were willing to buy fewer tanks in return for a speedier delivery of the systems. After hearing both sides, Defense Minister Dayan said that, though the army's case seemed stronger, he was not willing to overrule his entire MOD executive staff (the minister's assistant, the D-G, and the scientific adviser), especially as procurement is an MOD function, and therefore he was approving their recommendations. In this case, the IDF lost; in many other cases, the outcome was different.

A definite change in the relative balance of power between the CGS and the D-G occurred in the mid-1970s, with the pendulum swinging in the IDF's favor. This was largely the result of two factors: the combination of two very strong chiefs of staff (Gur, who served for four years, and Eitan, who served for five) with a rapid turnover in the post of D-G; and defense ministers who were deeply focused on other matters (Weizman with the peace process with Egypt, and Sharon with Lebanon) and were thus less involved in defense organization. It was only with the appointment of Rabin as defense minister in 1984, and especially with Ivri's appointment as D-G, that the pendulum swung back. With Arens as defense minister this trend continued.

The main bone of contention today between the CGS and the D-G is the central budget. In the past there was a substantial reserve budget that was neither divided nor allocated at the beginning of the fiscal year to the various users. This budget, over which the MOD had a meaningful degree of control, gave a certain flexibility to the system and enabled the heads of the defense establishment to give proper emphasis to long-range and overall needs and to an interservice approach. Eventually, however, increasing budget constraints led the IDF to press to have almost the entire budget allocated from the outset to the various elements and functions of the IDF. The result was that the budget lost its flexibility, and the role of the MOD was limited to technical administration with hardly any input in determining priorities. A concurrent result was an increase in the proportion of resources devoted to maintenance at the expense of development and new procurement. Today the only area where the D-G maintains some degree of budgetary flexibility and influence is the integrated function of R and D, but here, too, most of the funds are already divided among the various elements of the IDF—each, of course, interested in furthering its own pet projects. It is in this area that Ivri sees his major battle, and it is here that he is concentrating his efforts to increase the influence of the MOD.[64]

The Power of Appointment

The power of appointment is perhaps the secret to effective civilian control, second only to the power of the press. Not surprisingly, it is also a major source of tension and friction among the key actors, especially between the defense minister and the CGS.

The law deals only with the appointment of the CGS: "The chief of the general staff shall be appointed by the government on the recommendation of the minister of defense."[65] The practical consequence of this constitutional stipulation is that the appointment of a CGS must be coordinated and eventually agreed on by both the defense minister and the prime minister. The government cannot appoint a CGS on its own; it can only approve or fail to approve a recommendation by the defense minister. The recommendation itself can be put on the cabinet's agenda only by the prime minister, and there is little chance of the cabinet's approving a defense minister's recommendation if the prime minister opposes it. Which of the two wields more influence? It depends on the personalities involved and on the overall political situation.

Bar-Lev was the first CGS appointed after the two posts of prime minister and defense minister were separated in 1968. Prime Minister Eshkol favored Bar-Lev, and there was also considerable pressure from within Eshkol's party (Mapai) for the appointment.[66] Dayan may have had another first choice, but Bar-Lev, already deputy CGS, was the natural candidate and hardly had to be forced on Dayan.[67] This contrasts with the following appointment—that of Elazar in 1972—which was indeed forced on Dayan by Prime Minister Golda Meir. Meir and her close political colleagues (Sapir, Galili, and Alon) saw Elazar as someone closer to them politically and a potential check on the highly popular, highly independent, and highly unpredictable defense minister.[68] The two candidates for the job were the two victorious generals of the Six Day War—Elazar in the north and Gavish in the south—and although Dayan clearly preferred Gavish and was uncomfortable with Elazar, he yielded to the prime minister. The third appointment—that of Gur in 1974, immediately following the Yom Kippur War—was Dayan's choice, to which Golda Meir acquiesced. Given the unusual and difficult circumstances of the time, there seems to have been little alternative. Eitan—appointed CGS in 1978—was clearly the choice of Defense Minister Weizman. Begin questioned Weizman as to why he preferred Eitan over the other leading candidate, who had considerable support within the Likud Party, but accepted Weizman's reasons and supported him.[69] Begin intervened, however, to force Defense Minister Sharon to extend Eitan's tour of duty for a fifth year. Eitan, whom Begin admired immensely and in whom he had great confidence, is the only CGS in Israel's history to have served five full years, and there is good reason to suspect that Begin's appointment of Ariel Sharon as defense minister in 1981 was conditional on his agreement to a fifth year for Eitan. The appointment of Levy as CGS in 1983 was, once again, definitely a decision of Defense Minister Arens, with which Shamir went along.[70] The same probably holds true for Shomron's appointment by Rabin in 1987 and for Barak's appointment by Arens in 1991.

Which, if any, other appointments need the approval of the prime minister is unclear. It seems fair to say that two key appointments do need prime ministerial approval: that of the deputy CGS and that of the head of military intelligence, the former because he may be required, under certain circumstances, to act as the CGS and because he is considered the front-runner to succeed the current CGS, and the latter because of his role in presenting the national intelligence estimate to the government.[71] As far as other senior appointments are concerned, there are no set guidelines. Rabin's view is that the defense minister is obligated to notify the prime minister of all major appointments in the general staff—the chiefs of the services (the air force, navy, and FCH) and the O/Cs of the territorial commands—before they are finalized. Rabin followed this rule without exception. He would meet with the prime minister privately before such appointments were made, present him with the alternatives for each position, and explain the reasons for his choice.[72]

Ben-Gurion was responsible for establishing the procedure for all other appointments in the IDF. A matter of convention and practice, with no formal legal basis, this procedure has never been challenged, by either defense minister or CGS, and by now it has achieved the status of a constitutional convention. All appointments and promotions in the IDF are formally made by the CGS, with all those to the rank of colonel and above subject to prior approval by the defense minister.[73] Both defense minister and CGS thus have de facto veto power over appointments and dismissals: the defense minister cannot appoint anyone without the recommendation of the CGS; the CGS cannot make an appointment without the approval of the defense minister.

Dismissals of senior officers in the IDF are rare, and the guidelines for them are consequently far less institutionalized. They are, however, similar to those for appointments. Lack of agreement between defense minister and CGS can only lead to an impasse, to a continuation of the status quo, to a freeze in the rotation of senior officers—which is the hallmark and pride of the IDF—and to a general paralysis of the system.

Who, in the end, has the upper hand? As with the appointment of the CGS, a lot depends on the personalities and overall approaches of both sides. In many instances, it can turn into a battle of wills, and the one with stronger nerves who can hold out longer will win. In actual practice, the CGS presents his recommendations to the defense minister, usually at their weekly meetings, and tries to convince him to approve them.[74] If the defense minister refuses, the CGS can either present a new name at a future meeting or repeat his original recommendation—in effect refusing to accept no for an answer. This ritual has on occasion continued for months.[75] CGS Laskov once suggested to Ben-Gurion the same name three times. After the third refusal, Ben-Gurion explained privately to Laskov what his reservations were regarding this specific officer but added that if Laskov persisted in his recommendation, he would yield. Laskov made the appointment.[76]

Arens states that, in principle, he favored approving the recommendations of the CGS and did so unless he knew the nominee well and was convinced that he was unfit for the job. In his view, a defense minister should not try to dictate appointments to the CGS or even intervene overmuch since it is the CGS who has to work with these people. It would be unfair and unwise to prevent the CGS from choosing the small group of senior officers with whom he believes he can work most effectively. The instances when a defense minister should dictate or veto a senior appointment "should be few and far between." Levy, CGS under Arens and Rabin, not surprisingly, expresses the same opinion: "The minister determines policy, but it is the CGS who has to implement this policy, and, therefore, he should be permitted to choose the people with whom he wants to work."[77]

This proximity in view may explain why Arens and Levy maintained a relatively harmonious relationship, although the two still had differences in this area. Arens insisted that Levy keep both his contenders for the post of CGS—Dan Shomron and Ben Gal—in the army, and Levy had no choice but to agree. Arens suggested that Shomron be appointed O/C northern command—one of the most important positions in the IDF. Levy adamantly refused but compromised by appointing him commander of the FCH.[78] Levy suggested General Shachak as head of military intelligence. Arens put forth his own candidate: General Ehud Barak. The defense minister explained that since he had implemented the recommendations of the Kahn Commission of Inquiry (formed after the Sabra and Shatilla massacre) and dismissed the current head of military intelligence in the face of strong public criticism, he had to satisfy the public by appointing a well-known officer to this sensitive post—one who would inspire public confidence. Levy accepted the logic behind Arens's insistence and agreed to Barak's appointment.[79] Arens was less satisfied with certain other appointments, but he yielded to Levy, observing, "There is a limit to how much I can dictate to the CGS."[80]

Rabin, on the other hand, adopted a much more active approach, perhaps because of his military experience and familiarity with the IDF. Throughout his term of office, he had many confrontations, both with Levy and Shomron, over appointments.[81] The results of these confrontations confirm the thesis that if a defense minister is determined and adamant, he will, for the most part, have his way.[82] Rabin determined most of the senior appointments, especially with regard to the territorial commands. He was careful not to embarrass the CGS or overrule him in public, but he would meet with him privately three or four times—and even more, if necessary—until he convinced him.[83] Levy admits that, although he fought stubbornly, he ending up agreeing to many appointments with which he was quite unhappy.[84] Rabin forced Levy to appoint General Peled as O/C northern command and Shomron to appoint General Mordechai as O/C central command, even though in both cases the CGS recommended and strongly supported another candidate. Rabin also prevented Shomron for months from making any new appointments in the general staff until it was known who the next CGS would be.[85]

Regarding dismissals, there is a mutual veto. Rabin could not force the CGS to dismiss Drori. Equally, a CGS would find it impossible to remove a senior officer without the support of the defense minister. Eitan wanted to dismiss Shomron for giving an unauthorized newspaper interview that was critical of the IDF; Begin, as acting defense minister, refused to approve the request. Shomron wanted to dismiss General Bar Cochba for giving an unauthorized newspaper interview severely and personally attacking the CGS; again the acting defense minister—this time, Shamir—refused to approve the request.[86] Dayan, CGS in 1956, wanted to dismiss Ariel Sharon as commanding officer of the paratroop brigade for blatantly disobeying orders, but Ben-Gurion intervened and prevented Sharon's dismissal.[87]

Two final points need to be made. First, Peri claims that partisan politics frequently influence military appointments and considers this phenomenon a manifestation of permeable boundaries, the politicization of the IDF, and the inherent political-military partnership in Israeli civil-military relations.[88] This conclusion, however, does not characterize the system during the last two decades. The political factor may have been more dominant in the early years of the state, especially as a result of Ben-

Gurion's suspicion of those officers who had been associated in the past with the prestate independent or semi-independent military organizations (primarily the Irgun Zvai Leumi and the Palmach). But the last of these people left the IDF in the early 1980s. The three most recent chiefs of staff all began their military service as inductees in the IDF. There is, of course, political lobbying, as there is in every democratic state and open society, but it cuts across party lines, and its impact is limited.

Finally, the IDF has no service boards in the British sense, but it does have a permanent Appointments Forum. The forum, headed by the CGS, includes the deputy CGS, the chiefs of the three services, the O/Cs of the three territorial commands, and the head of the personnel branch of the general staff. The generals recommend various appointments to the CGS, and each nominee is discussed. The discussion is formal, and a transcript of the proceedings is prepared. The discussion is then summarized by the CGS, who has the final say.[89]

7 Civilian and Military Involvement in National Security

The three dimensions of civil-military interaction discussed in the preceding chapters manifest large differences in the degree of civilian control over national security matters. The operational dimension shows a very high degree of civilian involvement, comparable to that of any other advanced Western country. The dimension of strategic planning, on the other hand, shows a totally different picture: civilian involvement in the actual formulation of national security policy is minimal, and this area poses the most serious threat to civilian control in Israel. The dimension of force development—i.e., the allocation of resources—lies somewhere in the middle, showing a definite increase in civilian involvement over the last decade. My model, as shown in figure 2, identifies these three dimensions as those on which civil-military interaction takes place. In this chapter, I will attempt to illustrate and substantiate the statements I have just made above, as well as to examine in depth an instance or specific case representative of each dimension.

Operations

The principle that military operations can be undertaken only under the direction of the civilian authority and within the parameters determined by the civilian authority has never been questioned in Israel. As former

CGS Eitan puts it, "Not a single soldier crosses the border without the prior approval of the civilian echelon." I believe that this is a case not of nominal but of genuine instrumental control. This can be illustrated by an incident that occurred shortly after the Six Day War. One Saturday afternoon, there was a serious skirmish in the northern sector of the Suez Canal; Egyptian artillery shelled Israeli positions, and there were many casualties. Rabin, CGS at the time, tried to reach Defense Minister Dayan in order to receive approval for the use of the air force. Unable to reach Dayan, he ordered the air force to attack the Egyptian artillery. Dayan heard of the action on the radio and immediately called Rabin, asking him angrily, "Who gave you approval for the use of aircraft?" Rabin replied that he had made every effort to find Dayan, but not being able to reach him and in view of the heavy casualties, he had ordered the airstrike. Dayan responded, "Next time, if you can't reach me, call [Prime Minister] Eshkol"—in other words, you must receive permission from a civilian echelon before taking military action. Rabin, a strong CGS and the victorious commander of the IDF in the Six Day War, never even considered questioning Dayan's directive.[1]

Time and again throughout Israel's short history, the military has complied, without exception, with the operational directives of its civilian superiors—even when these directives were diametrically opposed to the recommendations, desires, and judgment of the military leadership. No doubt this owed something to the fact that the military commanders involved were deeply imbued with democratic values and ideologically committed to the principle of civilian control. Though he argued bitterly against the decision, Yigal Allon retreated from the Sinai in 1949, under orders from Ben-Gurion. Likewise, in 1956 CGS Dayan and the entire high command were aghast at the prospect of a total withdrawal from the Sinai. Ben-Gurion appeared personally before the general staff to explain the reasons behind the government's decision. There was never any question, however, that the decision was Ben-Gurion's and that it would be faithfully and fully implemented by the IDF.[2]

The twin cases of the waiting period before the Six Day War and the refusal to sanction a preemptive airstrike on the morning of the Yom Kippur War are prime examples of instrumental civilian control.[3] Very few civilian governments have ever faced such heavy pressure from the military to go to war as did Prime Minister Eshkol and his colleagues during the two-week period preceding the Six Day War. The general staff not only warned Eshkol that by not permitting the IDF to attack he was endangering Israel's security and would cause thousands of unnecessary casualties but went so far as to state that as a result of the government's procrastination the IDF would not be able to guarantee victory. Nevertheless, Eshkol and the Israeli government held their own. The decision to go to war eventually taken by the cabinet was not dictated by the army but grew from public opinion and certain political and diplomatic developments.

On the morning of October 6, 1973—when it became clear that Israel had been taken by surprise and would be attacked on two fronts within hours—CGS David Elazar strongly recommended a preemptive airstrike, especially against Syria, claiming that only such a move could neutralize the advantage of surprise held by the Arabs. Elazar and the air force commander both warned that failure to undertake such a strike could have disastrous consequences. Defense Minister Dayan and Prime Minister Meir were not moved and did not even bother to bring the issue before the cabinet.

Research in the field of civil-military relations has demonstrated that two major problems arise from time to time with regard to the operational dimension. The first occurs when the military broadens the scope and depth of an operation beyond the parameters determined by the civilian authority. This can result either from simple overeagerness or because the military's interests differ from the civilian agenda. Literature on civil-military relations records many such instances. In some cases, the field commander actually conducts unauthorized activities; in others, he presents the civilian echelon with a fait accompli, leaving it no choice but to agree. The behavior of both MacArthur and Lavelle, described in chapter 2, exemplifies this problem. The second major issue is that of micromanagement of the military by civilians. As Aubin and Englund put it, "History also teaches us that when the executive overinvolves itself operationally, disaster usually follows."[4]

As the earlier anecdotes of military obedience suggest, the first problem is hardly ever found in Israel. There have been instances where a military operation ended quite differently from the predicted conclusion originally presented to and approved by the civilian echelon, but these almost always resulted either from a flaw within the military system—i.e., insubordination by the commander in the field toward his military superiors—or from a lack of coordination within the civilian system—i.e., a defense minister exceeding his mandate. Examples of the former are a number of retaliatory raids in the 1950s, such as Kibiya and Kalkilia, or the ill-fated action at the Mitla Pass (when Israeli paratroopers advanced through the pass into the Sinai desert against orders and suffered very heavy casualties) and the introduction of armor earlier than planned during the Sinai operation in 1956. Incidentally, almost all these examples are connected in some way with Ariel Sharon, and the issue was a lack of military discipline, not one of the military circumventing civilian directives. Indeed, after the Kalkilia raid, CGS Dayan decided to dismiss Sharon for insubordination but was prevented from doing so by Ben-Gurion himself.[5]

Examples of the second problem are the Lebanon War in 1982 and the commando raid at Beirut International Airport on December 30, 1968. During the Lebanon War, Defense Minister Sharon acted at times without governmental authorization and even without the knowledge of the prime minister. He certainly exceeded the spirit, if not the letter, of many of the cabinet's decisions.[6] Most researchers in Israel point to this war as a major instance of severe breakdown in civil-military relations. This may be true, but the breakdown was not caused by overinvolvement by the military in the operational dimension: throughout the war, the IDF implemented the explicit instructions of its immediate civilian superior, i.e., the defense minister. What the war does appear to reflect is a breakdown in the relationship among the government, prime minister, and defense minister.[7]

The case of the raid on Beirut International Airport reflects a similar breakdown.[8] On December 26, 1968, Arab terrorists attacked an El Al plane and its passengers in Athens, killing two Israelis and wounding a number of others. The cabinet decided on a military response; Defense Minister Dayan and CGS Bar-Lev recommended an attack on Beirut International Airport and the destruction of Arab civilian aircraft on the ground. During the deliberations of the cabinet and the MDC, Dayan estimated that, on the basis of intelligence reports, four to five airplanes would be destroyed. The cabinet approved the raid, which was carried out with spectacular success: the Israeli force returned safely without a scratch and without causing any loss of life on the Lebanese side.

However, in the raid, which lasted for only thirty minutes, thirteen airplanes—almost the entire fleet of the Lebanese national airline—were blown up. Dayan was present at the command post during the entire operation, and when it became obvious that the number of aircraft on the ground far exceeded what had been expected, CGS Bar-Lev turned to Dayan for instructions. Dayan replied without hesitation: "Blow them all up."[9] Bar-Lev states that as far as he was concerned, Dayan's instructions constituted sufficient civilian approval for the broadening of the operation; he was unaware that Dayan had not received Eshkol's go-ahead.[10] Eitan also clearly remembers receiving orders both from Bar-Lev and Dayan to destroy all the civilian aircraft bearing the marks of Arab airlines.[11] Prime Minister Eshkol and the other ministers were astounded when they heard this news. Eshkol was evidently quite angry, feeling that something had been put over on him.[12]

An incident usually cited as an example of the military exceeding its mandate and presenting the civil authority with a fait accompli occurred during the Six Day War—specifically, when the IDF reached the Suez Canal contrary to Defense Minister Dayan's explicit directive. Two facts are clear: on the eve of the Six Day War, Dayan issued three basic guidelines to the IDF, one of which was *not* to reach the Suez Canal;[13] four days later, IDF officers were photographed bathing in canal waters. What is not so clear is how this happened. Dayan claims that the military did indeed present him with "an accomplished fact."[14] Were this true, this would be a classic example of a lack of civilian control—instrumental or even nominal—in the operational sphere.

The evidence, however, does not support Dayan's version of events. Rabin, CGS at the time, insists that Dayan changed his mind and approved the IDF's advance to the canal.[15] Rabin does not deny that he lobbied strongly with Dayan, emphasizing that he was speaking on behalf of the entire general staff when he stated that from a military point of view the canal was the ideal defense line for the IDF forces in Sinai, but he is adamant in his assertion that the IDF only advanced to the canal after it had received the defense minister's approval. In support of his version of the events, Rabin cites the fact that at one point, when it was thought that an IDF force had advanced to the canal, Dayan ordered it to turn back.[16] The chief of operations at the time, General Chofi, confirms that a force under Colonel Granit was ordered to return, but he adds that later in the same day Dayan demanded to know why the IDF had not yet reached the canal![17] Bar-Lev strongly supports Rabin's version, claiming that had an IDF force advanced beyond a line acceptable to Dayan, he would not have hesitated to order its return, as he did with that of Colonel Granit and with a small force that crossed one of the bridges on the Jordan.[18] It seems then that this is actually a case where the civilian echelon was convinced to prefer a tactical-military consideration to a strategic-political approach (not to threaten the Suez Canal): the decision rested squarely in the civilian court.

Micromanagement of military operations by civilians does pose a serious problem for Israeli civil-military relations, and it represents a potential source of tension and frictions within the overall system. Not surprisingly, micromanagement is characteristic of defense ministers with a military background and much less prominent among defense ministers who come from civilian life. It has been widely practiced by Dayan, Rabin, Weizman, and Sharon but hardly ever by Eshkol, Peres, or Arens or, for that matter, by Begin and Shamir when serving as acting defense minister. A few of the better-known examples will suffice to illustrate this phenomenon.

In 1971 a Sabena Airlines plane was hijacked by Arab terrorists and forced to land at Ben-Gurion Airport, where its passengers and crew were held as hostages to the demand for the release of the terrorists held by Israel. The plane was finally taken over by Israeli commandos in a daring operation in which the terrorists were killed and the hostages freed. From the moment the plane landed in Israel until all the passengers were freed, Dayan took direct command over all Israeli forces, coordinated all activities in the area from the emergency command post at the airport, gave all the orders, and, in effect, acted in place of the chief of staff—perhaps even in place of the O/C central command.[19] Likewise, when terrorists infiltrated across the Lebanese border and took control of a children's home in the Misgav Am kibbutz, demanding to negotiate the release of fellow terrorists from Israeli prisons, Defense Minister Weizman arrived at the scene by helicopter, took charge of the situation, and assumed personal command over the rescue operation.[20]

Micromanagement is not limited to instances of terrorism, where civilian targets and lives are usually involved. When two Israeli soldiers were abducted by Hizballah terrorists in Lebanon, Defense Minister Rabin, standing by a map in the IDF central command post in Tel Aviv, gave orders as to exactly where the army should set up checkpoints and ambushes in an attempt to interdict the abduction.[21] During the War of Attrition (1968–1971), there were cases when Dayan would determine the exact number of shells to be fired by the artillery in response to a certain incident; in one instance, Dayan ordered Acting CGS Weizman to fire exactly five shells at the Jordanian town of Irbid.[22] During the Lebanon War, Defense Minister Sharon not only usurped the function of chief of staff, but in many instances acted as a de facto O/C northern command.[23] Micromanagement is especially prevalent with regard to noncombat activities of the IDF. Thus it was Yitzhak Rabin, not CGS Shomron, who for many months, if not years, commanded operations against the intifada,[24] and it was Ariel Sharon, not CGS Eitan, who personally directed the IDF efforts to remove the Jewish settlers from Yamit.[25]

In contrast, Eshkol, as both prime minister and defense minister, did not intervene directly in operational matters but gave Rabin a free hand. Thus Rabin made the operational decisions regarding the struggle with the Syrians over water rights from 1965 to 1967, as well as regarding the scope of the reserve call-ups and emergency mobilization before the Six Day War.[26] Similarly, when terrorists took over Bus Number 300 from Tel Aviv to Ashkelon, Defense Minister Arens left the rescue operation to the commanders in the field, arriving at the scene only after the hostages had been released. During a seaborne PLO attack on Israel's southern border in May 1990, it was CGS Shomron, not Acting Defense Minister Shamir, who decided not to clear the beaches of the thousands of civilians; such an occurrence would have been inconceivable if Rabin had been defense minister.

The IDF, while certainly not happy with the extent of micromanagement, has resigned itself to the facts of life and rarely puts up a serious fight. One such rare occasion occurred during the Lebanon War. Sharon, who maintained a notoriously high degree of micromanagement, had ordered Chief of the Air Force David Ivri to execute a bombing mission in a certain way. Ivri was convinced that Sharon's method would lead to unnecessary civilian casualties and cause morale problems among his pilots. He went to CGS Eitan, saying that he could fulfill the mission but that the method put forth by Sharon was unacceptable. Eitan supported Ivri, and the mission was executed as proposed by him (precision target bombings instead of carpet bombing).[27]

The following incident from recent American history illustrates the power of civilian control in the operational sphere in Israel. During the Cuban missile crisis in 1962, Defense Secretary McNamara visited the chief of naval operations (CNO) in order to explore the organization of the naval blockade and the procedures for the first interception. CNO Anderson replied that he had outlined his procedures at the National Security Council meeting and that there was no need for further discussion. McNamara continued to question CNO, until at one point Anderson picked up the Manual of Naval Regulations and, waving it in McNamara's face, shouted, "It's all in there." The encounter finally ended with the CNO's remark: "Now, Mr. Secretary, if you and your Deputy will go back to your offices, the Navy will run the blockade."[28] True, this occurred in 1962 and probably could not happen now; nevertheless, the anecdotes related above hardly suggest that similar events could ever have taken place in Israel.

Case Study: The Bombing of the Iraqi Nuclear Reactor

On June 7, 1981, at 5:30 P.M., eight Israeli F-16 fighter aircraft attacked the Iraqi Osirak nuclear reactor, situated on the outskirts of Baghdad. Within less than two minutes, sixteen bombs had been dropped on the target, and the nuclear reactor, known as Tammuz I, was completely destroyed. The rising flames from the atomic installation brought to an end Saddam Hussein's first attempt to produce an atomic bomb. A careful analysis of the Israeli decision to undertake this complex and daring military operation can shed a great deal of light on the intricate interaction between the civilian and military echelons in the area of military operations. This case also illustrates the complex relationships among the key actors as outlined in chapter 6.[29]

Israel began worrying about Saddam Hussein's nuclear ambition as early as the mid-seventies, when Iraqi-French discussions on cooperation in the field of nuclear energy seemed to be on the verge of practical implementation. On November 17, 1975, France and Iraq signed a secret agreement for cooperation in the peaceful use of atomic energy, under which France would supply Iraq with a nuclear reactor, known as Osirak, fueled with weapons-grade enriched uranium. Under the agreement, France agreed not only to deliver and install the Osirak reactor but also to supply Iraq, over time, with eighty kilograms of highly enriched uranium. In the first stage, the reactor, along with a smaller twin, would be supplied and fueled with twenty-six kilograms of weapons-grade uranium—a quantity sufficient for the production of one or two atomic bombs. On August 26, 1976, a detailed agreement for the sale and installation of the reactor, as well as for the supply of the fuel, was signed.

Israel's main concern was not that Hussein would use the enriched uranium to make atomic bombs, although this possibility could not be excluded, but rather that he would use the reactor as a means to produce large quantities of plutonium, which would enable him to build up an arsenal of nuclear weapons. This concern took on dramatic proportions in February 1978, when the Italian and Iraqi Atomic Energy Commissions signed an agreement under which Italy would build laboratories, known as "hot cells," in which plutonium could be separated, thus giving

Iraq access to a continuous supply of fissionable material—the essential ingredient of nuclear weapons.

Israel's initial efforts to thwart Hussein's plans were limited to the political and diplomatic arena, coupled with a media campaign. The planned date for the installation of the Osirak reactor was sometime during 1979–1980, so Israel still had ample time to lobby. First, Israel approached the French at the highest levels, urging them to cancel the project. Their representations increased in frequency and urgency as the target date for the project's completion neared and were augmented by an intense effort to arouse French public opinion against the grave danger and inherent immorality of their government's policy. All these efforts failed to bring about any change in French policy.

Israel's best hope to prevent the actual delivery of the reactor to Iraq lay with the United States. Aware of America's traditional strong antiproliferation policy—especially that of the Carter administration—and of its success in convincing France to cancel its agreement to supply Pakistan with a plutonium-separation plant, Israel used its influence in Washington to bring American pressure to bear on the French and the Italians. The Americans agreed with the Israeli appraisal of the danger posed by Iraqi efforts and interceded with both France and Italy. The United States intensified its diplomatic efforts to convince the French to cancel the deal or, at least, to supply a different type of reactor, one based on low-grade enriched uranium. At the same time, it pressured the Italians not to deliver the hot cells to Iraq. The administration even leaked secret information to the American press in order to create both congressional pressure in the United States and negative public opinion in France as well as in Italy. Ultimately, however, the United States was no more successful than Israel in convincing either France or Italy to change its policy.

In the early morning hours of April 6, 1979, an explosion took place in the facility near Toulouse where parts of the Osirak reactor were being assembled. Although an unknown organization by the name of Guardians of the Environment took responsibility for the explosion, almost everyone assumed that the Israeli Mossad was behind the action; no traces of the perpetrators were ever found. The actual damage was limited, resulting in a delay of only a few months. Having failed to achieve a positive result by political or diplomatic means—or, perhaps, by sabotage—it was now amply clear that the only viable option left to Israel was a military strike against the nuclear installation itself.

It should be noted that the initiative for the military operation came not from the military but from the civilian echelon. The driving force behind the Israeli attack was none other than Prime Minister Menachem Begin, who had the strong support of a number of key ministers, chief among them Ariel Sharon, who was to become the defense minister only two months after the successful strike. In the eighteen-month period preceding the bombing of the reactor, the concept of a military attack on the Iraqi reactor was a source of deep division both within the IDF and the government and beyond—to a degree perhaps unprecedented in Israel's history. There is no question that had it not been for Prime Minister Begin's deep conviction, underlined by his memories of the Holocaust, that the destruction of the Osirak reactor was for Israel a question of survival, the operation would never have come about.

In October 1979, following a number of high-level meetings of the MDC, Begin directed CGS Lieutenant General Eitan to start planning a military strike against the Iraqi reactor and to present the civilian echelon with viable military options. From the beginning, Eitan was a strong advocate of the operation. The IDF presented two options: a commando raid on the ground or a bombing attack from the air. On January 18, 1980, Defense Minister Weizman heard arguments on both sides and decided in favor of the second option. A number of observations should be made with regard to this development. The first and most important is that although the CGS supported the air option, believing that it was less risky and potentially less costly than the ground alternative, it was the defense minister who made the decision. In other words, the choice between the military options was made by the civilian echelon, even though the pros and cons were essentially of a military and operational nature. At the same time, the military echelon took pains to present a military option that was palatable to the civilian authority, in that it minimized the twin risks of high casualties and severe political repercussions.

The second point is that an operational decision, in the early stages of planning, was made by the defense minister on his own, and not by the prime minister or the MDC, although had CGS Eitan disagreed with Weizman, he undoubtedly would have appealed the decision to the prime minister. This supports a point made throughout this book: when the CGS and the defense minister agree on operational questions, the issue is usually determined at the first level of the civilian echelon, and not higher. There is reason to believe, however, that had the prime minister had a military background—as Yitzhak Rabin does, for instance—he would have been far more involved in a decision of such importance, its operational nature notwithstanding.

Finally, one should note that Weizman, who subsequently left his post as defense minister and resigned from the government, became one of the most vocal and intense opponents of the plan, believing that it would destroy the peace with Egypt. Judging by this behavior, there is reason to assume that when he made the decision in favor of an air attack, he never intended for it to be carried out, probably counting on subsequent developments to allow him to derail it. Indeed, had Weizman remained defense minister throughout, it is difficult to imagine that the Israeli attack on the reactor would have been implemented. This is a classic example of a defense minister avoiding a head-on collision with the prime minister on a key security issue yet hoping that by biding his time and playing his cards carefully, he would eventually prevail.

On May 19, 1980, the MDC reviewed the situation. It soon became apparent that the idea of an airstrike against a nuclear installation deep in Iraq faced stiff opposition from many quarters. Those opposing the plan included the DMI and the head of the Mossad, the two individuals responsible for all intelligence assessment and evaluation, as well as Deputy Defense Minister Zipori. More important, however, were the strong opposition expressed by Deputy Prime Minister Yigal Yadin, who was also the leader of the second-largest coalition party, as well as a former CGS, and the growing reservations of Defense Minister Weizman. Their concerns notwithstanding, Prime Minister Begin instructed the IDF to continue its preparations for the operation.

On May 28, 1980, Ezer Weizman resigned his post as defense minister and left the government as a result of serious differences with the prime minister regarding the defense budget and the autonomy negotiations with Egypt. Prime Minister Begin took over the defense portfolio, a position he held until the establishment of a new government in August 1981. For the first time in thirteen years, Israel had reverted to the arrangement that had characterized it until 1967—namely, the concentration of the prime ministership and the defense portfolio in the hands of one individual. The hub of Israeli civil-military relations—the relationship among the prime minister, the defense minister, and the CGS—ceased to exist; the civilian echelon and the command authority over the IDF were now represented by one man: Menachem Begin. As the plan for the Israeli operation took shape and the controversy and debate within the government, the IDF, and the defense establishment intensified, this factor became increasingly significant.

During the latter half of 1980, Israel stepped up its diplomatic efforts in Paris, Rome, and Washington, while at the same time moving forward with the military planning for the airstrike. These new diplomatic efforts were no more successful than their predecessors had been. In late 1980, however, a momentous development introduced a new factor into the situation. On September 17, 1980, Saddam Hussein unilaterally canceled the Iranian-Iraqi border treaty and launched a full-scale attack against Iran: the first Gulf War had begun. On September 27 and again on September 30 Iranian aircraft attacked the Iraqi nuclear installation near Baghdad. Both airstrikes failed to cause significant damage, but they did impel the French to recall many of their technicians from Iraq, leaving only a skeleton crew. Yet, although this set back the Iraqi nuclear program a number of months, the following weeks showed that France, Italy, and Iraq remained determined to go ahead with their plan, the war notwithstanding. Begin remained convinced that the reactor had to be attacked and destroyed before it went into operation; once it became "hot," the danger of an air attack causing radioactive fallout and subsequent civilian casualties would render a strike almost impossible. For Israel, the moment of truth appeared to be fast approaching.

The fact that this moment of truth lasted close to eight months is testimony to the intense involvement of the civilian echelon in the operational dimension. On October 14, 1980, Begin brought the issue before the MDC. The committee was deeply split, with six ministers in favor and four opposed to the attack. Facing such a division, the prime minister decided not to take a vote but instead to bring the issue before the entire cabinet, as well as to consult with leaders of the opposition (Rabin and Peres). On October 28, Begin put the issue to the cabinet. Again, wide divisions within both the IDF itself and the defense establishment as a whole—the CGS strongly in favor, the deputy defense minister against; the DMI against, his deputy in favor; the head of the Mossad against, his deputy in favor—made the decision difficult. After a long discussion, the cabinet voted ten to six in favor of the operation and empowered Begin to order its execution at the earliest possible date (following the American elections in early November).

The involvement of the civilian echelon—at the governmental level— did not end here, however. Following the vote, Deputy Prime Minister Yigal Yadin announced that he was not willing to accept collective responsibility for the action and thus would resign from the government. At this point, although armed with authorization from the cabinet and heading a government that enjoyed a majority in the Knesset even without Yadin's party, Begin declared that he was not willing to go ahead with the operation at the expense of Yadin's resignation. He convinced Yadin not to resign for the time being, promising him that he would not authorize the airstrike without giving Yadin ample advance notice so that he would be able to resign without giving away the impending attack.

From a formal point of view, the cabinet decision to attack remained in effect and the prime minister and defense minister were obligated to implement it. Yet no one in the cabinet questioned Begin's stated intention not to do so. This is interesting evidence of a point made earlier: the cabinet is very unlikely to force a military operation on a reluctant prime minister and defense minister, especially when both (in this case, one individual) are of the same opinion. Had Begin requested the cabinet to rescind its decision, no doubt it would have done so; instead, he simply acted as if it had done so.

Begin, however, was not ready to give up; he continued to pressure Yadin. New intelligence data confirmed that the damage caused by the Iranians had been repaired and that France and Iraq had jointly set the end of July 1981 as the date for full activation of the reactor. Begin asked CGS Eitan and the DMI to meet privately with Yadin in an attempt to convince him. He authorized them to show Yadin all the raw intelligence data. (Here is a classic example of a prime minister and defense minister using the military in an advocacy role to gain support from other members of the government.) The CGS was only too willing to cooperate. Had he and the military been more circumspect, history might have been different. As it was, the efforts bore fruit: on December 28, 1980, Yadin informed Begin in writing that while he remained firmly opposed to the proposed action, he was withdrawing his threat to resign.

But events continued to postpone the operation, and time dragged on. The lack of unanimity within the IDF and the defense establishment, as well as within the government, had had an effect. By the time Yadin removed his veto, the United States was on the eve of inaugurating a new president (Ronald Reagan), and Begin realized that such a time was inopportune for carrying out an attack on Iraq. After the inauguration, Israel was awaiting a visit from the new United States secretary of state, Alexander Haig. The fact is that even if the military and civilian echelons agree on a common goal, the civilian perspective remains different from that of the military. Begin was totally committed to the action; nevertheless, he could not ignore certain political constraints. Such diplomatic niceties meant very little to the CGS or the commander of the air force; for them the weather over Baghdad was probably much more important. Meanwhile, hundreds of French technicians returned to the nuclear site near Baghdad, complicating the matter even further. On March 15, 1981, Begin once again brought the issue before the MDC. This time the committee was tied five to five. Begin supported a resolution under which the CGS would continue to plan the airstrike and the committee would reconsider the matter in one month.

At this juncture, a new complication arose in the form of increased tension between Israel and Syria in Lebanon. On April 1, 1981, heavy fighting broke out in East Lebanon, near the Christian city of Zachle, between the Syrian army and the Christian forces under Bashir Gemayel. The Syrians used helicopters against the Christian forces. Gemayel sent a special emissary to Jerusalem with an impassioned plea to Begin for help. Begin convened the MDC to discuss the situation in Lebanon and to evaluate the Christian request for Israeli military intervention. During the meeting, Begin proposed Sunday, April 12, as the date for the air attack on the Iraqi reactor; however, even the ministers who supported the action suggested that it would be unwise for Israel to take on both the Syrians and the Iraqis at the same time. Begin agreed, once again, to postpone the action.

The Christians' calls for help became more and more desperate. The cabinet approved limited air action in their support, and the Israeli air force shot down two Syrian helicopters that were transporting Syrian troops to the Zachle area. Within twenty-four hours, Syria moved SAM 6 anti-aircraft missile batteries into Lebanon. This represented a clear challenge to Israel and a change in the accepted rules of the game. Israeli aircrafts' freedom of action in Lebanese skies was now severely curtailed, a situation that Israel had often declared would be unacceptable. Begin immediately announced that the IDF would act against the SAM 6 missile batteries, and on April 30 he ordered the air force to attack the missile sites. Bad weather prevented the air force from operating effectively in the area, and the attack was postponed, but tension remained high.

At this point, the future of the air attack on the Iraqi nuclear reactor hung in the balance. The crucial question was, what should come first—the missiles or the reactor? The DMI and the O/C northern command, as well as other members of the general staff, demanded that the IDF first take out the missiles, which, in their opinion, represented a direct and immediate danger to Israel's security and to its deterrent posture. Had they had their way, the threat of widespread Israeli-Syrian hostilities would have become very real. This would have resulted in international criticism of Israel and intensive American mediation (which took place even in the absence of an Israeli airstrike against the missiles). Would Israel have been able, in such a climate and only six weeks away from a national election, to undertake—in blatant violation of Iraqi sovereignty as well as Jordanian and Saudi airspace—an air attack against a French-built nuclear reactor on the outskirts of the Iraqi capital? The question remains academic, but it is reasonable to assume that Israel would have thought twice before striking out in all directions at the same time. In all probability, the reactor would have become hot, and the attack would never have taken place.

The choice was in the hands of CGS Eitan. Had he supported an immediate attack on the missiles, the government almost certainly would have authorized the attack. Eitan, however, surprised almost everyone and, although known for his anti-Syrian stance and deep enmity towards Syria (both of which were decisive in his strong support of the Lebanon War a year later), came out openly against an attack on the missile sites. He made it clear in subsequent interviews (including one for this book) that his position was motivated solely by his strong support for the attack on the Iraqi nuclear reactor and his understanding and appreciation of the diplomatic and political limitations and restraints of his civilian superiors—already manifested in his conscious attempt to present a plan for destroying the reactor that would answer most of the major concerns of the civilian echelon. For Eitan, the existential if less immediate threat to Israel came from Iraq's nuclear reactor; the Syrian missiles could be dealt with afterward (as indeed they were, one year later, when they, together with many additional Syrian batteries, were destroyed in the early days of the Lebanon War in June 1982). An air attack on the missile sites would have meant the cancellation of the plan to destroy the Osirak reactor—an outcome Eitan was determined to avoid.

One can only imagine what might have happened had the CGS been someone with less political savvy and less understanding of the concerns, restraints, psychology, and workings of the civilian echelon. True, the attack was Begin's idea, and the decision was plainly that of the civilian echelon, but the military's input remained crucial, its ability to influence events never negligible. Eitan's stature here also exemplifies the predominance of the CGS within the military echelon, illustrating that, in the final analysis, it is the CGS who speaks on behalf of the IDF.

The saga of the attack on Iraq's nuclear reactor was now fast approaching its climax. The final episode, played out during the month of May 1981, demonstrates the complexities of the civilian echelon, which, as pointed out in chapter 3, is not limited to the government but includes the Knesset as well. On May 3, 1981, Begin once again convened the MDC and proposed that the attack against the reactor be carried out during the month of May, the exact date to be determined by the prime minister and minister of defense (Begin) and the CGS (Eitan) in consultation with the foreign minister (Shamir). The resolution was passed by a vote of six to three. Begin and Eitan agreed on Sunday, May 10, as the final date for the attack. At this point, however, the opposition made a last-ditch attempt to prevent the operation. Former defense minister Weizman, who somehow got wind of what was about to happen, appealed to key ministers and even to the commander of the air force, beseeching them to prevent what he called "an act of lunacy." Late on Saturday night, May 9, the leader of the opposition, Shimon Peres, sent a top-secret note to Begin, asking him not to go ahead with the operation, or at least not at this time (referring to the fact that May 10 was the date of the French presidential election).

Peres's letter was delivered to Begin in the middle of the cabinet meeting on the morning of May 10. At exactly the same time, at an air force base in southern Israel, CGS Eitan, his deputy, and the commander of the air force were meeting with the pilots who, later in the afternoon, were to take part in the attack on the Osirak reactor. Eitan and his entourage ate lunch with the pilots, wished them good luck, and headed back to the air force command post in Tel Aviv.

Immediately following the cabinet meeting, Begin convened the MDC and read them the note from Peres. He informed them that the attack was scheduled for the late afternoon but that since he wanted a national consensus and did not want the Knesset to be split on this issue, he was proposing a two-week delay. A number of ministers, notably Ariel Sharon, objected, claiming that any further delay would jeopardize the entire mission; however, the majority still sided with Begin. Begin immediately informed CGS Eitan, who was still in the air on his way to Tel Aviv, that the mission was to be postponed. The pilots were already in their cockpits when the CGS phoned the head of air operations and ordered him to scratch the mission. Two interesting points should be noted. First, Begin brought the issue before the MDC, not the cabinet, even though the cabinet had held its regular weekly meeting that very morning. Second, and even more important, Begin and the MDC took a key operational decision at a meeting where no senior military person was present—in other words, without any input from or consultation with the military. This further demonstrates the predominance of the civilian echelon and the high degree of civilian involvement in the operational area.

Begin was to postpone the mission twice more. The attack was rescheduled for May 17 but postponed to May 31. This was to be the *final* date. CGS Eitan bitterly complained to Begin that the "civilians were driving the air force crazy" and that things could not continue this way any longer. But despite Eitan's demands that the mission either take place on May 31 or be canceled, on May 30 Begin ordered a further postponement of one week, because of the summit meeting between him and Sadat scheduled for June 4. The military's fulminations notwithstanding, the civilian echelon did not hesitate to postpone again and again a crucial and complex military operation when it was convinced that this was the right thing to do politically.

Finally, the word was given. On June 3, 1991, CGS Eitan informed the commander of the air force that the mission was set for Sunday, June 7. This time it was for real. At 4 P.M., the eight F-16 fighter aircraft took off for Iraq. An hour and a half later, Saddam Hussein's nuclear dream went up in smoke.

As this case study demonstrates, in Israel the operational dimension shows a high degree of civilian involvement and control coupled with a substantial military input. In short, this area manifests a healthy and satisfactory balance and systematic interaction between civilian and military involvement.

Strategic Planning

The most serious flaw in Israeli civil-military relations can be summed up in the words of Samuel P. Huntington: "In many countries strategic planning is effectively dominated, if not totally monopolized, by the military acting through a central military staff. What is often lacking is an effective civilian counterweight to the strategic advice the military provides the government."[30] Yariv writes, "There is a most conspicuous weakness in the Israeli governmental system, with regard to the development of overall strategy. In the past . . . only the military possessed the staff requisite for strategy development."[31] Perlmutter adds, "The heart of the matter is that the IDF is the institution that formulates Israel's grand strategy and makes its tactical decisions, although not necessarily the decision to go to war. . . . Again, with the exception of the Soviet military, the IDF can be said to be the only military organization in the world that wields almost complete power over strategic and tactical questions."[32]

The total monopoly of strategic planning by the planning branch of the IDF general staff and the total lack of any "civilian counterweight" has been amply detailed in the preceding chapters. The only possible exception was David Ben-Gurion, who, although lacking any policy-planning body, to a large degree determined the strategy of the newly born state. His personal contribution to national security policy was immense; indeed, it has been claimed that Ben-Gurion's direction of the War of Independence was guided by an overall strategic concept that he kept secret from both the cabinet and the army.[33] This influence can perhaps be explained by Ben-Gurion's towering personality, as well as by his unique working habits. Ben-Gurion kept his list of appointments to a bare minimum and at times would meet with only two or three people during a day's work. When I asked what he did with all that free time, the answer was "Think."[34]

Most of those interviewed agree that this dimension is characterized by heavy overinvolvement by the military and underinvolvement by civilians. Meron, a former D-G of the MOD, admits that with regard to strategic issues, the minister of defense is completely dependent on the military. Former CGS Bar-Lev states that "unlike most other countries, in Israel the planning branch has come to dominate the entire area of national planning." D-G Ivri, confirming the fact that the planning branch is the only body dealing with strategic planning, adds that the branch does not have the necessary tools with which to prepare a national policy "because it lacks an overall comprehensive national view and has neither the requisite level of accessibility nor of responsibility."[35]

The lone dissenting opinion comes from former CGS Mordechai Gur. He claims that while the military does enjoy a strong input into strategic thought, and this is as it should be, it is not a one-way street. In his opinion, the prime minister or defense minister can avail themselves, if they genuinely want to, of other sources of input besides the military, and this is so even in the absence of formal institutionalized staff facilities. Such sources could include members of the scientific and academic communities, as well as former senior officers.[36] Yet although from a purely theoretical point of view, this may be so, in reality it is both unworkable and impractical: unworkable because the ability of outside experts to contribute meaningfully to strategic policy is severely limited inasmuch as they are not privy to classified information and do not have at their disposal all the necessary data; impractical because of the incessant demands on the working time of modern-day political leaders, which inevitably result in the outside experts' appearances being postponed again and again in favor of institutionalized bureaucratic structures and domestic political priorities.

According to the definition developed in chapter 2, a radical imbalance between military and civilian involvement indicates a lack of civilian control. Yariv claims that the civilian-political authority has completely abdicated responsibility, and the military has simply stepped in to fill the vacuum thus created. For example, he recalls that when serving as Golda Meir's adviser on terrorism from 1972 to 1973, he requested that the prime minister hold a high-level meeting on the overall strategy for the war against terrorism; Meir declined. Only after Yariv hinted that he would resign was such a meeting convened. Schiff points out that as both prime minister and defense minister, Rabin opposed the creation of a civilian body for strategic or policy planning, preferring to work alone directly with the military.[37]

Nowhere is this abdication more evident than in the crucially important and eminently civilian area of war aims. In the tradition of Clausewitz's famous dictum that war "is a continuation of political relations . . . by other means," it is universally accepted that a prime responsibility of the civil authority is to determine the goals of war, leaving it largely to the military to decide on how they are to be achieved. The Israeli paradox is that while the civilian echelon intervenes quite actively in deciding on the *how*, it fails dismally to meet its primary responsibility to determine the *what*. In the absence of clearly defined war aims and/or national security goals, the military, having to cope with rapidly changing situations and new scenarios, has no choice but to produce these aims and goals on its own. Not only does the government fail to take an active part in the initial formulation of national goals and interests, but the cabinet rarely even troubles to conduct a serious review of the formulations prepared by the military—formulations that form the basis both for IDF operational plans and for force development programs.[38]

When the IDF set out in 1966 to prepare a long-range plan for developing its order of battle, it laid down a number of political-strategic assumptions that formed the basis for the five-year plan, among them: (a) the state of Israel can realize its national aspirations within its present boundaries; (b) the battle must be transferred to the enemy's territory in order to bring about political negotiations; (c) Israel will retain all captured territory until full peace is achieved; and (d) in the peace negotiations, Israel will demand changes in the cease-fire lines of 1949.[39] Although all these assumptions are plainly of a political nature, they were approved by CGS Rabin and were not even the focus of any serious discussion at the political-civilian level.

There are many other examples of strategic issues being determined by the military. The initiative in 1970 to draw the Russian pilots in Egypt into a trap in order to shoot them down—a strategic move aimed at limiting Russian intervention—originated with the IDF.[40] Benjamini, in his analysis of the Six Day War, points out that "the outcome of the war was more a result of an initiative on the operational level than the outcome of a civilian political strategic 'goal definition' on the institutional level." He claims that the cabinet never made a decision to conquer the entire West Bank; rather, Defense Minister Dayan approved the occupation of the West Bank on a piecemeal and ad hoc basis, giving in to military pressures from the field. Emphasizing that nominal civilian control was not compromised but that effective instrumental control was lacking, Benjamini concludes, "Instead of disobeying political policies, the military organization was forced to initiate them."[41] Perhaps the most extreme example of military influence on strategy is the claim that the 1956 Sinai Operation was forced on Ben-Gurion by the defense establishment. According to this view, Ben-Gurion was not happy about the idea of going to war and had serious reservations about the entire operation. Under heavy pressure from CGS Dayan and D-G Peres, he stipulated a host of difficult conditions (specifically his demands for active French and British participation and for a joint Anglo-French ultimatum to both sides), firmly believing that they would never be met. When, to his complete surprise, all his demands were accepted by Eden and Mollet (prime ministers of Britain and France, respectively), he had no choice but to go along with the operation.[42]

There are, however, some exceptions. One such was the strategic decision, taken in late 1968, to adopt a defensive approach to terrorist attempts to cripple Israel's national airlines and to launch an intensive and expensive security effort to protect El Al planes and passengers. The originator of this plan was Deputy Prime Minister Yigal Allon.[43] On another occasion, the cabinet rejected CGS Gur's approach to an interim agreement with Egypt in 1975, preferring that of Prime Minister Rabin and Defense Minister Peres.

With the assumption of power by the Likud in 1977, a conscious attempt was made by both Begin and Weizman to increase civilian involvement in strategic planning. On his first visit to the IDF general staff as prime minister, Begin informed the generals that the government's new political guidelines for the army were that Israel's permanent borders would be the El-Arish–Ras-Muhammed line in the south and the Jordan River in the east and that operational plans and the order of battle were to be built accordingly. CGS Gur asked to receive these guidelines in writing, and Begin complied.[44] As time passed, however, the Likud leadership lost its enthusiasm, and the situation more or less reverted to what it had been previously. Nevertheless, two key strategic decisions stood out as being the product of civilian initiative: the peace initiative with Egypt in 1977 and the maintenance of the IDF deployment in Lebanon during 1984.

During Rabin's tenure as defense minister, he took an increasing interest in strategic planning.[45] This interest, however, was limited to the ministerial level, and although he demanded changes in formulations and strategic assumptions presented by the planning branch, the formulations themselves were still performed by the military.

The central point of this section is best summarized in the words of Yechezkel Dror:

> If the civilian has only the option offered by the military, it is an unacceptable situation. Ben-Gurion created options for himself and forced them on others. . . . Ben-Gurion's great contribution, from a historical-theoretical view, was in his ability to create an option, i.e., his conceptual independence from the existing military. . . .
>
> However, Ben-Gurion failed to institutionalize this ability. He did not build a system that guarantees instrumental civilian control of defense—the creation of options. Today, we do not have a Ben-Gurion. Even Ben-Gurion would not have been able, in the far more complicated circumstances of today, to develop significant options alone. In the absence of civilian staffs for politico-military thinking, the civilian echelon does not have genuine options at his disposal, and thus the [existence of nominal civilian control] does not solve the problem that Ben-Gurion solved by virtue of his personality— the problem of instrumental civilian control through the existence of options not necessarily acceptable by the military. Ben-Gurion

succeeded, but he failed to build the necessary infrastructure so that we, too, could succeed.[46]

Case Study: The Lebanon War

A few minutes before midnight on Thursday, June 3, 1982, as the Israeli ambassador to Great Britain, Shlomo Argov, was leaving the Dorchester Hotel in London, he was shot and seriously wounded by an Arab terrorist. The bullet that penetrated Argov's skull was, in effect, the first shot in the disastrous Lebanon War. Sixty hours after the attempted assassination of Israel's ambassador, the IDF invaded Lebanon in an all-out attack against the PLO state-within-a-state in south Lebanon. What was supposed to be a seventy-two-hour blitzkrieg turned into a four-month war and a three-year Israeli military presence in Lebanon. The Lebanon War, in which Israel suffered six hundred fifty dead and thousands of wounded was, by far, Israel's most tragic military engagement. It caused extensive damage to Israel's image in the world and to its international standing, for years had a negative impact on the morale, motivation, and training of the IDF, resulted in a deep chasm in Israeli society, and left scars whose effects, like those of the Vietnam War in America, can be felt to this very day.[47]

The individual directly responsible for the Lebanon War and its dire consequences was the defense minister, retired major general Ariel Sharon. The war was Sharon's brainchild: he conceived it and was its midwife. The war would never have taken the negative course it did, and events in Lebanon would never have developed so adversely if not for Sharon's relentless striving—by almost any and every means—to realize his grand design. True, as defense minister Sharon was officially part of the civilian echelon, but he took personal control of the entire strategic planning apparatus of the IDF and subjugated the military involvement in the formulation of national security policy to his own will, using the military, at times unscrupulously, to achieve his own agenda.

Contrary to much of what has been written, Sharon was not an adventurist or a militarist. He certainly was not a warmonger. The war was not an action taken lightly or in anger; it was not an act of revenge. The Lebanon War represented the implementation of a grand design—that of Sharon and the IDF. Unlike the Six Day War, it did not suffer from a lack of aims or strategic planning. In fact, the Lebanon War was probably the most thoroughly planned military operation in Israel's history, intended to achieve ambitious strategic objectives.

The seeds of the tragic Lebanon War were planted in the seventies. In September 1970, in what became known as Black September, King Hussein of Jordan cracked down on the Palestinian presence in Jordan and on the independent PLO activity in his kingdom. Killing hundreds of Palestinians and imprisoning thousands, Hussein put an end to the use of Jordanian territory as a launching ground for attacks against Israel and eradicated the PLO presence in West Jordan. Many of the Palestinian terrorists fled to southern Lebanon, where there were a number of large Palestinian refugee camps—the only remaining area bordering Israel in which they could enjoy some degree of freedom of movement. In 1975, civil war broke out in Lebanon between the Christians and Moslems, a war that lasted over fifteen years and cost over one hundred thousand lives. The war led to the disintegration of the Lebanese army as an effective fighting force and to the breakdown of the central government in Beirut.

The PLO was quick to fill the vacuum that opened up in southern Lebanon—which had become, in effect, a no-man's-land—and created a state-within-a-state. The entire southern portion of Lebanon became known as the Fatahland (after the terrorist group within the PLO) and served as a staging area for attacks against Israel. The northern area of Israel, known as the Galilee, suffered for years from terrorist incursions across the Lebanese-Israeli border, both by land and sea, and the hostage taking of children, adults, and entire families, as well as from mortar, artillery, and especially Katyusha rocket attacks from South Lebanon. Israel responded from time to time with retaliatory attacks against PLO bases in southern Lebanon, but to no avail.

After an especially daring and damaging terrorist attack in early 1978, Israel undertook Operation Litani, in which an area extending three to five kilometers north of the Lebanese border was occupied by the IDF and established as a security zone, policed by local Lebanese villagers. This action, too, did not solve the problem. In May 1981 heavy fighting broke out, and for over a week Israeli towns and villages in the Galilee were subject to serious and sustained mortar and Katyusha rocket attacks causing significant casualties and extensive damage. A cease-fire was eventually arranged by American negotiator Philip Habib, but the situation remained tense. The PLO increased its attacks against Israeli and Jewish targets throughout the world, holding the entire Galilee hostage to prevent Israeli retaliation. It was becoming more and more clear that Israel could not continue indefinitely to live with the situation.

Ariel Sharon became defense minister in August 1981. Within a few months, his grand design for Lebanon—subsequently known as the Grand Plan, code-named Oranim—was completed. It represented a radical shift from all previous Israeli strategic thinking. Until the Grand Plan, Israel's main preoccupation was with protecting its northern border; hence, its main concern was the ever-growing PLO presence in and increasing takeover of south Lebanon. Sharon, however, set his sights much higher. His goal was to create a major strategic realignment in the Middle East. Israel would no longer be satisfied with the removal of the PLO from south Lebanon, or even with its removal from all of Lebanon.

The only way to guarantee that the PLO would never return to Lebanon, argued Sharon, was to turn Lebanon into a pro-Western country aligned with Israel. The way to achieve this was to ensure that the leader of the Christian Maronites and Israel's ally, Bashir Gemayel, was elected president. Sharon intended to become kingmaker in Lebanon, backed up as needed by Israeli bayonets. But this was impossible with the Syrian army in the country: Assad would do everything in his power to thwart the designs of his implacable enemy, Israel. Thus the forced removal of the Syrian army from Lebanon, or at least from Beirut and its surroundings, as well as from south and central Lebanon, became a major element in the Grand Plan. The civilian echelon was never aware of this. Had the cabinet known of Sharon's intentions, the Lebanon War would probably not have happened, because the last thing the Israeli government wanted was a major battle with the Syrian army, even if limited to Lebanon.

This became quite obvious in December 1981. On December 14, 1981, the Israeli cabinet decided to annex the Golan Heights, and on the very same day, the Knesset enacted legislation applying Israeli law, jurisdiction, and administration to the Golan. The reaction of the Arab world, as well as of the international community was, not surprisingly, quite severe. The United States responded by suspending its strategic cooperation agreement with Israel, as well as temporarily interrupting the scheduled delivery of advanced fighter aircraft to the IDF. On Sunday, December 20, Begin convened the weekly cabinet meeting at his residence, where he was recuperating from a broken hip. His mood was grim. There was a possibility of a Syrian reaction, he said, and Israel had to be ready. He then surprised his ministers by stating that the IDF had prepared a detailed plan for a far-reaching military operation in Lebanon. He further astounded them by demanding that the cabinet approve the plan at that very meeting, empowering him and Defense Minister Sharon to put it into effect with no further consultation with the cabinet, as there might not be time.

Sharon, CGS Eitan, and other senior officers proceeded, with the aid of maps, to present the Grand Plan—Oranim. Arrows clearly showed the IDF reaching the main Beirut-Damascus highway. Sharon emphasized that the IDF would not enter Beirut itself, as it was a capital city full of foreign embassies, including those of the United States and the Soviet Union, but alluded to the possibility of an Israeli amphibious landing at the Christian stronghold of Juneih, north of Beirut. Neither Sharon nor Begin mentioned the strategic concept behind the proposed action. Oranim was presented as a response to be implemented in retaliation for Syrian provocation or any further acts of terrorism by the PLO. The discussion thus was held in a strategic vacuum; no attempt was ever made to clarify the war's aims or the strategic thinking behind it.

The ministers were aghast: the cabinet was being asked to approve a major military operation, if not an all-out war, with no apparent justifiable reason or immediate cause. Two key ministers spoke, both expressing strong opposition to the plan. Then the deputy prime minister, who was also number two in Begin's Likud Party, asked for the floor, muttering, "This is impossible." Noting rather bitterly that "the atmosphere is quite clear, and there is no point in continuing," Begin abruptly halted the discussion, announced that he was withdrawing his proposal, and adjourned the meeting.

These events illustrate an important point regarding the relationship between the prime minister, the defense minister, and the cabinet, albeit one relevant primarily for the operational rather than the strategic dimension. In certain instances, the cabinet will refuse to agree to proposals for military action even if they are supported jointly and adamantly by both the prime minister and the defense minister. Thus, although these two individuals are the key civilian actors in civil-military relations, at times the cabinet can play a crucial role in the area of military operations. Indeed, since 1948 cabinets have repeatedly braked the military activism of prime ministers and defense ministers, despite their efforts to coerce agreement.

Begin and Sharon reached different conclusions from the stormy December 20 cabinet meeting, although both certainly recognized that the government was not going to approve the Grand Plan. Begin decided that he would have to settle for a watered-down Oranim—a military operation whose limited goal would be the destruction of the expanding PLO infrastructure throughout southern Lebanon—and this Small Plan, as it came to be known, was what he presented to the cabinet (and to the leaders of the opposition) in the months to come. Sharon, on the other hand, had no intention of abandoning his grand strategic design merely because of the hesitation and weakness of his colleagues. Instead, he decided that he would have to resort to subterfuge and clever manipulation to achieve his ends. For the next five-and-a-half months, he went along with Begin in presenting the Small Plan to the cabinet and the leaders of the opposition (Peres and Rabin). But while the government heard and deliberated on one plan, the IDF planners, following Sharon's instructions, were working on something altogether different.

Had there been significant civilian involvement—beyond that of the defense minister—in the planning stages of the Lebanon War, Sharon and the IDF would never have been able to keep their preparations secret. A planning facility or staff unit dealing with strategy or national security in the prime minister's office or attached to the cabinet would have informed the prime minister and the MDC that the IDF was planning a major military operation based on assumptions and designed to achieve aims that had never been approved by the government and were almost totally unacceptable to it. As it was, Sharon managed to isolate the prime minister's military secretary (who was a new appointment and thus lacked experience, senior rank, and prestige) and to a certain degree even the head of the Mossad.

On Friday morning, June 4, 1982, only hours after the attack on Ambassador Argov in London, Begin convened the cabinet in Jerusalem. On his suggestion, the cabinet approved a major airstrike on PLO targets in the heart of Beirut, to which there was little doubt the PLO would respond. Begin then announced that the cabinet would meet at his residence on Saturday night in order to decide on Israel's future moves. It was clear to all those present that the cabinet would be asked to approve a major military ground action in Lebanon. As was to be expected, the PLO responded to Israel's heavy airstrike by shelling the northern Galilee and by firing Katyusha rockets into Kiryat Shmona and other cities and towns along Israel's northern border. On Saturday night, June 5, Sharon and CGS Eitan presented the cabinet with the Small Plan, a military operation whose declared aim was to take over an area of southern Lebanon extending approximately forty kilometers north of the Israeli-Lebanese border, thus putting the Israeli north outside the range of the PLO rockets and artillery. Begin proposed a four-point resolution, which the cabinet approved almost unanimously.

The resolution, which was published on Sunday, June 6, 1982, read:

> The government has decided as follows:
>
> A. The IDF will be instructed to remove all the towns of the Galilee from the range of fire of the terrorists, who are concentrated, together with bases and headquarters, in Lebanon.
>
> B. The name of the operation will be Peace for the Galilee.
>
> C. In implementing this resolution, the Syrian army is not to be attacked unless it attacks our forces.
>
> D. Israel continues to strive for the signing of a peace treaty with an independent Lebanon, which will preserve her territorial integrity.

No member of the civilian echelon present at the meeting seemed to be aware of the inherent contradiction in the resolution. No member of the military echelon took the trouble to inform them that it would be impossible to remove all the Galilee from the range of the terrorists' fire without a direct confrontation with the Syrian army, because in the eastern section, the forward positions of the Syrian army were fifteen kilometers from the Israeli border. It was a catch-22, and it was exactly what Sharon needed to give him room for maneuvering.

Initially, the IDF halted its advance three kilometers from the Syrians' forward position. But Sharon kept emphasizing that if the IDF did not advance, it could not carry out the mission set for it by the cabinet decision. By Monday, the second day of the war, Sharon was convincing the cabinet to authorize a pincer movement around the Syrian forces that would supposedly convince them to withdraw without a fight. Had the cabinet had the advantage of an honest intelligence assessment, or had there been a civilian function—independent of the defense minister—dealing directly with strategy and planning, it would have been quite obvious to the cabinet that such a scenario bordered on the absurd. As it was, the movement took place, but Assad did not withdraw; instead, he moved into Lebanon a large number of SAM 6 anti-aircraft missile batteries to protect his troops.

On Wednesday, Sharon, supported by Begin, asked the cabinet to approve an all-out attack on the Syrian missile batteries by the Israeli air force. A number of ministers balked at going along with the move, for it was clear that a massive blow to Syria's air defense system could only lead to a Syrian-Israeli military confrontation. Sharon countered by warning that failure to cripple the Syrian missile batteries without further delay would severely limit the Israeli air force's freedom of action, leaving the Israeli troops on the ground without air cover or support. No Israeli government would willingly assume such a responsibility; the cabinet reluctantly approved the strike. What was supposed to have been a cleanup operation against the PLO turned into a major military confrontation between Israel and Syria—an outcome to which the government had been consistently and firmly opposed, and one that it would never have knowingly approved.

This is a typical example of the military echelon under explicit instructions from the minister of defense creating a fait accompli in the field and thereby maneuvering the civilian echelon into an impossible position. It must be emphasized that the inherent contradiction in the cabinet's June 5 decision was quite evident to the military echelon. On May 13, 1982, three weeks before the outbreak of the war, a special meeting of the general staff had been convened for a final review of the upcoming operation. At this meeting, DMI General Saguy warned his fellow generals of the serious and even dire consequences of the proposed operation. Scoffing at the idea that the Syrians would withdraw on their own, he said there was no way the IDF could clear the terrorists out of the forty-kilometer zone in the eastern sector of southern Lebanon without a direct military confrontation and heavy fighting with the Syrians. Saguy also warned that the Syrians would bring up missile batteries; the IDF would then have no choice but to attack and destroy them, and the inevitable result would be that the confrontation would become an all-out war in Lebanon.

The DMI is responsible not only to the IDF but also to the government for overall intelligence assessment; he is almost a permanent guest at cabinet meetings. Yet Saguy never presented this assessment to the cabinet, certainly not in such concise and unambiguous terms and definitely not on the fateful Saturday night of June 5, 1982. This was a direct result of Sharon's high-handed tactics with the IDF and its senior officer corps. As mentioned previously, Sharon took control of the IDF's entire strategic planning apparatus and systematically subjugated the general staff to his will. Although willing to tolerate officers speaking out openly against his plans and assessments in closed deliberations of the military echelon, he made it clear that doing so before the civilian echelon would be considered an unacceptable act of disloyalty and that he would do his best to isolate and even ostracize any offending officers. Quite simply, Saguy was afraid of Sharon, and in Sharon's presence he was not willing to speak his mind to the ministers.

The Kahn Commission—established after the Sabra and Shatilla massacre of September 1982—condemned Saguy for not presenting his dissenting views before the civilian echelon. In its view, he was derelict in his duty to his civilian superiors. The commission has thus established a basic norm in civil-military relations: namely, that senior IDF officers do not owe their loyalty to the minister of defense but rather to the government as a whole. It would, however, be a grave mistake for the civilian echelon to depend solely on this norm and on the IDF's compliance with it in the future. It can never substitute for direct civilian involvement in the strategic dimensions.

The tragedy of the war was that the strategic objectives were totally unachievable. The source of the tragedy lay in a planning process entirely concentrated in the hands of the IDF under the orchestration and direction of Sharon; there were no checks and balances, no contending civilian oversight or review. Not only was Sharon's grand design never subjected to external civilian review, but it was never even presented to the ultimate civilian authority. The cabinet approved military action aimed at achieving strategic goals of which it was totally ignorant. In the absence of independent sources of information and any high-ranking civilian body or staff institution dealing specifically with national security or strategic planning, Sharon controlled the flow of information from the IDF to its civilian masters—even Prime Minister Begin. Sharon was always careful not to lie outright to the cabinet, but he withheld some information, was very cavalier with his use of facts, and thus presented a highly selective, tainted, and one-sided picture of the situation.

Begin was fully aware of Sharon's reputation for manipulating the truth and of his readiness in the past to use unscrupulous methods to achieve his ends. However, instead of creating a civilian body to deal with strategy and monitor information, which would serve as a counterweight to Sharon, Begin placed his trust in the chief of staff, General Eitan—with whom he had a very close relationship—believing that Eitan would remain loyal to him and the government and prevent Sharon from taking over the IDF. As mentioned earlier, Begin had made it clear to Sharon when he appointed him defense minister that he would maintain a direct channel of communications with the CGS. Begin did retain such a channel throughout the war; unfortunately, he failed to realize that, despite the basic level of mistrust between Sharon and Eitan, they would have no problem joining forces to achieve a common goal.

Eitan did not fully support Sharon's grand design—he had his own agenda—but he was a fervent advocate of the action in Lebanon throughout the war and thus was willing to go along with Sharon's manipulations. Eitan himself stated that he was often aware that Sharon was not reporting the whole truth to Begin, and while he adamantly claims that when questioned directly by Begin he always gave accurate and objective answers, he openly admits that, on his own initiative, in most cases he would not correct one-sided information and biased impressions given by Sharon. Once Sharon succeeded in gaining the CGS's cooperation—which is tantamount to the cooperation of the entire IDF—the civilian echelon was rendered helpless.

The Lebanon War was a colossal failure of civilian oversight of strategic planning. All the inherent weaknesses, drawbacks, and pitfalls of Israeli strategic planning outlined in this book merged, leading naturally to a disastrous result. No better example than the Lebanon War can be found to illustrate military monopolization of strategic planning and the IDF's almost complete dominance over the formulation of national security policy. Indeed, a glaring feature of the Lebanon debacle was civilian abdication of its prime responsibility to formulate and determine the goals of war. It was a classic instance of nominal, but not instrumental, civilian control.

Force Development

Unlike the operational dimension, which has always manifested a high degree of civilian control, and unlike the strategic dimension, which to date has been characterized by highly limited civilian involvement, the dimension of force development has been undergoing an evolutionary process of change. During the early years of the state, the structure and organization of the IDF as well as priorities in the allocation of resources within the armed forces were almost the private domain of the military; civilian involvement—to the degree that it was present—was limited to the defense minister (or to the prime minister and defense minister when both posts were combined). As time passed, and especially during the eighties, the role of the defense minister became much more prominent and decisive, and there was a slow but perceptible increase in the involvement of the cabinet.[48]

The heart of the acute problem in the strategic area is also the major limitation on effective civilian involvement in force development—namely, the lack of a civilian body or staff facility that can create independent options for the civilian echelon.[49] All decisions on major weapons systems, all long-range development plans of the IDF (five-year and ten-year plans), the major order of battle of the armed forces, and the allocation and distribution of the budget among the key elements of the IDF are subject to approval by the defense minister. However, the only alternative to approval is for the minister to reject proposals (as Rabin has done more than once) and send them back to the military for reworking. He does not have the option of presenting an alternative proposal of his own, and no civilian bureaucratic structure (such as the Office of the Secretary of Defense [OSD] in the United States) can prepare one for him.

One important factor works strongly in the defense minister's favor in this arena: interservice rivalry. In vivid contrast to the strategic dimension—where the defense minister usually faces military unanimity—in the area of force development, the existence of quasi-independent services means that the defense minister is often presented with different options. There is fierce competition between the air force and, to a lesser degree, the navy and the ground forces over the size of each one's share of the limited resources, which became even more scarce during the eighties, when the defense budget was cut in real terms by hundreds of millions of dollars. The disagreements are too severe and too basic to be resolved within the confines of the IDF and are invariably brought to the attention of the defense minister—who can then arbitrate among the conflicting views. True, the various options all originate with the military, and the minister still lacks a genuine civilian option; nevertheless, the conflict within the military increases the degree of freedom available to the civilian echelon and the scope of instrumental civilian control.[50]

A recent example of this phenomenon was the decision in 1989 to acquire the Apache attack helicopter. The FCH favored the procurement of a large number of less sophisticated helicopters (mainly the Cobra, which was already in the service of the IDF), while the air force lobbied strongly for acquisition of the Apache. The FCH emphasized the ground support mission of the attack helicopter and hence its preference for larger numbers, whereas the air force concentrated on the need to maintain Israel's qualitative edge. Rabin held three discussions on this issue before deciding in favor of the air force. His decision was guided by an overall view of national security interests and of the strategic threats facing Israel—threats that could be met more effectively by the Apache (mainly because of its extended range and night flying capabilities). Rabin's opinion happened to coincide with that of the CGS, so in effect he approved the recommendation of the highest level in the IDF, but still there was no doubt that the decision was his.[51]

A second factor working in favor of increased civilian involvement in this dimension is the Israeli media's ever-increasing tendency to deal openly with these issues. Indeed, it would be fair to say that, by and large, development of civil-military relations in Israel on this dimension has followed the American pattern, with a time lag of twenty to twenty-five years. Until the Yom Kippur War, this entire area was considered out of bounds to public debate, and the media cooperated fully in the conspiracy of silence. Major R-and-D projects as well as the procurement of important weapons systems were kept secret from the Israeli public until long after—in some cases, even years after—they had become operational. As a result of the Yom Kippur War, however, the defense establishment lost its aura of inviolability, and the Israeli public as well as the media were much more willing to question the wisdom of decisions made by the general staff. It soon became clear that the military censor's attempts to cast a veil of secrecy over all IDF plans in the area of weapons acquisition served mainly to shield the IDF from public scrutiny and potential criticism. The media thus refused to continue cooperating with the censor, and as a result controversy on these topics within the IDF became the subject of intense public debate. Politicians began to feel heavy pressure to deal more effectively with these issues, lest they be accused of squandering public funds.[52] For just one example, the bitter controversy over the acquisition of new submarines for the navy was brought before the MDC, and the project was the subject of a public lobbying effort by members of the Knesset.[53] The classic example, of course, is the Lavie project, which I analyze in depth at the end of this section.

Force development, priorities among the various elements of the military, and the overall battle order of the armed forces should reflect, to a large degree, war objectives and possible politico-military-strategic scenarios. These objectives and scenarios should be handed down to the military by the civilian authority. But in view of the Israeli government's abdication of its responsibilities in this field, the military has no choice but to determine by itself and for itself the basic assumptions that form the strategic infrastructure for force development.[54] These assumptions are usually subject to approval by the defense minister, who may request or demand some modifications, but they remain largely a military product. Rabin, as defense minister (1984–1990), made a serious attempt to alter the status quo by formulating for the military the key elements of a national security policy that would underlie all IDF long-range planning.[55] However, his formulations were presented orally, and it fell to the military to put them in writing; moreover, this civilian involvement was perforce limited to the ministerial level. Rabin himself admits that the fact that these guidelines never reached the MDC for discussion reflected a basic flaw within the system.[56]

Perhaps the system's original sin can be traced to Ben-Gurion's maxim that the *what* was to be determined by the military, whereas the *how* was to be dealt with by the civilian MOD. This approach is no longer viable in the complex, high-tech economic and military systems of the eighties and nineties. The D-G of the MOD, David Ivri, points out that in almost all advanced Western states today major decisions on the *what* are made by civilians, and this is as it should be, because such decisions have long-range consequences beyond the responsibility of the current military leadership, as well as far-reaching consequences for the national economy. Thus maintenance and running budgets (manpower, upkeep, spare parts, and so on) are divided among the various services, but R-and-D and procurement budgets are within the authority and control of central civilian bodies.[57] In Israel, by contrast, almost the entire budget is divided among the various services and branches of the IDF, with almost no central budget at all.

De facto military control over the budgets and de facto military supervision of key projects explain why it is so difficult for the civilian echelon to implement or enforce even the decisions it does take regarding the overall size of the defense budget. On assuming the post of defense minister in 1977, for example, Weizman announced his intention to reduce the defense budget by almost two hundred million dollars to stem the tide of rising inflation (fueled by large-scale budget deficits). CGS Gur bitterly opposed the idea, claiming that it was unfeasible, and demanded that the proposed cuts be delayed for at least three months to allow in-depth study and discussion of the issue. Gur, together with the rest of the general staff, stalled for time, raised objections, and created as many obstacles as possible; in the end, the IDF won, and nothing came of the proposed cuts.[58]

The defense minister isn't alone in having a problem in this area. Even when the cabinet itself decides on cuts, implementation is not a foregone conclusion. Unlike other countries, the government never decides where to make the cuts but leaves this formidable and unenviable task to the defense establishment, i.e., to the IDF. It thus limits its involvement to determining the size of the defense budget but does not follow up on its decisions by requiring that the IDF make the necessary parallel changes in its long-range force development plans. The government is supposedly relying on the defense minister to ensure that the IDF'S plans are updated to reflect the new, lower anticipated spending levels. This faith, however, is not always justified. The defense minister himself may be very unhappy with the deep cuts in the budget, and he may not always be able or ready to withstand pressures from the military. The IDF generally is reluctant to make changes in its battle order or to scrap its pet projects, preferring either to increase a plan's time span—spreading certain projects over many years and thus increasing their overall cost and negatively effecting their economic viability—or to make cuts that it knows will cause intense political and public pressure on the government to increase the budget.[59]

During the 1980s, the lack of effective independent civilian control and supervision over R-and-D and procurement decisions led to many instances where the IDF invested considerable sums in projects for which there never was an adequate budget. As a result, many projects had to be canceled because of lack of funds; some of these were later reinitiated and then canceled once again, with a lot of money being wasted along the way. Large sums of the Israeli taxpayers' money have been spent on ambitious R-and-D projects, only to have the IDF realize, on successful completion of the systems, that it had no money with which to buy them.[60] In 1981 Defense Minister Sharon and Finance Minister Aridor reached agreement on the defense budget framework and on spending levels for the coming five years. Sharon approved a five-year development plan commensurate with the agreed-upon spending levels. However, it was not long before decisions were made that deviated from the approved plan and had no support in terms of the budget estimates. These included the Lavie, a new artillery gun to be developed by Soltam in Israel, the new Sa'ar 5 missile boat, and the acquisition from the United States of hundreds of armored personnel carriers (APCs).[61] Arens admits that his approval of CGS Eitan's request for the purchase of the APCs, which was presented to him during his very first weeks in office, was a grave mistake and was given without adequate study.[62]

It is important to keep in mind that, although this dimension is characterized by strong military involvement, there are a considerable number of instances where decisions are genuinely made by civilians—

instances that have become more frequent in the last few years. These include: Ben-Gurion's decision to cut the defense budget drastically in 1957; his decision in favor of a unified armed service and against an independent air force; Prime Minister Eshkol's decision in 1965 to diversify Israel's arms suppliers and to move toward an American orientation instead of a French one (deciding in favor of the military, headed by Rabin, and against the MOD, headed by Peres), his decision on arms procurement, and especially his compromise regarding the number of Mirage aircraft;[63] Rabin's intensive involvement, as prime minister (1974–1977), in the area of arms procurement, especially from the United States;[64] Defense Minister Dayan's appointment of Zur as assistant to the minister with a strong say in the budget, R-and-D, and procurement areas; decisions made by defense ministers Sharon, Arens, and Rabin regarding priorities among the services;[65] Arens' decision to stop procuring tanks from abroad and put greater emphasis on attack helicopters;[66] the establishment of the FCH by Arens; Rabin's implementation of deep budget cuts in 1985; Rabin's rejection of CGS Shomron's recommendation in 1989 to cancel the navy's submarine program;[67] and Rabin's decision to put greater emphasis on the surface-to-surface missile threat to Israel.[68]

Finally, it should be noted that there are two civilian bodies outside the defense establishment that exercise a control function over the defense budget and thus, to a certain degree, over force development and allocation of resources: the Department of the Budget in the Finance Ministry, and the State Comptroller's Office. However, the actual impact of both these organizations is quite limited. The State Comptroller's Office only reviews past activities and expenditures of the various ministries; its efforts thus suffer from a serious time lag, which limits its influence on ongoing activities. As for the Department of the Budget, it suffers from quite limited human resources, and although its people benefit from various leaks within the military and the MOD, it is not equipped to challenge the IDF effectively.

Case Study: The Rise and Fall of the Lavie

On February 8, 1980, Defense Minister Ezer Weizman decided on the development and production by Israel Aircraft Industries (IAI) of a single-engine fighter aircraft that would be the mainstay of the Israeli air force through the nineties and into the twenty-first century. Seven years and one billion dollars later, the Israeli cabinet voted to cancel the Lavie project. Three milestones marked the seven-and-a-half year history of the ill-fated program: the initiation of the program in February 1980, the fateful decision on the Lavie's engine in May 1981, and, of course, the cancellation of the project on August 30, 1987. Civilian involvement in the first stage was minimal and only slightly greater in the second; by the final stage, however, it reached major proportions, equaling if not exceeding that of the military.[69]

The deliberations that preceded the defense minister's decision in February 1980 were limited almost exclusively to the Defense Ministry, although some civilian input on the political level did occur, primarily in a recommendation by the Foreign Affairs and Defense Committee of the Knesset that Israel develop its own advanced fighter aircraft. The chair of the committee, Moshe Arens (later to become defense minister and foreign minister), himself an aeronautical engineer and a former vice president of IAI, lobbied strongly in favor of the recommendation, as did IAI itself. Even so, the issue was essentially determined by the minister of defense and the air force.

The Israeli air force was initially opposed to the Lavie, preferring to purchase the latest American fighter planes off the shelf—particularly the F-16 and F-18 aircraft. But Defense Minister Ezer Weizman—himself a former commander of the Israeli air force for many years—espoused a different plan. In his view, the air force should procure a small number of highly advanced and expensive aircraft, such as the F-18, and complement its order of battle with a large number of smaller, less sophisticated, and less expensive single-engine aircraft. Weizman envisaged the Lavie as fitting this description. He succeeded in convincing the air force to go along with his approach and eventually, with the concurrence of the air force and the IDF, made his decision on February 8, 1980.

On February 20, 1980, the MDC approved Weizman's decision, although it did not engage in any serious discussions beforehand and made no attempt to evaluate its ramifications. The MDC's decision did not mention the Lavie's engine, size, cost, or basic mission; it simply rubber-stamped the defense minister's original plan. In fact, the civilian echelon never made an independent assessment of the R-and-D costs of the Lavie program or of the eventual procurement price of each aircraft. The only figures presented to the minister of defense were those prepared by the air force and supplemented by IAI; in other words, the only information came from the two organizations that had a vested interest in the project. No other options, such as procurement or joint production of American planes, were presented systematically, either to the defense minister or to the MDC. The MDC did add a rider to its approval of Weizman's decision, calling for joint examination by the defense minister and the finance minister of the economic aspects of the Lavie project, as well as of other projects related to the overall order of battle of the air force, the results of which were to be brought before the committee; however, this decision was never implemented. Repeated attempts by the senior level of the Finance Ministry to be involved fully in the decision-making process regarding the Lavie—attempts that enjoyed the complete support of the finance minister—were rebuffed by the Defense Ministry and, especially, by the IDF.

Weizman's approval of the Lavie had been based on his unique conception of the proper order of battle for Israel's air force. In line with his view, he envisioned the Lavie as a small, relatively inexpensive aircraft that would be produced in relatively large numbers. Unfortunately, however, he did not tie the go-ahead for the Lavie to the implementation of his overall concept; nor, for that matter, did the MDC. Consequently, when Weizman resigned the government on May 28, 1980, and Prime Minister Begin took over the defense portfolio (a position he held until the establishment of a new government in August 1981), all decisions regarding details of the Lavie—most notably, that concerning the plane's engine—were laid squarely in Begin's lap.

Although the civilian echelon, including the Finance Ministry, was nominally involved in the decision-making process, the military echelon called the shots. Ultimately, Begin's decision was clearly shaped by the air force, and no sooner had Weizman left the Defense Ministry than the air force had begun to change its tune. It was no longer willing to accept a small Lavie but instead wanted a larger and stronger Lavie—an advanced first-line fighter aircraft, capable of carrying state-of-the-art avionics. Thus, while it was widely assumed that Weizman would have supported the choice of the General Electric F-404 engine for the plane, the air force rejected that engine as too small, instead opting for the as-yet-not-fully-developed Pratt and Whitney PW 1120 engine, which was larger, stronger, and, of course, much more expensive. IAI had initially supported the smaller engine but, fearful of antagonizing the air force and the IDF, it, too, switched its support to the PW 1120 engine.

Begin hesitated before making a decision, recognizing that he lacked not only personal expertise but also a sound, objective, and comprehensive evaluation of the various options. In December 1980 he postponed the decision for a few months in order to secure more civilian involvement in the decision-making process. He asked the economic adviser of the defense establishment—a civilian employee of the Defense Ministry (unlike the financial adviser, who is an IDF general)—to assess the economic implications of the proposed upgrading of the Lavie. He also moved to involve the Finance Ministry in the process. And as a result of Begin's prodding, on January 4, 1981, the senior echelons of the defense and finance ministries met to discuss the Lavie.

It is only reasonable that a defense minister with no military background and lacking personal knowledge or expertise in the area of weapons systems would advocate more extensive and systematic civilian involvement in the area of force development. At the same time, however, this defense minister—who also happened to be the prime minister and thus endowed with the full personal authority of the civilian echelon— was unwilling to override the military. For its part, the military echelon was quite unhappy with Begin's preference for more civilian involvement, especially from outside the defense establishment, and at times even acted to circumvent it. For example, only a few days before the final decision on the Lavie engine, Deputy Defense Minister Zipori, himself a former IDF general, convened a meeting on the issue to which only the IDF, IAI, and senior Defense Ministry staffers were invited.

On May 29, 1981, Begin called a meeting to decide the issue; senior echelons of the IDF and the air force and representatives of the Defense Ministry, the Finance Ministry, and IAI attended. The air force gave a comprehensive presentation on its view of the Lavie's role in enabling it to execute its mission and explained in detail its reasons for supporting the PW 1120 engine. The economic adviser's initial reports had been negative concerning the PW 1120 engine, stating that a large Lavie would be more costly than the F-16 option; however, on the very day of the meeting, he revised his figures. According to the revised figures, even a large Lavie would still be cheaper than the F-16 alternative, and the R-and-D cost of the project and the life-cycle costs of the aircraft would be much the same regardless of which engine was used.

After listening to the air force's presentation, Begin gave each participant a few minutes to state his preference. The D-G of the Finance Ministry claimed that his people had not been provided with the necessary information to prepare an in-depth economic analysis of the two alternatives and that the economic estimates presented were speculative and

lacked a solid foundation. Since the issue would have far-reaching consequences for the defense budget particularly and the overall budget in general and since the Finance Ministry was not privy to the economic analysis presented by the Defense Ministry, he requested that the decision be
postponed to permit a thorough comparison of all the options—including the purchase of F-16 aircraft from the United States. He was supported by the finance minister.

Begin, in his dual capacity as prime minister and defense minister,
summed up the meeting first by stating that there would be no further
delay. The issue, in his view, was not economic but operational, i.e., relating to the Lavie's ability to function and prevail on the future battlefield.
On such an issue, no one was better equipped to give a definitive answer
than the air force. Begin concluded by stating that the commander of the
air force knew best what airplane he needed; therefore the PW 1120
would be the Lavie engine, and the project was to go forward without further delay. Begin made this decision on his own and did not bring the
matter before the cabinet or even the MDC. For that matter, the debate
regarding the choice of the engine for the Lavie was largely hidden from
the public eye, and the decision-making process kept shrouded in secrecy.
Both these facts were to change dramatically during the final stage of the
Lavie saga.

The final chapter of the Lavie was written on August 30, 1987, but its
roots can be traced to late 1984 and 1985. In late 1984, the National
Unity Government was founded, with Shimon Peres as prime minister,
Yitzhak Shamir as deputy prime minister and foreign minister, and
Yitzhak Rabin as defense minister (in late 1986, Shamir and Peres
exchanged positions). The new government's main goal was to tackle
Israel's hyperinflation, which had reached 400 percent a year. On July 1,
1985, the government introduced a comprehensive economic program
designed to combat inflation. (The plan, incidentally, was a great success: within a year, the inflation was reduced to 16 percent.) A major element of the new program was a deep cut in the defense budget, which
was forced on the IDF by Defense Minister Rabin. Faced with budgetary
constraints whose likes it had not known since 1967, the IDF had to
cancel many of its pet projects. The Lavie project—whose costs, as
could have been expected, had risen far beyond the 1981 estimates—
was consuming almost all available R-and-D funds, and its full-scale
continuation would kill virtually every other military R-and-D project.
Not surprisingly, the IDF began to turn against the Lavie. Even within

the air force, which formally remained in favor of the Lavie, serious doubts were being raised about the utility and wisdom of the Lavie; a number of senior officers openly called for the scrapping of the entire project and for the replacement of the Lavie with the advanced F-16C fighter.

A major public debate on the future of the aircraft erupted. Had the military fought intensely against the Lavie in February 1980, it probably could have prevented its inception. Had it opposed the PW 1120 engine in 1981, it certainly would have had its way and so could have ensured a less grandiose and risky project; indeed, it might have been able, even at that late stage, to kill the program altogether. This, however, was not the case in 1985–1987. Times had definitely changed. The Lavie had gone public, and for many in Israel it had become a symbol of national pride, national independence, and national commitment. Between 1981 and 1986, a major pro-Lavie civilian lobby sprang up throughout the country, backed by supporters in the political establishment, the press, industry, and labor—and especially by IAI and its powerful Workers Committee. The age of the military-industrial complex had finally reached Israel, but the military and industry were at loggerheads. By 1986 even the formidable IDF could not shoot down the Lavie on its own.

In March 1987, Lieutenant-General Dan Shomron was appointed chief of staff of the IDF. On assuming office, Shomron publicly declared his intention to streamline the IDF and prepare it for the battlefield of the future. He spoke of a smaller but smarter army, based on high-tech weapons systems and smart munitions. None of this could be achieved, however, as long as the Lavie continued to swallow the major part of a shrinking R-and-D budget. Aware of this, Shomron set as his first and primary goal the cancellation of the Lavie project and was ready to put all his prestige (Shomron had an illustrious battle record and had been the commander on the ground of the famous Entebbe rescue operation in July 1976) on the line. He was strongly supported in this effort by the head of the planning branch of the general staff, an air force general (Avihu Bin Nun) who was later to become commander of the air force.

But gone were the days when the IDF, especially a strong and popular CGS, could dictate the major issues of force development and weapons systems acquisition. These areas were now open to public scrutiny: civilian involvement had come of age. The military realized that it had no chance of killing the Lavie project without the strong support of Defense Minister Rabin. Not only did it have to convince Rabin that its goal was correct, it had to persuade him to undertake a major political battle to achieve it. Rabin had harbored doubts about the Lavie from the beginning and was easily convinced that the project was a gross mistake and an unbearable drain on the defense budget; he was unsure, however, that its cancellation was politically feasible. But by mid-1987 Rabin became convinced that there was no alternative and declared publicly that the Lavie had to go. The battle lines were now clearly drawn.

The IDF, supported by its civilian superior, called for cancellation of the Lavie project, notwithstanding the billion dollars that had already been invested in it. By now, though, the question had become an issue of such paramount national importance that it could only be decided by the government—i.e., the full cabinet—and it was highly questionable whether a majority would favor cancellation. The Likud (Labor's chief partner in the National Unity Government) turned the issue into a political one. For them, the Lavie was not only a symbol of Israel's scientific, technological, and industrial capability but a major element in reducing Israel's military dependence on the United States and thus increasing its ability to withstand American pressure with regard to the territories. Workers, facing major layoffs in the event of the Lavie's cancellation (in IAI alone, three thousand would be fired following the government's August 30 decision), not only threatened massive demonstrations but warned that they would bring the entire country to a standstill.

In one of the rare instances of a prime minister and defense minister utterly disagreeing on a major national security issue, Prime Minister Shamir came out strongly against the Lavie's cancellation. In the face of his opposition, Rabin and the military realized they needed another strong civilian ally, whom they found in the person of the finance minister, himself a senior member of the Likud and a close confidant of Shamir. The professional echelon of the Finance Ministry had opposed the Lavie at the beginning and had fought it almost all along the way. Now it joined ranks with the IDF and the defense establishment to bring about its downfall. Finance Minister Nissim went along with the unanimous advice of the senior level of his ministry, broke ranks with Shamir, and fully supported Rabin in demanding that the government cancel the project. As it was, the decision was a cliff-hanger. The cabinet met on August 30, 1987, and, after hours of debate, voted twelve to eleven, with one abstention, to terminate the Lavie. The abstention came from a junior Labor minister who supported the Lavie: after strong pressure from her Labor colleagues during a recess in the meeting, she had broken down in tears and then abstained.

This case study supports the conclusion that civilian involvement in the dimension of force development has rapidly and steadily grown over the last ten to fifteen years. The driving force behind the demise of the Lavie may have been the IDF, but it was no longer the only player in the field. Not only was the civilian echelon of the Defense Ministry more involved and more forceful in the decision-making process, but key decisions generally arose from broader civilian participation, including that of the Finance Ministry, the cabinet, the political establishment, the press, and public opinion. In this sphere, Israel has come of age.

8 | Civilian Control Revisited

The theoretical approach to civilian control developed in chapter 2 enables one to undertake a much more detailed evaluation of civilian control in Israel, examining it from many different perspectives. A broad definition of civilian control emphasizing the maximization of civilian involvement and the minimization of military involvement would certainly find civilian control in Israel quite lacking. A much narrower definition of civilian control would be the noninvolvement of the military in the area of political affairs (represented by the dotted line in figure 1 in chapter 1). Using this yardstick, hardly anyone would argue with the conclusion that Israel manifests the highest degree of civilian control.

There is no instance in Israel's history of military intervention or even of a veiled threat of military intervention in the electoral process or in the political institutions of the state. This holds true not only for blatant interference but for minimal involvement—such as influence on political appointments or interference in the decision-making process—as well. Even Mordechai Gur, who as CGS balked at taking action against the Greater Israel activists at Sabastia, made it clear to them that he would not hesitate to use maximum force if they attempted to undermine the government's freedom of decision.[1] As Perlmutter points out: "General Dayan was appointed Defense Minister in the crisis of June 1967, not because he had great influence with Zahal, but because it was the will of the Israeli electorate."[2]

Some believe the expanding role of retired senior military officers in government and the entrance of ex-generals into politics represent indirect military intervention in the political and electoral process. In their opinion, these phenomena denote a dangerous convergence of the military and civilian sectors of society and thus pose a definite threat to civilian control. This practice can be found in other Western countries, especially in the United States, which has a long history of military heroes running for and being elected to the presidency. In the Israeli context, however, it may give rise to a greater degree of concern, primarily because of the large number of former senior IDF officers active in government and politics and the informal nature of Israeli society.

The IDF is committed to a rapid rotational system, as a result of which its most senior officers leave the army in their mid-forties or early fifties. These officers are encouraged to enter active civilian life—whether government, politics, or business—there to benefit from the high prestige enjoyed by the IDF. As a result, an inordinate number of ex-generals can be found occupying key positions in public service. Six of Israel's thirteen former chiefs of staff entered politics; at one time or another, all of them have served as cabinet ministers. In 1984, the National Unity Government's MDC counted among its ten members four ex-generals, two of whom were former chiefs of staff. The Israel Electric Corporation, the Israel Military Industries, the Antiquities Authority, the National Water Authority, the Rails and Port Authority—all government corporations or agencies—are or recently were headed by ex-generals. Some of the country's leading mayors are former senior IDF officers.

This picture becomes even more problematic when one takes into consideration the informal nature of Israeli society. Israel is a tiny country, where it is quite easy to maintain friendships and contacts. After serving for twenty to thirty years in the IDF and being a member of the general staff, one's circle of close friends will inevitably include many of those currently serving in the general staff and/or occupying other senior military positions. Such closely knit social networks, supported by a commonality of interests and experiences, can easily become a major avenue for strong, albeit indirect, military influence in political affairs and, under certain circumstances, could pose a serious challenge to effective and genuine civilian control.

An in-depth examination of this issue in the unique Israeli context must await further study, inasmuch as it comes under the general heading of military involvement in domestic affairs—a topic not dealt with directly in this book. A superficial examination of this issue, however, shows that the extensive role played by retired IDF officers in government and politics does not seem to contribute to increased military involvement in political affairs. There is little, if any, evidence that, on entering civilian life, ex-generals tend to serve military interests or even to advocate positions supported by the IDF. On the contrary, the defense ministers who instituted, or at least attempted to institute, the most far-reaching cuts in defense spending and in the IDF budget—forcing them on the CGS and the general staff—were all ex-generals (Weizman, Sharon, and Rabin). Ex-generals are among the strongest and loudest critics of the IDF in the Knesset and in its Foreign Affairs and Defense Committee. It would seem that on entering civilian life, and especially politics, former generals tend to adopt civilian perspectives.

More careful examination, however, points to at least two subtle, yet significant, effects of this phenomenon on civil-military relations. First, most chiefs of staff as well as most officers of the general staff hope to attain, on leaving the service, key positions in politics, government, or industry and business, much of which is controlled directly or indirectly by those in government; such an unhealthy dependence on the goodwill of politicians may compromise the professional integrity of these soldiers. This represents a subtle case of politicization of the military. Second, the integration of so many senior IDF officers into the higher echelons of civilian activity and decision making after they have spent twenty to thirty years in the armed forces results in a massive transfer of manners, work habits, nomenclature, norms, and values from the military to civilian society, i.e., a militarization of the civilian sphere. Both effects are difficult to recognize and virtually impossible to quantify, yet both can be quite impressive.

Interestingly enough, one of the very few hints ever uttered regarding possible military involvement in political appointments may have been issued by the highest civilian authority, Prime Minister Shamir. Press reports of a closed meeting of the Likud ministers after the general elections of 1988 and on the eve of the establishment of the National Unity Government maintained that Shamir responded to a claim by Sharon that the Defense Ministry must be in the hands of the Likud by saying: "If the Defense Ministry is in the hands of the Likud, there will be serious problems in the army." This was understood to imply that the IDF would refuse to accept Sharon as defense minister. Sharon replied immediately that Shamir's approach was a danger to Israel's democratic system of government and asked: "Since when does the army determine the composition of the government?" Shamir retorted that he would not satisfy Sharon's curiosity and that anything further said would be detrimental to Israel's security.[3] Although Shamir never denied it publicly and explicitly, there are no independent confirmations of this press report, and it should be taken with a grain of salt. What Shamir probably meant to imply was that Sharon's appointment as defense minister would meet with severe public criticism and would be highly divisive for Israeli society, not that the appointment would be seriously opposed by the IDF.

The narrow definition of civilian control based on lack of military involvement in the political electoral process falls short of encompassing the full scope and meaning of the concept. A different approach puts the emphasis on the question of who exercises ultimate control, i.e., on the readiness of the military to comply with civilian authority. The interviewees in this study all agreed that from the formal point of view the IDF has always complied with civilian authority, and all expressed their solemn conviction that the senior officer corps in the IDF was fully committed to the principle of civilian supremacy. Weizman states that in all his military experience he cannot think of even one instance where a senior officer in the IDF suggested that the military do what it wanted and "the hell with the civilians." Even Peri writes that "never since the establishment of the State was there any expression of the army's desire to question the roles the political national institution allotted to it, to take part in the process of power transition, or to usurp political power."[4]

Yet this definition, too, was shown in chapter 2 to be inadequate. The more modern position is that the crux of civilian control lies in who in fact, not theory, establishes national security policy and determines the allocation of finite resources to fulfill security needs. Civilian control thus refers to the appropriate balance between civilian and military involvement in all relevant areas—a balance that varies from country to country and from time to time—and this book has described this balance in the Israeli case, as well as the changes that have occurred over the years. The picture that emerged is complex; in some areas there exists a very fine balance, whereas others manifest a high degree of military or civilian over-involvement. The main point made in chapter 2 is that civilian control is not a standard by which countries are to be judged but rather a sliding scale along which societies adjust themselves. No given point can be defined a priori as signifying civilian control or a lack of civilian control. Effective civilian control depends on the mechanisms available to society and on the means it employs to cope with the diverse dangers that may from time to time threaten the principle of civil supremacy over the military. In chapter 2 I defined four key factors or variables that determine the ability of any state or society to maintain civilian control. I will now review these factors, examining the degree to which each is present and effectively employed in the Israeli context.

The first factor is the determination of the civilian echelon to uphold its authority and to guard its privileges and prerogatives. Here, the Israeli system shows a definite weakness, especially in the area of strategic planning. The civilian authority's abdication of its responsibility for the formulation of national security policy has been amply illustrated in these pages. But Peri is mistaken when he singles out Israel as a country where the military is highly influential in the determination of government policy and where civilian supervision is not always sufficiently effective.[5] After all, such a state of affairs can be found, on occasion, in every Western democracy, especially in times of war—the case of the United States during World War II being merely one example. One must constantly recall that Israel is in a state of war with most of its neighbors and has fought at least one war every decade of its existence. The IDF is a fighting army—an army constantly called on to engage in military operations—and this accounts for its inordinate influence on strategic planning and policy formulation.

A lack of determination by the civilian echelon to uphold its authority and to maintain a proper balance between the defense establishment as a whole—including its civilian component—and other branches of government is also manifested in the oft-found phenomenon of military usurpation of the conduct of foreign affairs. Lawyer wrote in 1980 that "there has been a growing feeling in some quarters that military participation in international relations is an unwarranted incursion that can only lead to the militarization of United States foreign policy." He claimed that while in the fifties and sixties military officers seldom ventured further into international diplomacy than to conduct base rights negotiations or work out military assistance packages, in the 1970s the military assumed active roles in such major international negotiations as the SALT talks and the Law of the Sea Conference. Although "direct military influence . . . has declined since its peak in World War II, when the military virtually ran U.S. foreign policy," indirect influence has "tended to grow."

Lawyer points out that there are no less than six separate staffs in the Pentagon directly concerned with foreign policy, with a combined budget and manpower exceeding that of the State Department itself.[6]

Lawyer's portrait of extensive military involvement in international relations and in the conduct of foreign affairs certainly holds true for Israel. This began with the armistice negotiations in 1949, continued with the arms deals negotiations of the 1950s and 1960s, and reached its peak during the negotiations with Egypt in the 1970s.[7] In certain instances, the military came to dominate the process—at times even to the exclusion of the Foreign Ministry. In 1956, when the IDF occupied the Gaza Strip in the course of the Sinai Operation, the Foreign Ministry asked to send a representative to Gaza. CGS Dayan reacted negatively, and the representative who eventually went met with a total lack of cooperation on the part of the IDF. During the 1971 incident with the Sabena Airlines plane that was hijacked to Ben Gurion Airport, two representatives of the director-general of the Foreign Ministry arrived at the command post at the airport only to be summarily sent home by Defense Minister Dayan.[8]

The tendency of the defense establishment—through both its military and civilian arms—to conduct its own independent foreign policy behind the back of the Foreign Ministry is a constant feature of—and basic fault in—Israeli civil-military relations. It has often caused serious friction within the system. Not only did Peres, as D-G of the Defense Ministry, take personal charge of the rapidly developing defense relationship between France and Israel in the early 1950s, but he sidestepped the Foreign Ministry and kept the Israeli embassy and the Israeli ambassador in Paris in the dark. Such a state of affairs could never have come about without the prime minister's approval. Indeed, not only did Ben-Gurion condone Peres's abuse of Foreign Minister Sharett, but he countenanced the same conduct toward Foreign Minister Golda Meir, even though she was one of his closest confidants and staunchest political supporters.[9] Issar Harel, former head of Israel's Mossad and a trusted associate of both Ben Gurion and Golda Meir, reports that Meir bitterly complained to him about the independent activities of the Defense Ministry in the international arena, saying that "she simply couldn't take it any more."[10] This unwillingness on the part of Israel's prime ministers to control the imperialist tendencies of the defense establishment is a recurrent feature of Israeli politics. Thus Ariel Sharon, as defense minister, traveled extensively, conducting political and diplomatic negotiations with many foreign leaders—all under the guise of arranging defense exports and security matters. Foreign Minister Shamir complained to Begin—but to no avail.[11] The problem exists in other countries, but it appears to be far more serious in Israel's case.

Although the civilian echelon in Israel abdicates its responsibility in certain areas, it zealously maintains its authority and prerogatives in others, especially the conduct of military operations, the naming of senior appointments, and the activities of the IDF in the Administered Territories. Moreover, legislation passed in February 1991 creating a statutory National Security Ministerial Committee and compelling the prime minister to appoint and to operate a permanent professional team to advise the government on national security affairs, as well as efforts by defense ministers Rabin and Arens to increase their involvement in strategic planning, may signify a determination of the civilian echelon to reassert its authority in these all-important areas.

The second factor or variable that determines the extent of civilian control is a firm ideological commitment to democratic government and unshakable belief in the principle of civilian supremacy. Indeed, this factor seems to be one of the most effective forces guaranteeing civilian control. While at times the military has used all the means at its disposal in a free and open society to influence the civil authority to accept its opinion and/or to yield to its will, these efforts have never deviated from the normal constitutional channels and procedures. Thus in June 1967, O/C northern command General Elazar openly orchestrated a major civilian lobby to pressure the cabinet to approve an attack on the Golan Heights and in so doing may have gone beyond the normal constraints on a senior military officer, but he never challenged civilian authority, and he did nothing to undermine the government's freedom of decision. Many of Elazar's successors have actively instigated civilian pressure groups among the kibbutzim and other outlying settlements in the north, but again such efforts have been strictly limited to the level of influence.

There is much in Israeli society to strengthen the military's ideological commitment to democratic government. As I pointed out in the introduction, the democratic character of the state of Israel and of Israeli society in general reflects the age-old tradition of the Jewish people, which goes back thirty-five hundred years. That tradition is also manifest in the high degree of internal democracy within the IDF itself. Very few, if any, military organizations in the world maintain an atmosphere as open as the IDF's. This democratic style is a direct result of the IDF's popular character: it is a genuine people's army, evidenced not only in the fact that three-quarters of the IDF's order of battle are reservists but also in the rapid rotation system, the early retirement program, the universal draft, the lack of elitist officer training programs, as well as in the existence of a young, inquisitive, and intelligent officer corps.[12] Yariv reports that in 1971 when the general staff discussed proposals for reopening the Suez Canal, CGS Bar-Lev put the various positions to a vote in the full general staff forum.[13] Although this was, and remains, a definite exception to the rule, it still suggests an egalitarian attitude not found in other Western armies. Former CGS Levy comments that on a number of occasions he requested the defense minister's permission to bring to various cabinet forums generals who differed with his own view, so that they could present their contrary views directly to the government.[14] Former CGS Gur emphasizes the freedom enjoyed by officers of every rank to express their own views openly and to appeal decisions before a higher authority.[15] There have been instances where officers have stood up in formal gatherings and demanded the resignation of their superiors, even the defense minister. Arens also stresses the lack of monolithic positions in the IDF and the fact that on most issues there is a lively, open, and free debate within the IDF itself.[16]

The third factor critical for civilian control is the political leadership's respect for the professional autonomy of the military and trust in the high command of the armed forces. There can be no doubt that the IDF high command enjoys the confidence not only of the Israeli government but of the public at large. Public opinion polls consistently show that the IDF and the judiciary are the two national institutions that enjoy the highest degree of public confidence. As in any other democracy, such strong public support must necessarily be reflected in the opinion, attitude, and behavior of the government. Israel is a characteristic example of the fusionist theory of administration. In line with this theory, the IDF exercises influence in defense and foreign policy and is a partner in the formulation of national security policy. Indeed, it enjoys inordinate influence and is, perhaps, the senior partner in the process. While it is true that in the operational sphere civil-military relations suffer from an overdose of micromanagement and some defense ministers have functioned as super chiefs of staff, in terms of the overall picture, it is fair to say that the IDF enjoys a high degree of professional autonomy. Its voice is always heard, and its positions are respected; in many areas, there is a healthy environment of mutual deference. The special status enjoyed by the CGS and his right of access to the prime minister is another strong manifestation of the professional autonomy of the IDF. Of the five roles that can be taken by the military in politico-military affairs—advisory, representative, executive, advocacy, and substantive—it is clear that the IDF plays the first four roles, including, at times, an exaggerated advocacy role. But it does not engage in the prohibited substantive role.[17]

The fourth and last factor determining civilian control is a clear constitutional framework and precise legal guidelines regarding the functions, authority, and responsibilities of the civilian and military echelons—both notably lacking in the Israeli context. Herein lies one of the gravest threats to civilian control. This area, more than any other, is in dire need of correction.

9 | Conclusions and Recommendations

Recognition and appreciation of the complex and evolving nature of Israeli civil-military relations is perhaps the central conclusion of this study. Certainly, it does not support Peri's argument that these relations are characterized by a unique partnership between the generals and the politicians and by nominal civilian control. Yet the contention of many scholars that Israeli civil-military relations are modeled along the lines of the major Western democracies seems equally lacking in insight. Both characterizations suffer from oversimplification and fail to do justice to the subtleties of the relationship.

The overall picture of Israeli civil-military relations that has emerged in this book is positive, reflecting an essentially healthy and balanced system. Although Israeli civil-military relations have known many a crisis, they have never broken down, nor has civilian control ever faced a serious challenge. This book is replete with examples of actual, not nominal, civilian control; the record is impressive, especially in view of Israel's unenviable position of being in a state of war virtually constantly since its inception. If there has ever been a case of a democracy being ripe for the development of Lasswell's "garrison state," it is Israel; yet Israel shows no signs of becoming such a state.

In line with the theoretical model adapted for this study, this book has focused primarily on the relative involvement of the civilian and the military in two spheres of national activity: the armed services and national security. The results are mixed. The data presented clearly lead to the conclusion that in certain areas, at certain times, civilian involvement is maximized beyond what is accepted and common in Western countries. This is especially so with regard to the actual conduct of military operations. At the same time, civilian involvement is barely present in other areas. In particular, strategic planning and, to a lesser degree, force development suffer from military overinvolvement and domination at both the decision-making and organizational levels. Yet this conclusion, too, must be viewed against the backdrop of Israel's unique circumstances. Israel has known six wars in its short history, and the IDF is a fighting army. Most scholars in the field, as well as many of those interviewed for this book, point out that the profile of civil-military relations is quite different in war than in peace. Overinvolvement of the military in the armed forces and national security areas during wartime is common in most Western democracies. Thus, although military involvement in Israel in strategic planning, force development, or foreign affairs is beyond what is currently accepted in the United States, it is not much different from what prevailed in the United States during World War II.

I have identified three main trouble spots in Israeli civil-military relations, all of which are in definite need of reform: the lack of constitutional and legal clarity as to the formal aspects of the system, the lack of civilian input in strategic planning, and the lack of a proper balance between the military and civilian echelons of the defense organization. Although none of these three issues poses, at present, a serious threat to effective civil-military relations, they are all potentially dangerous and could, at some future time, be the source of a major crisis, particularly in light of the social, political, and demographic changes outlined in the introduction. For this reason, it is important to deal with these issues now, in an atmosphere of positive and more or less tranquil relations.

Chapters 3 and 4 showed that the absence of clearly defined roles and spheres of authority, as well as certain legal anachronisms and lacunae, continues to plague the system and is a major source of potential trouble and friction. The lack of a clearly defined national command authority, conflicting views as to the degree of authority wielded by the defense minister over the chief of staff and the IDF, and the failure to deal specifically with the role of the prime minister vis-à-vis the IDF are examples of nonconstructive ambiguity that needs correction. Add to this the total disregard of the question of succession, which could assume crucial importance in a nuclear Middle East or in war involving strategic attack on the centers of government.

Matters have improved somewhat since the early years of the state, when there was hardly any legislation in the area of civil-military relations, and almost everything was a matter of constitutional convention. Major steps were taken following the Yom Kippur War in 1973, and in early 1992 a new law regarding direct elections of the prime minister—a constitutional act of legislation scheduled to go into effect in 1996—stipulated explicitly that the government, and the government alone, is empowered to declare or initiate war. The law states further that the prime minister shall notify the Knesset, as soon as possible, of such a decision and that speedy notification of any military activities shall be given to the Knesset's FADC. There remains, however, an acute need for further legislation in order to overcome the ambiguities and conflicting views described in chapters 3 and 4. Following are a number of concrete suggestions to achieve this end.

1. *Instructions of the High Command.* The law should be amended to stipulate that instructions of the high command are to be issued by the defense minister, with the approval of the prime minister, and that both the Ministerial Committee on National Security (MNSC) and the FADC shall be informed of such instructions. Such legislation would correct the present anomaly whereby the military determines its own organization and administration, albeit with civilian approval. It would also clarify the roles of the prime minister, the government (through the MNSC), and the legislature (through the FADC).

2. *The National Command Authority.* The law should be amended to spell out the national command authority clearly and to define more precisely the roles of the three key actors. The positions of the defense minister vis-à-vis the CGS, the prime minister vis-à-vis the defense minister, and the cabinet vis-à-vis the prime minister and the defense minister should all be enhanced. The national command authority should run from the cabinet or the MNSC to the prime minister, from him to the defense minister, and from the defense minister to the CGS.

The authority of the defense minister over the CGS should be absolute and unequivocal but not exclusive. This is the heart of the Israeli system. The relationship between the CGS and the defense minister should be hierarchal, with no area—be it tactical, operational, or administrative—in which the CGS is independent of the minister; the CGS must carry out all the defense minister's orders, excepting, of course, any that are patently illegal. On the other hand, the right of access and appeal by the CGS to the prime minister, as well as the prime minister's ultimate authority, should be rooted in law. Inasmuch as the CGS can be dismissed only by the cabinet, it should be made clear by law that, under extraordinary circumstances, the civilian authority—i.e., the prime minister and the defense minister, acting jointly—can assume the powers and functions of the CGS and issue orders directly to IDF commanders, subject to speedy approval by the government. The law should also be amended to make it clear that in case of general hostilities or a major military operation, the instructions and orders of the prime minster and defense minister should be subject to general guidelines determined by the cabinet or the MNSC.

3. *Succession.* The law should be amended to specify clearly the order of succession both with regard to the defense minister and the prime minister. No room should be left for doubt as to who is the effective civilian authority. The CGS must know, at any point in time and under any set of circumstances, to whom he is subordinate and who is authorized to issue him orders.

4. *Appointments.* The procedures and regulations regarding the appointment of senior officers should be codified into law. The current convention by which every appointment to the rank of colonel needs the defense minister's approval seems anachronistic, given the growth in size of the IDF since the days of Ben-Gurion; such appointments and promotions should be left to the discretion of the CGS. On the other hand, the role of the defense minister and the prime minister regarding very serious appointments should be enhanced. Not only should all promotions to the ranks of brigadier general and major general and appointments to positions occupied by officers of such rank need the approval of the defense minister, but certain key appointments should be subject to prime ministerial approval. Such positions could include the deputy chief of staff, head of military intelligence, and the commanders of the air force, navy, and FCH. Furthermore, the law should state clearly that officers appointed with the approval of the defense minister may be dismissed by him after consultation with the CGS or by the CGS with the approval of the defense minister.

Chapter 5's detailed description of the defense organization in Israel pointed up a number of important flaws and structural weaknesses in this organization. Many functions that rightly belong to the civilian echelon are performed by the military echelon. There is a lack of significant civilian input at the central defense organization level, which undermines de facto civilian control. The central conclusion is that while Israel is far advanced along the road to unification and centralization, perhaps even leading the way in these areas, it lags behind in the realm of integration. Greater integration in the system would likely resolve many of the problems plaguing the central defense organization, and this presents the most promising means for rapid and significant improvement. The United States' response to the challenges of military domination of central defense organization—the creation of a parallel civilian staff, namely, the Office of the Secretary of Defense—is clearly inapplicable in the Israeli case. Israel is a small country with quite limited resources and cannot afford the luxury of two parallel staffs. An integrated civilian-military staff system at the central organizational level being the optimum solution for Israel, I recommend that the MOD gradually implement an integrated civilian-military staff system along the lines of those in Great Britain and Canada. In addition to budget and R-and-D functions, which are currently integrated in whole or in part, planning, legal advice, information, and intelligence should also be wholly or partially integrated. Among the specific steps that should be taken are the following:

1. The FA-HB should be a civilian with a military deputy. Alternatively, the position should rotate between a senior civil servant from the MOD and a senior IDF officer, with a deputy from the other side.

2. The planning branch (G5) of the general staff should be restructured as an integrated civilian-military structure reporting jointly to the CGS and the D-G. Here, too, the headship of the facility should rotate between a civilian and a soldier, with a deputy from the other side. As a first step, the head of the strategic planning division within the planning branch should be a civilian.

3. The office of the IDF spokesperson should also be restructured as an integrated civilian-military structure, reporting jointly to the CGS and the D-G and headed by a civilian with a military deputy.

4. The legal advice and legislature section within the advocate general's office in the IDF should be abolished, and all its functions transferred to the legal division of the MOD.

Thought should also be given to organizational reform within the IDF itself. It is clear that the multipurpose general staff, combining staff and command functions, serves Israel's interests; however, chapter 5 did note the lack of a balanced three-service structure. The time seems ripe for the IDF to create such a structure at the staff level. The general staff would then serve a single staff function, acting as a genuine joint defense staff dealing with overall planning and operations, while all staff functions for the ground forces would be transferred to an augmented FCH.

A final word regarding strategic planning. The central conclusion from chapter 7 was that the dimension of strategic planning is by far the most problematic and poses the most serious threat to civilian control in Israel. Civilian involvement in the actual formulation of national security policy is minimal. This area, more than any other, is in urgent need of far-reaching reform. Integrating the planning function in the MOD, which would lead to increased involvement of civilians, would contribute meaningfully to correcting the problem; however, it is not enough. The best solution would be to create a strategic planning and analysis function at the governmental level, under the authority and guidance of the prime minister. Only such a staff facility enjoying the prestige of the prime minister's office and working from a broad outlook free of particularistic interest could become an effective counterbalance to the IDF's domination of the strategic planning process. Legislation enacted in 1991 calls for just such a facility. One can only hope that this legislation will be put into effect as soon as possible.

Appendix A
Theoretical Perspectives

Civil-military relations, in their broadest sense, have been a topic of great interest at least since the beginning of recorded history. The relationship between the soldier and the state he is sworn to serve has always fascinated scholars, thinkers, and philosophers. The essence of the issue, as summed up in the much-quoted aphorism from the first-century Latin national poet Juvenal is "Quis custodiet ipsos custodes?" (Who is to guard the guards themselves?).

In ancient times, as well as in premodern days, a nation's leader and military commander were in many instances one person—as was the case with Judas the Maccabee, Alexander the Great, Genghis Khan, Napoleon, Frederick the Great, and many others—making the question of civil-military relations seem irrelevant. However, even biblical times saw blatant instances of the military undermining the express desires and policies of the supreme political leadership. A dramatic example is the case of King David and his chief of staff, Yoav, son of Zeruyah.

The Bible tells how King David strove to unite the kingdom of Israel and to effect a reconciliation with the House of Saul. He met with Avner, the chief of staff of Saul's son, and they concluded an agreement by which David would be recognized as king of all Israel. This constituted a clear-cut decision of state, a policy determination of the highest order, taken by the ultimate authority in the kingdom. However, on hearing of these events, David's chief of staff expressed his violent opposition. Unable to change David's mind, Yoav secretly invited Avner to meet with him and then killed him.[1] The superhawkish and aggressive Yoav, whose personal loyalty to David was absolute and beyond question, remained chief of staff for almost forty years, until David's death, and continued to act independently, not hesitating to undermine David's policies aimed at containing war and limiting bloodshed as much as possible. It was only on his deathbed that David commanded his son and heir, Solomon, to settle accounts with Yoav, telling him that Yoav had chosen war over peace and should not be permitted to go to his grave peacefully.[2]

The truly interesting, almost incredible aspect of the story is that the all-powerful David was unwilling or unable to relieve Yoav of his command. It is difficult to understand why the king who put so many men to death for minor misgivings publicly reprimanded his chief of staff repeatedly yet took no action against him. Why was the greatest Jewish hero of all time, who enjoyed almost unlimited authority and power over his kingdom, unable to impose his will on his chief military officer? The answer can only be that King David faced the same grave problem that has beset so many leaders after him: namely, the great difficulty and high price involved in replacing a highly popular military commander. There is no doubt that Yoav, for all his insubordination, was a soldier's general, a natural leader extremely popular with the troops.[3] Despite the tremendous differences in time, place, and system of government, King David's dilemma closely resembles the conflicts so many kings, presidents, and prime ministers have confronted over the centuries, when they must decide whether to relieve a popular military hero from his command.

Civil-military relations have a long history, but most researchers agree that they have acquired new significance in our day and age. People date the beginning of modern civil-military relations from different periods. Many suggest that the rise of the modern nation-state toward the end of the eighteenth and during the nineteenth century heralded the new era. Huntington claims that "the emergence of a professional officer corps created the modern problem of civil-military relations in Europe and North America," yet he lists the growth of the nation-state as one of the three key factors underlying the rise of military professionalism. Still other researchers point to the twentieth-century phenomenon of large-scale standing armies as the main source of civil-military interaction. Janowitz writes that until World War I the military was small, functioning as a self-contained, socially distinct force. It was only after World War

I and especially with the onset of World War II that there was a definite trend toward the emergence and dominance of the "mass army" or, more precisely, the "mass armed force." Sweetman emphasizes that the standing armed forces states create for their self-protection "possess at the same time the potential to destroy them." Hendrickson draws attention to the deep-rooted Anglo-American tradition that always saw a basic danger to internal freedom and democracy in the mere existence of large standing armies over long periods of time.[4] This tradition focuses attention on another factor contributing to the rise in importance of civil-military relations in the nineteenth and twentieth centuries: the emergence of democracy. Democratic government places major emphasis on government by the people and thus on the subordination of the military to the will of the people as represented by their elected civilian leaders; it is also particularly suspicious of the military mind with its emphasis on the concentration of authority, command, and resources.

Clearly, then, the roots of modern civil-military relations are to be found, more or less, in the nineteenth century. That century also saw the emergence of a new science of war, whose most notable spokesman was Karl von Clausewitz, author of the first comprehensive and explicit formulation of the new theory of war, *Vom Kriege* (*On War*), first published in 1831. Clausewitz's famous dictum that war "is a continuation of political relations . . . by other means" underlines the need and justification for civilian control over the armed forces. Clausewitz stressed that war was a genuine instrument of state, the political goal being the end and war merely the means. As he expressed it, "While war has its own grammar, it has no logic or purpose of its own." Huntington claims that "in formulating the first theoretical rationale for the military profession, Clausewitz also contributed the first theoretical justification for civilian control."[5] Different and contrary approaches were, however, also offered.

The military theorists of the nineteenth and early twentieth centuries did deal with aspects of modern civil-military relations, but only within the wider context of an overall military science. Their work was paralleled by that of democratic theorists such as Jefferson and de Tocqueville, as well as that of a new school of scientific political scientists early in the twentieth century. Nevertheless, the emergence of civil-military relations as an independent field of research and study is regarded, almost universally, as a post–World War II occurrence. Huntington writes that "it is . . . fair to say that prior to World War II civil-military relations received little attention from social scientists and historians, at least in the English-language literature and certainly in American writing." Edmonds writes that "civil and military relations . . . as a field of study is relatively new. . . . The approach to the study of armed forces and society today cannot benefit greatly from looking at scholarly works written before the Second World War. Even then, not much of great analytical value was accomplished until the middle to late 1950s." The end of the 1950s saw the appearance of three classic works—all within a period of five years and all three having a major impact on the study of civil-military relations. Lissak writes that the publication of these three books represented a turning point in the study of the social and political aspects of the armed forces and of the politico-military establishment.[6]

The first work, published in 1957 and certainly one of the best known, is Samuel Huntington's theory of professionalism, first outlined in his book *The Soldier and the State*. Huntington's fundamental thesis is that "the principal form of civil-military relations is the relation of the officer corps to the state" and that "the modern officer corps is a professional body and the modern military officer a professional man."[7] For him, the concept of professionalism was central to an understanding of civil-military relations, and maximizing military professionalism was the key to objective civilian control.

Huntington defined a profession as a special type of vocation characterized by expertise, responsibility, and corporateness. It is expertise that separates the professional from the layperson, and responsibility for performing a service essential to the functioning of society that separates the doctor from the research scientist. Corporateness refers to the self-perception of the members of a given profession as belonging to that profession, i.e., to their group identity (8–10). Officership in a modern army and in a modern state meets these three principal criteria of professionalism, and thus the "fundamental character [of the officer corps] as a profession is undeniable" (11). Huntington defined the central skill common to all military officers as "the management of violence" (11); this, in contradistinction to the enlisted man, who is a "specialist in the application of violence" (18) but not in its management, and who has neither the responsibility nor the corporateness of a profession—hence his vocation is merely a trade.

A major element in Huntington's theory is the differentiation between "subjective civilian control" and "objective civilian control." Subjective civilian control is achieved through maximizing the power of civilian groups—in practice, usually only a particular group or groups—in relation to the military. Objective civilian control minimizes military power by professionalizing the military, thus rendering them politically sterile and neutral; its essence is the recognition of autonomous military professionalism (80–84). Huntington also distinguishes between the operating and institutional levels of national security policy. The first deals with the actual means taken to meet security threats, while the second relates to the manner in which the aforementioned policy is formulated and executed. Civil-military relations is the principal institutional component of national security policy. While public debate usually focuses on the operational issues, Huntington draws our attention to the importance of the institutional level, for "in the long run the nature of the decisions . . . is determined by the institutional pattern through which the decisions are made. . . . The ordering of its civil-military relations . . . is basic to a nation's military security policy" (1–2).

The second work, published in 1960, was *The Professional Soldier*. In it, Morris Janowitz addressed very much the same concerns as Huntington—namely, the long-range effects on American civil-military relations of the far-reaching changes in America's military posture as a result of World War II and the ensuing Cold War—and reached similar conclusions. Detailing the professional character of the American officer corps, he concluded that the armed services had indeed retained their professional distinctiveness and integrity and that the professional ethic was adequate to maintain civilian political supremacy without destroying required professional autonomy.[8]

The emphasis on professional autonomy has brought a sense of balance to the study of civil-military relations. While for many scholars, and for all too long, the problem of civil-military relations has been interference by the military in civilian affairs, the principle of professional autonomy focuses attention on the opposite side of the coin—overinvolvement by civilian authorities in military matters. This aspect of civil-military relations has been neglected (indeed, it is hardly mentioned in any of the studies on Israeli civil-military relations). In recent years, however, it has received considerable attention. Segal and Schwartz, for instance, write that "controversies regarding civil-military relationships focus on the issue of professional autonomy: the degree to which the professional nuclei of the armed forces are constrained by political and organizational forces external to the military." They go on to state that while some are concerned about "insufficient control by the civilian sector of military power and autonomy," others are concerned about a reverse problem, namely, "excessive loss of a singularly military sense of purpose, of military autonomy, and of internal control." Janowitz recognizes that there are two sides to the equation and emphasizes that "civilian supremacy is effective because the professional soldier believes that his political superiors . . . are prepared to weigh his professional advice with great care."[9] The balanced approach is basic to this book, which seeks to give due consideration to both sides of the equation.

Huntington and Janowitz dealt mainly with the Western world and saw the development of civil-military relations as a function primarily of the nature and character of the armed forces. The third work, Sam Finer's *The Man on Horseback*, published in 1962, focused on the Third World and viewed civil-military relations as essentially reflecting the nature and character of society.[10] The problem Finer addressed was of central concern to most students of civil-military relations, especially in the fifties and sixties—the intervention of the armed services in civilian affairs and, more specifically, in government. The main impetus for this concern, as well as for Finer's work, was the high incidence of military coups throughout the world and the growing number of countries under military rule.

The importance of Finer's work lies in his analyses of the various levels and types of military intervention. This conceptualization and classificatory system represents a genuine contribution to the field because Finer has given us a methodological tool for categorizing and evaluating military intervention. The level of military intervention is, in effect, an intervening variable, with the antecedent independent variable being the level of a society's political culture and the resultant dependent variable is the type of regime in the state. Finer's central thesis is that the level of military intervention in a given country is a direct function of that society's level of political culture. The level of respect, support, and importance accorded by a population to the institution and processes of government—the degree to which a regime's legitimacy is basic to its acceptance—is highly correlated with the extent and depth of civilian organization—the degree to which there exist in the society interrelated and cohesive voluntary organizations, such as trade unions, labor and professional organizations, religious institutions, and political parties. Both factors together determine the level of the political culture in any given society. The lower the level of political culture, the higher the level and degree of military intervention in public affairs.[11]

Amos Perlmutter, building on the work of his predecessors, attempted to present a theory of civil-military relations that would encompass all the nations of the world. His work reflects newer thinking and a more complex approach to the relationship between the civil and military spheres.[12] Perlmutter rejects the previously accepted view that drew a clear-cut distinction between the civil and military functions of the state, emphasizing that in the modern state there is a wide area of overlap between the two.[13] The assumption "that professionalism removes the military from politics" was based on "the classical tradition of administrative theory" that is built on the premise that politics can be separated from administration, i.e., "that policy making (the responsibility of politically elected officials) is distinguished from policy implementation (the responsibility of appointed officials)." Today that theory no longer holds, and the new administrative theory is fusionist, recognizing that "bureaucracy and politics . . . are all symbiotically connected."[14]

Firmly adopting the fusionist approach, Perlmutter claims that even in nations where the principal of civilian rule is deeply rooted, "the military exercises influence in defense and foreign policy."[15] Echoing Janowitz, he states that "the authorities of the modern industrial state have imbued the professional military organization with a sense of belonging. The military professional understands that he shares with the authorities not only the formulation of strategy and the maintenance of the bureaucratic-hierarchical system, but also participation in the making of national security policy." He agrees with Huntington's statement that politics is beyond the scope of military competence in the sense "that the military takes no active role in the electoral system" but maintains that "the military's role in the formation and implementation of national security policy forces it to espouse a political attitude."[16]

Perlmutter introduces two concepts, which are central to his theoretical framework: *corporatism* and *praetorianism*. Following in Huntington's footsteps, he views professionalism as the hallmark of all modern armies but regards the corporate nature of modern armies—specifically, of the modern officer corps—as the key factor in determining the military's involvement in politics. Challenging Huntington's definition of professionalism, Perlmutter claims that "the concept of corporatism should be extracted from the concept of professionalism and treated as an independent variable."[17] Furthermore, in clear contradistinction to Huntington, his central thesis is that corporatism, an outgrowth of professionalism, "furnishes [the] motive for political intervention by the military" (x). "Modern professionalism," writes Perlmutter, "is corporate; that is, it

includes group consciousness and a tendency to form corporate professional associations."[18]

Praetorianism refers to the military's tendency to intervene in the
affairs of state. The term is borrowed from the Roman guard that made
and unmade emperors.[19] Praetorianism is a direct corollary of the fusionist theory of administration and of the corporate nature of government,
including both the armed forces and the civilian bureaucracy. All states
are praetorian to a certain degree, although in nonpraetorian states the
military organization is motivated not to replace the civilian regime—as
is the case in praetorian states—"but to play a key role (even to supersede
other groups) in the making of national security policy."[20]

Perlmutter's main contribution, and the one most relevant to this
book, is his classification of modern nation-states and their armed forces
into three broad groupings. A unique advantage of Perlmutter's classificatory system is that he does not categorize states into conventional
groupings, such as the Western democracies, communist countries, and
the Third World, but adopts different criteria, according to which the Red
Army is treated together with the French and Prussian armies, while the
Israeli army is placed in the same category as that of Communist China.[21]
The three types of armies are the professional army, found mainly in
industrial states that enjoy civil-military relations notable for the primacy
of the civilian over the military; the praetorian army, which exercises
independent political power and is found mainly in Third World countries where civilian authority is weak; and the professional revolutionary
army, which is neither a bureaucratic agent of the regime nor a menacing
praetorian guard but rather an independent and coequal part of the government in a country where a strong ideological component encompasses
the whole of society.[22] In contrast to both the professional and praetorian
soldier, "the orientation, organization and inclination of the revolutionary soldier are anticorporate or noncorporate."[23]

Perlmutter cites two examples of the professional revolutionary soldier: the Chinese People's Liberation Army (PLA) and the IDF. The key
characteristic of the professional revolutionary soldier is that he is the
instrument of an ideological movement: in the case of the PLA, he is a
servant of the Maoist Communist revolution; in the case of the IDF, he is
an instrument of Zionism and part of a Zionist-oriented military.[24] Perlmutter emphasizes that

> the revolutionary soldier is more ideological than the professional
> or the praetorian. His ability to cope with the revolutionary envi-

ronment and his influential role in the realm of foreign and defense policy are partial explanations of his failure to intervene. He is subordinate to a movement, party, or regime that is certainly more resilient than the military, even if the latter is a major factor in the making of the revolution. (21)

Echoing the concept of professional autonomy, he states that "the autonomy of the military organization in Israel and China has guaranteed both its high professionalism and its political subordination" (21).

Perlmutter stresses the fact that in both China and Israel, the military forces were created by their ideological masters—the Communist Party and the Labor Party, respectively—in order to accumulate and eventually to win complete political power (22).[25] With the success of the revolution, the military becomes nationalized yet retains its ties with the party.[26] Perlmutter claims that although tension and conflict do develop in this postrevolutionary period, both within the military and between soldiers and civilians, they are resolved in favor of the civilians—thus "setting the professional revolutionary apart from the praetorian soldier" (484). An important hallmark of the revolutionary army—in clear contrast to the other two types—is the fact that recruitment to the officer class is universal and based on a system of moving up in the ranks. "A revolutionary army is a mass army—a nation-in-arms."[27] The revolutionary soldier seldom aspired to be a soldier; rather, he became one as a loyal servant of the revolutionary movement (226). These qualities are highly characteristic of the IDF, and have a significant bearing on civil-military relations in Israel.

Theories of Israeli civil-military relations are rooted, to a large degree, in the general theoretical formulations cited here. Perlmutter himself has written extensively on Israel;[28] those studies constitute, by and large, a more detailed and elaborate application of his general theoretical assumption to the Israeli case. Yoram Peri's incisive work *Between Battles and Ballots: Israeli Military in Politics* is a major in-depth study and an important contribution to the field.[29] Peri's central thesis that Israel's civil-military relations constitute a partnership between the military (i.e., the IDF) and the dominant political establishment (i.e., the Labor Party) can be seen as a further development and refinement of Perlmutter's concept of the professional revolutionary soldier. Indeed, using the conventional classification of states according to their political systems—praetorian (military dictatorship), professional (liberal Western democracies), and communist—Peri claims that Israel does fall somewhere between the last two—a category, once again, quite similar to Perlmutter's professional revolutionary type.[30]

Building on Perlmutter's model and on some of Janowitz's work, Dan Horowitz and Moshe Lissak have further developed the theory of permeable boundaries between the military and civilian sectors as the cornerstone of civil-military relations in Israel. "Broad civilian participation in national security tasks, vague boundaries between military and political institutions, and social networks including members of both military and civilian elites" are some of the key characteristics of Israel's unique pattern of civil-military relations.[31] Borrowing a term used by many theorists, they see Israel as "coming closer than any other society to the model of a 'nation in arms'" (14). Horowitz and Lissak emphasize the point that Israel's experience poses a strong challenge to the contention, stated by many scholars, that there is a direct relationship between an increased salience of security concerns and a growing proportion of resources devoted to security and the dominance of the military elite over civilian elites; yet, at the same time, organization patterns and modes of operation have emerged "that permit a high level of involvement by the military in shaping policy in foreign affairs and defense" (17). An important expression of the permeable boundaries between the two spheres is the expansion of the military's role, which has led to "militarization of the civilian sector and the 'civilianization' of the military," although certain civilian areas remain strictly off limits (23–31).

The last three decades of research on civil-military relations have followed a trend characteristic of other branches of the social sciences—namely, the differentiation of the discipline as a whole and the delineation, within it, of subareas of specialization. Lissak lists some of these substantive subareas, including such topics as the military as a profession, organizational aspects of the military system, the social results of wars, and the relationship between the armed forces and the state and between the armed forces and society. Lissak further differentiates the last topic into a number of subtopics: analysis of the phenomenon and concept of militarism; division of authority and the nature of the boundaries between the civil administration and the military command; and the conditions and reasons for the intervention and/or involvement of military officers in the process of political, economic, and social decision making.[32]

The aim of this book has been to give a detailed and broad overview of the actual ongoing relationship between the civilian and military authorities in Israel. It falls squarely into Lissak's last subarea: the relationship between the armed forces and the state. This book has dealt primarily with the division of authority and the nature of the boundaries between the civil administration and the military command but also has touched on such issues as the phenomenon and concept of militarism and the conditions for the intervention or involvement of military officers in the process of political, economic, and social decision making.

Appendix B
People Interviewed

Meir Amit, head of the Mossad, 1963–1969.

Moshe Arens, defense minister, 1983–1984; foreign minister, 1988–1990; defense minister, 1990–1992.

Chaim Bar-Lev, chief of the general staff, IDF, 1968–1971; minister, 1972–1977, 1984–1990.

Yitzhak Chofi, head of the Mossad, 1975–1982.

Uzi Eilam, head of the Research and Development and Infrastructure Directorate, Ministry of Defense, 1987–.

Rafael Eitan, chief of the general staff, IDF, 1978–1983; minister of agriculture, 1990–1992.

Mordechai Gazit, director-general, Ministry of Foreign Affairs, 1972–1973; director-general, Prime Minister's Office, 1973–1975.

Mordechai Gur, chief of the general staff, IDF, 1974–1978; minister of health, 1984–1988; deputy minister of defense, 1992–.

Eitan Haber, media adviser to the minister of defense, 1984–1990; director, prime minister's bureau, 1992–.

Issar Harel, head of the Mossad, 1953–1963.

David Ivri, director-general, Ministry of Defense, 1987–.

Moshe Levy, chief of the general staff, IDF, 1983–1987.

Menachem Meron, director-general, Ministry of Defense, 1983–1987.

Shimon Peres, director-general, Ministry of Defense, 1953–1959; deputy minister of defense, 1959–1965; defense minister, 1974–1977; prime minister, 1984–1986; foreign minister, 1986–1988, 1992–.

Ephraim Poran, military secretary to the prime minister, 1975–1981.

Yitzhak Rabin, chief of the general staff, IDF, 1964–1968; prime minister, 1974–1977; defense minister, 1984–1990; prime minister, 1992–.

Zeev Schiff, military correspondent, *Ha'aretz.*

Avraham Tamir, chief of planning branch, general staff, IDF, 1974–1979; national security adviser to the defense minister, 1979–1981; national security adviser to the defense minister and head of the National Security Unit, Ministry of Defense, 1981–1983; director-general, Prime Minister's Office, 1984–1986; director-general, Ministry of Foreign Affairs, 1986–1988.

Ezer Weizman, defense minister, 1977–1980; president of the state of Israel, 1993–.

Aharon Yariv, director of military intelligence, IDF, 1964–1971; minister of information, 1974–1976; head of the Jaffee Center for Strategic Studies (JCSS), Tel Aviv University, 1977–1993.

Chaim Yisraeli, director of the defense minister's bureau, 1953–.

Notes

Introduction

1. Personal communication.

2. Samuel P. Huntington, *The Soldier and the State* (New York: Vintage Books, Random House, 1957), p. 80; John Sweetman, ed., *Sword and Mace* (London: Brassey, 1986), p. ix; and John P. Lovell, "Civil-Military Relations: Traditional and Modern Concept Reappraisal," in Charles L. Cochran, ed., *Civil-Military Relations: Changing Concepts in the Seventies* (New York: Free, 1974), p. 11. See also Amos Perlmutter and William La Grande, "The Party in Uniform: Toward a Theory of Civil-Military Relations in Communist Political Systems," *American Political Science Review* 76, no. 4 (Dec. 1982): 779–80; and Yehoshafat Harkabi, *War and Strategy* (in Hebrew) (Tel Aviv: Ma'arachot, 1990).

3. Amos Perlmutter, *Military and Politics in Israel* (London: Cass, 1969), p. 126. See Edward Luttwak and Dan Horowitz, *The Israeli Army* (London: Allen Lane, 1975), p. 203; Moshe Lissak, "Paradoxes of Israeli Civil-Military Relations," *Journal of Strategic Studies* 6, no. 3 (Sept. 1983): 1–2; Yoram Peri, *Between Battles and Ballots: Israeli Military in Politics* (Cambridge: Cambridge University Press, 1983); and Yoram Peri, "Patterns of the IDF's Relations with the Political Establishment in Israel," in Joseph Alpher, ed., *A War of Choice* (in Hebrew) (Tel Aviv: Hakibbutz Hameuchad, 1985).

4. Perlmutter, *Military and Politics in Israel*, p. 128.

5. Amos Perlmutter, *The Military and Politics in Modern Times* (New Haven: Yale University Press, 1977), pp. 14, 205, 251–53.

6. Interview with Rafael Eitan.

1. The Scope of the Study: A Theoretical Model

1. See Samuel P. Huntington, *The Soldier and the State* (New York: Vintage Books, Random House, 1957), pp. 163–64, 177–79, 191–92, 400–412.

2. Dan Horowitz, "Is Israel a Garrison State," *The Jerusalem Quarterly*, serial no. 4 (summer 1977): 58–65.

3. John Sweetman, ed., *Sword and Mace* (London: Brassey, 1986), pp. ix, xv.

4. Huntington, *Soldier and State*, p. 20. See John P. Lovell, "Civil-Military Relations: Traditional and Modern Concept Reappraisal," in Charles L. Cochran, ed., *Civil-Military Relations: Changing Concepts in the Seventies* (New York: Free, 1974), pp. 11, 14–15.

5. Martin Edmonds, *Armed Services and Society* (Boulder: Westview, 1990), pp. 94, 99.

6. See ibid., 56–57.

7. One can, of course, categorize the various functions of state or areas of society in many different ways. The one chosen here was deemed the most relevant for a model of civil-military relations.

8. See Amos Perlmutter, *Military and Politics in Israel* (London: Cass, 1969); idem, *Politics and the Military in Israel 1966–1977* (London: Cass, 1978); Edward Luttwak and Dan Horowitz, *The Israeli Army* (London: Allen Lane, 1975); Moshe Lissak, "The Israeli Defense Forces as an Agent of Socialization and Education: A Study of Role Expansion in a Democratic Society," in M. R. von Gills, ed., *The Perceived Role of the Military* (Rotterdam: Rotterdam University, 1971), pp. 325–40; and Tom Boudan, *Army in the Service of the State* (Tel Aviv: Tel Aviv University Publishing Project, 1970).

9. Edmonds, *Armed Services and Society*, p. 175. See Samuel P. Huntington, *The Common Defense: Strategic Programs in National Politics* (New York: Columbia University Press, 1961).

10. *The Basic Law: The Military, Laws of the State of Israel*, vol. 30 (Jerusalem: Government Printer, 5736–1975/76), pp. 150–51.

2. Civilian Control

1. Samuel P. Huntington, *The Soldier and the State* (New York: Vintage Books, Random House, 1957), p. 80.

2. Lyman L. Lemnitzer, James L. Holloway, Louis Wilson, John W. Vogt, Leslie M. Fry, Robert Cockrill, and J. Russel Blanford, *A Report by the Committee on Civil-Military Relations* (Indianapolis: Hudson Institute, 1984), pp. 2–3.

3. Quoted in U.S. Senate Committee on Armed Services, *Defense Organization: The Need for Change* (staff report) (Washington, D.C.: U.S. Government Printing Office, 1985), p. 25.

4. Trevor N. Dupuy, "Civilian Control and Military Professionalism: A Systematic Problem," *Strategic Review* 8, no. 1 (winter 1980): 39–40.

5. John P. Lovell, "Civil-Military Relations: Traditional and Modern Concept Reappraisal," in Charles L. Cochran, ed., *Civil-Military Relations: Changing Concepts in the Seventies* (New York: Free, 1974), p. 13.

6. See Harold Lasswell, "The Garrison State," *American Journal of Sociology* 46 (1941), pp. 455–68.

7. Committee on Armed Services, *Defense Organization*, p. 46.

8. Ibid., pp. 36–37. See also Huntington, *Soldier and State*, pp. 315–25.

9. Committee on Armed Services, *Defense Organization*, pp. 42–43. See also Robert Murphy, *Diplomat Among Warriors* (New York: Doubleday, 1964).

10. Elmer J. Mahoney, "The Constitutional Framework of Civil-Military Relations," in Charles L. Cochran, ed., *Civil-Military Relations: Changing Concepts in the Seventies* (New York: Free, 1974), p. 39; David R. Segal and Janet S. Schwartz, "Professional Autonomy of the Military in the United States and the Soviet Union," *Air University Review* 32, no. 6 (Sept.–Oct. 1981): 22, 24.

11. Committee on Armed Services, *Defense Organization*, p. 25.

12. Amos Perlmutter and V. P. Bennett, eds., *The Political Influence of the Military* (New Haven: Yale University Press, 1980), p. 14. For a good description of civilian control in India, see Veena Kukreja, "Civilian Control of the Military in India," *The Indian Journal of Political Science* 50, no. 4 (Oct.–Dec. 1989): 469–502. For a comparison of civil-military relations in totalitarian and democratic states, see Alexander J. Groth, "Totalitarianism and Democrats: Aspects of Political Military Relations 1939–1945," *Comparative Strategy* 8 (1989): 73–97.

13. The most acute example in Britain would be the Curragh mutiny in 1919 and in the United States the MacArthur episode in 1950–1951.

14. See Committee on Armed Services, *Defense Organization*, p. 75; and Perlmutter and Bennett, *Political Influence of the Military*, p. 206.

15. Amos Perlmutter, *The Military and Politics in Modern Times* (New Haven: Yale University Press, 1977), p. 14.

16. Ibid.

17. Quoted in Huntington, *Soldier and State*, pp. 106, 109. See also ibid., pp. 98–139.

18. From a speech to the Massachusetts legislature on July 25, 1951, reported by the *New York Times*, July 26, 1951, p. 12, and quoted in Huntington, *Soldier and State*, p. 353.

19. Martin Edmonds, *Armed Services and Society* (Boulder: Westview, 1990), p. 175.

20. For Lincoln, see Committee on Armed Services, *Defense Organization*, p. 33. For Jackson, see ibid., pp. 31–32. For MacArthur and Lavelle, see ibid., pp. 38–39. See also William Manchester, *American Caesar* (Boston: Little, Brown, 1978), pp. 599–600.

21. See Groth, "Totalitarianism and Democrats."

22. Allan Montgomery, *The Memoirs of Field Marshall The Viscount Montgomery of Alamein, K.G.* (New York: World Publishing, 1958), pp. 213–14, quoted in Groth, "Totalitarianism and Democrats," pp. 81–82.

23. John Sweetman, "Historical Perspectives: From Waterloo to the Curragh," in John Sweetman, ed., *Sword and Mace* (London: Brassey, 1986), pp. 14–15.

24. Ibid., p. 15.

25. Committee on Armed Services, *Defense Organization*, p. 38. See also Manchester, *American Caesar*, pp. 599–600.

26. Committee on Armed Services, *Defense Organization*, p. 37; Ernest May, *The Ultimate Decision* (New York: George Braziller, 1960), pp. 138–39, quoted in Committee on Armed Services, *Defense Organization*, p. 36.

27. Huntington, *Soldier and State*, p. 316, 317, 336; quotation is from p. 324.

28. See ibid., pp. 157–62.

29. Groth, "Totalitarianism and Democrats," 82.

30. Huntington, *Soldier and State*, p. 106.

31. See, for example, David C. Hendrickson, *Reforming Defense: The State of Ameri-*

can Civil-Military Relations (Baltimore: Johns Hopkins University Press, 1988), p. 116; and Morris Janowitz, *The Professional Soldier* (New York: Free, 1960, 1971), p. lv.

32. See Manchester, *American Caesar*, pp. 600–650; Committee on Armed Services, *Defense Organization*, pp. 37–39.

33. Mahoney, "Constitutional Framework," pp. 37, 38. For Fremont, see Committee on Armed Services, *Defense Organization*, pp. 32–33. Fremont issued a proclamation ordering all rebel slaves to be seized and freed. This order clearly exceeded the "Confiscation Act" that authorized only the seizure of slaves used by the rebel military.

34. Manchester, *American Caesar*, p. 645.

35. Bruce Catton, *Terrible Swift Sword* (Garden City, N.Y.: Doubleday, 1963), p. 478, quoted in Committee on Armed Services, *Defense Organization*, p. 35. See also Committee on Armed Services, *Defense Organization*, p. 33–35.

36. Committee on Armed Services, *Defense Organization*, p. 30.

37. Thomas Flexner, *Washington: The Indispensable Man* (Boston: Little, Brown, 1974), pp. 174, 175, as quoted in Committee on Armed Services, *Defense Organization*, p. 30. For a full description of the incident, see Committee on Armed Services, *Defense Organization*, pp. 29–30.

38. Hendrickson, *Reforming Defense*, pp. 57–58.

39. Groth, "Totalitarianism and Democrats," p. 70, 81; John Grigg, *1943: The Victory that Never Was* (New York: Mill and Wang, 1980), p. 227, quoted in Groth, "Totalitarianism and Democrats," p. 74. See also Alex Danchev, "The Central Direction of War, 1940–41," in John Sweetman, ed., *Sword and Mace* (London: Brassey, 1986), pp. 57–78. For more on micromanagement and bureaucratic bypass exercised by Hitler and Stalin, see Groth, "Totalitarianism and Democrats," pp. 77–81.

40. Sir Ewen Broadbent, *The Military and Government: From MacMillan to Heseltine*, Royal United Services Institute Defence Studies Series (London: Macmillan, 1988), pp. 122, 121, and 124. See *Laws of the State of Israel*, vol. 30 (Jerusalem: Government Printer, 5736–1975/1976), pp. 150–51. Civilian positions comparable to the chiefs of staff would be the director-general of the Ministry of Defense in Israel, the permanent secretary or permanent under secretary (PUS) in Britain, and the deputy secretary in the United States.

41. See John R. Probert, "Vietnam and United States Military Thought Concerning Civil-Military Role in Government" in Charles L. Cochran, ed., *Civil-Military Relations: Changing Concepts in the Seventies* (New York: Free, 1974), pp. 142–43, 146–49.

42. Groth, "Totalitarianism and Democrats," p. 80.

43. See Dupuy, "Civilian Control," p. 36.

44. Goldwater-Nichols Reorganization Act—PL 99–433, Section 153; *Time*, Nov. 12, 1990, p. 30. See Hendrickson, *Reforming Defense*, p. 114.

3. The Israeli System: Constitutional Principles

1. See Aharon Yariv, "Military Organization and Policymaking in Israel," in Robert J. Art, Vincent Davis, and Samuel P. Huntington, eds., *Reorganizing America's Defense* (Washington: Pergamon-Brassey's, 1985), p. 108.

2. See, for example, Samuel P. Huntington, *The Soldier and the State* (New York: Vintage Books, Random House, 1957), pp. 315–44, where he describes in great detail

the nature of civil-military relations in the United States during World War II, which were radically different from pre- and postwar relations.

3. For an excellent review of Israel's constitutional system, see Amnon Rubinstein, *Constitutional Law of Israel* (in Hebrew), 3d ed. (Tel Aviv: Shoken, 1980).

4. Sections 1, 3, 4, 5(a), 27, 29, 31(a) and (e), of *The Basic Law: The Government, Laws of the State of Israel*, vol. 22 (Jerusalem: Government Printer, 5728–1967/68), pp. 257–64.

5. *Cabinet* used in the British sense should not be confused with the *Kabinet*, a uniquely Israeli creation first established in 1984.

6. The Supreme Court espoused this position even before enactment of *The Basic Law: The Government*, basing it on constitutional convention. See C.A. 131/67, *Kamiar v. State of Israel, Piskey Din* (in Hebrew), vol. 22(2), p. 85.

7. See Shimon Shetreet, "The Grey Area of War Powers: The Case of Israel," *The Jerusalem Quarterly*, serial no. 45 (winter 1988): 31–32.

8. Section 18 of *The Law and Administration Ordinance, Laws of the State of Israel*, vol. 1 (Jerusalem: Government Printer, 5708–1948), p. 10. See Shetreet, "Grey Area of War Powers," p. 37.

9. This view was expressed by Attorney General Aaron Barak in 1976 and was published in "Guidelines of the Attorney General," quoted in Shetreet, "Grey Area of War Powers," p. 36 n. 31. In Israeli practice the attorney general doubles as the legal adviser of the government, and his legal opinions—unless overturned by the courts—are binding on the government. As there has been no judicial decision to the contrary, the guideline of the attorney general represents the established view. There are, however, different views; for these and for a discussion of this question, see Rubinstein, *Constitutional Law*, p. 310.

10. Shetreet, "Grey Area of War Powers," p. 36.

11. *Laws of the State of Israel*, vol. 13 (Jerusalem: Government Printer, 5719–1958/59), p. 328. See also Shetreet, "Grey Area of War Powers," p. 36.

12. *Laws of the State of Israel*, vol. 30 (Jerusalem: Government Printer, 5736–1975/76), pp. 150–51.

13. For a brief review of the history of the MDC during Israel's first two decades, see Michael Brecher, *The Foreign Policy System of Israel* (New Haven: Yale University Press, 1972), pp. 213–15. See also Yariv, "Military Organization and Policymaking," p. 122. For Begin and Shamir's MDCs, see Yehuda Ben Meir, *National Security Decision Making: The Israeli Case* (Tel Aviv: Jaffee Center for Strategic Studies, 1980), pp. 97–98.

14. The coalition agreement also mandated that, at the demand of the prime minister or the vice prime minister, any issue before the full government or cabinet—in which a number of small parties were included—would be referred to the *Kabinet*. This was done in order to prevent any important political decisions from being made against the united stand of either of the two major parties. However, the coalition agreement had no basis in law and was not legally binding; indeed, it was not always upheld.

15. See Shetreet, "Grey Area of War Powers," p. 34.

16. See *Laws of the State of Israel* (Jerusalem: Government Printer 5751–1990/91), p. 86.

17. *Laws of the State of Israel*, 1:10. For *The Law and Administration Ordinance 1948*, see ibid., p. 7. For the Israel Defense Forces Ordinance, see ibid., pp. 15–16. See also sec-

tion 4 of the Laws and Administrative Ordinance [Further Provisions] 1948, ibid., p. 26. Section 1 of the Proclamation of 5th Iyar 5708 (May 14, 1948), issued together with Israel's Declaration of Independence, enabled the Provisional State Council to delegate some of its legislative power to the Provisional Government for the purpose of urgent legislation. See Shetreet, "Grey Area of War Powers," p. 36.

18. *Laws of the State of Israel*, 1:15–16.

19. For the Defense Service Law of 1949, see *Laws of the State of Israel*, vol. 3 (Jerusalem: Government Printer, 5709–1949), p. 112. This law has undergone many amendments and changes over the years. See Defense Service Law (Consolidated Version), 1959, *Laws of the State of Israel*, 13:328. For the Military Jurisdiction Law of 1955, see *Laws of the State of Israel*, vol. 9 (Jerusalem: Government Printer, 5715–1954/55), p. 184.

20. See section 26 of the Defense Service Law (Consolidated Version) 1959, *Laws of the State of Israel*, 13:328.

21. *Laws of the State of Israel*, 9:195–96.

22. See Zvi Hadar, "The Commanding Power of the Chief of Staff and the Defence Minister Over the IDF" (in Hebrew), *Hapraklit* 31 (1978): 20.

23. "The Army's Structure and Way," a lecture delivered by David Ben-Gurion on Oct. 27, 1949, published in Hebrew in *Ma'arachot* (Oct. 1955): 141, and quoted in Yariv, "Military Organization and Policymaking," p. 109; interview with Avraham Tamir.

24. *Agranat Commission Report* (in Hebrew) (Tel Aviv: Am Oved, 1975), pp. 25–26. See also Shetreet, "Grey Area of War Powers," pp. 27–28.

25. *Laws of the State of Israel*, 30:150–51.

26. For the amendment to the Military Justice Law, see *Laws of the State of Israel*, vol. 33 (Jerusalem: Government Printer, 5739–1978/79), pp. 133–35.

27. Ibid.

28. Ibid.

29. See Ben Meir, *National Security Decision Making*, pp. 96–97.

30. *Laws of the State of Israel*, 22:257. See also sections 5(b) and 23, ibid., 22:257, 261.

31. According to the law, the prime minister tenders his resignation to the president of the state.

32. See *The Basic Law: The Government (Amendment no. 3)*, 5741–1981, *Laws of the State of Israel*, vol. 35 (Jerusalem: Government Printer, 5741–1980/81), p. 339.

33. For the primacy of the prime minister, see Ben Meir, *National Security Decision Making*, p. 97. Details concerning the difficulties in monitoring and firing ministers are from my interview with Ephraim Poren.

Ariel Sharon was compelled to relinquish his post as defense minister in 1983, in the wake of the Kahn Commission of Inquiry, primarily as a result of Prime Minister Begin's implicit threat to fire him. Prime Minister Shimon Peres forced Finance Minister Modai out of the National Unity Government by threatening to fire him under the authority of section 21a. Shamir fired Ezer Weizman in early 1990 for alleged contacts with the PLO, although he later retracted this action—accepting, instead, Weizman's resignation from the Ministerial Security Committee.

34. For an extensive description of that debate and its political overtones, see Yoram Peri, *Between Battles and Ballots: Israeli Military in Politics* (Cambridge: Cambridge University Press, 1983), pp. 152–55.

35. See notes 18, 19, and 25 above.

36. Amos Perlmutter, *Military and Politics in Israel* (London: Cass, 1969), p. 80; *Agranat Commission Report*, p. 26, quoted in Shetreet, "Grey Area of War Powers," p. 35.

37. From a document entitled "Subservience of the Chief of Staff and the IDF— Legal Position," quoted in Peri, *Battles and Ballots*, pp. 140–41. The Agranat Commission had recommended that the chief of staff, head of military intelligence, officer in command of the southern command, and other senior officers should be removed from their posts.

38. *Davar*, April 20, 1976, quoted in ibid., p. 140.

39. *Agranat Commission Report*, p. 26, quoted in Shetreet, "Grey Area of War Powers," p. 31. For the failures of *The Basic Law: The Army*, see Yariv, "Military Organization and Policymaking," p. 110.

40. Interview with Shimon Peres.

41. See Yariv, "Military Organization and Policymaking," p. 110.

42. Personal communication.

43. Section 2(b) of *The Basic Law: The Army, Laws of the State of Israel*, 30:150.

44. Interview with Shimon Peres.

45. Perlmutter, *Military and Politics in Israel*, p. 115.

46. See Peri, *Battles and Ballots*, p. 146. See also Hadar, "The Commanding Power of the Chief of Staff," p. 219.

47. See section 1 of the original law and section 2A of the law as amended in 1979, *Laws of the State of Israel*, 9:195–96; 33:133.

48. The word *regulations* translates the Hebrew *takanot*, which refers to secondary legislation, i.e., legally binding directives issued usually by government ministers by virtue of authority to do so under existing law.

49. For the Emergency Defense Regulations of 1945, see *The Palestine Gazette* 1, supp. 2 (1946): 148–66.

50. See note 25 above.

51. The original text read: "The chief of staff is appointed subordinate to the civilian authority as provided by the law." The change was introduced in order to strengthen the power of the defense minister; ironically, it strengthened the CGS instead. See Shetreet, "Grey Area of War Powers," p. 33.

52. From an interview by Mordechai Gur in *Ma'ariv*, April 14, 1978, quoted in Peri, *Battles and Ballots*, p. 149.

53. Interview with Shimon Peres.

54. Interview with Mordechai Gur.

55. Interviews with Mordechai Gur and Moshe Levy.

56. Section 1 of *The Basic Law: The Knesset, Laws of the State of Israel*, vol. 12 (Jerusalem: Government Printer, 5718–1957/58), p. 85. See Peri, *Ballots and Battles*, p. 175. For a good description of the Knesset, its authority, and its workings, see Shevah Weiss, *The Knesset, Its Role, and Functions* (in Hebrew) (Tel Aviv: Achiasaf, 1977).

57. For the Knesset's influence on executive activities, see Yariv, "Military Organization and Policymaking in Israel," p. 122. For its lack of war powers, see Shetreet, "Grey Area of War Powers," pp. 36–37. For the 1992 legislation, see note 13 of chapter 4.

58. For the various statutes, see Yariv, "Military Organization and Policymaking in Israel," p. 123; and Peri, *Ballots and Battles*, p. 179.

59. *Laws of the State of Israel* (in Hebrew) (Jerusalem: Government Printer, 5746–1985/86), p. 107.

60. For budget regulations, see Section 3 of *The Basic Law: The State Economy, Laws of the State of Israel*, vol. 29 (Jerusalem: Government Printer, 5735–1974/75), p. 273. The Finance Committee and the Foreign Affairs and Defense Committee are the Knesset's two most prestigious committees, and the Finance Committee is, by far, the most powerful. This is due primarily to its wide-ranging mandate: it deals with all fiscal and monetary matters, the budget, banking, and all legislation dealing with taxation and other state revenues. It is thus a combination of the Finance Committee, Budget Committee, Appropriations Committee, Banking Committee, and Ways and Means Committee of the United States House of Representatives.

61. See *The Basic Law: The State Economy (Amendment no. 2)*, 5743–1982/83, *Laws of the State of Israel*, vol. 37 (Jerusalem: Government Printer, 5743–1982/83), p. 58.

62. Personal communication.

63. Quoted in Peri, *Ballots and Battles, pp. 182, 226.*

64. Personal communication. See also Peri, *Ballots and Battles*, p. 226.

65. Personal communication

66. See Peri, *Ballots and Battles*, pp. 181–84.

67. Section 13(a) (4) of the *Knesset Procedural Code*, July 1981.

68. Interview with Zeev Schiff. See also Yariv, "Military Organization and Policymaking in Israel," p. 123. For a slightly less rosy view, see Peri, *Ballots and Battles*, ch. 8.

69. Quoted in Peri, *Ballots and Battles*, pp. 185, 182. See Lissak, "Paradoxes of Israeli Civil-Military Relations," p. 4.

70. Personal communication.

71. See Yariv, "Military Organization and Policymaking in Israel," p. 123.

72. Personal communication.

73. Personal communication.

74. Personal communication. See also *Jerusalem Post*, Aug. 7, 1987, p. 8.

75. Quoted in Elmer J. Mahoney, "The Constitutional Framework of Civil-Military Relations," in Charles L. Cochran, ed., *Civil-Military Relations: Changing Concepts in the Seventies* (New York: Free, 1974), p. 50.

76. *Laws of the State of Israel*, vol. 35, p. 104.

77. HCJ 27/48, *Lahis v. Minister of Defense, Piskey Din* (in Hebrew), vol. 2, pp. 153, 155.

78. HCJ 7/48, *El-Karbotly v. Minister of Defense, Piskey Din* (in Hebrew), vol. 2, p. 5.

79. See note 23 in chapter 4.

80. HCJ 358/88. *The Israeli Association for Civil Rights v. O/C Central Command, Piskey Din* (in Hebrew), vol. 43(2), p. 579.

81. HCJ 425/89. *Tchafan v. the Advocate-General, Piskey Din* (in Hebrew), vol. 43(4), p. 718.

82. HCJ 910/86, *Ressler v. the Defense Minister, Piskey Din* (in Hebrew), vol. 42(2), p. 441. A yeshiva is a school for higher Jewish studies conducted in a strictly orthodox environment. Ben-Gurion promised Israel's chief rabbis in 1948 that students who devoted their time to Torah studies would be exempt from military service in the IDF, which is normally applied universally to all able-bodied males.

83. HCJ 680/88. *Shnitzer v. the Chief Military Censor, Piskey Din* (in Hebrew), vol. 42(4), p. 617.

84. HCJ 561/75, *Moti Ashkenazi v. Defense Minister, Piskey Din* (in Hebrew), vol. 30(3), p. 309; HCJ 13/82, *Kooper v. Defense Minister, Piskey Din* (in Hebrew), vol. 36(3), p. 245; and HCJ 676/82, *The General Labour Federation (Histadrut) v. the CGS, Piskey Din* (in Hebrew), vol. 37(4), p. 105.

85. Interview with Yitzhak Rabin.

4. The National Command Authority: Who Commands the IDF?

1. Interview with Aharon Yariv.

2. Yoram Peri, *Battles and Ballots: Israeli Military in Politics* (Cambridge: Cambridge University Press, 1983), p. 143.

3. The various aspects of the constitutional issue are summarized in a hitherto unpublished confidential legal opinion of the IDF's adjutant general's office: "Constitutional Aspects of Relations Between the Cabinet–Defense Minister–Chief of Staff," *Compendium of Legal Opinions*, vol. 40 (Tel Aviv: Adjutant General's Office, 1980), legal opinion 10.0101. The discussion in the text is based primarily on this document, as well as on a number of other sources.

4. For the government's authority, see sections 2(a) and 3(b) of *The Basic Law: The Army, Laws of the State of Israel*, vol. 30 (Jerusalem: Government Printer, 5736–1975/76), pp. 150–51. Section 3(c) of *The Basic Law: The Army* stipulates that the CGS is appointed by the government on recommendation of the defense minister (ibid.). Section 14 of *The Interpretation Law*, 5741–1981, states: "Any empowerment to make an appointment implies empowerment to suspend the validity thereof, to revoke it, to dismiss the person appointed or to suspend him from office." See *Laws of the State of Israel*, vol. 35, p. 372. See also Shimon Shetreet, "Grey Area of War Powers: The Case of Israel, *The Jerusalem Quarterly*, serial no. 45 (winter 1988)", p. 33. For the U.S. president as commander in chief, see U.S. Constitution, art. 2, sec. 2. For the prime minister as commander in chief, see Shetreet, "Grey Area of War Powers," p. 35, n. 29.

5. Interviews with Chaim Bar-Lev, Rafael Eitan, Mordechai Gur, Moshe Levy, Shimon Peres, Yitzhak Rabin, Ezer Weizman, and Aharon Yariv. Bar-Lev takes exception to absolute governmental authority in the operational sphere. In his opinion, the chief of staff may refuse to execute the cabinet's operational orders if they go against his professional integrity—although he must be ready to pay the price and face summary dismissal by the government. There is little support for his position, although one could compare it to that of a captain of a naval craft or aircraft in distress, who may issue orders regarding the rescue of the craft or of the lives of those on it to anyone—even someone higher in rank. See Zvi Hadar, "The Commanding Power of the Chief of Staff and the Defence Minister Over the IDF" (in Hebrew), *Hapraklit* 31 (1978) p. 221.

6. Sections 2(a) and 2(b) of *The Basic Law: The Army, Laws of the State of Israel*, 30:150–51.

7. Personal communication.

8. For the 1981 amendment to section 4 of *The Basic Law: The Government*, see note 32 of chapter 3.

9. See Shetreet, "Grey Area of War Powers," pp. 30, 37.

10. Interview with Moshe Levy.

11. Interview with Yitzhak Rabin.

12. Interview with Chaim Bar-Lev.

13. *Laws of the State of Israel* (in Hebrew) (Jerusalem: Government Printer, 5752–1991/92), p. 214.

14. See Shetreet, "Grey Area of War Powers," p. 11. This information also derives from a personal communication.

15. See Ron Ben Yishai, "Who Approves Military Operations" (in Hebrew), *Yediot Aharonot*, May 15, 1988.

16. Ibid.

17. See *Ha'aretz*, May 6, 1988, p. 1; *Ma'ariv*, May 6, 1988, p. 1; *Jerusalem Post*, May 7, 1988, p. 1.

18. See *Ma'ariv*, May 6, 1988, pp. 1–2.

19. See *Ha'aretz*, May 6, 1988, p. 1.

20. Interview with Lt. Gen. Dan Shomron in *Yediot Aharonot*, May 6, 1988, magazine sec., p. 2.

21. See *Ha'aretz*, May 5, 1988, p. 1; *Ha'aretz*, May 6, 1988, p. 1; *Ha'aretz*, May 7, 1988, p. 1; *Jerusalem Post*, May 7, 1988, p. 1; *Ma'ariv*, May 7, 1988, p. 3.

22. See *Ha'aretz*, May 9, 1988, p. 1; *Ma'ariv*, May 9, 1988, p. 3.

23. HCJ 390/79, *Dwikat v. Government of Israel*, *Piskey Din* (in Hebrew), vol. 34(1), p. 10, quoted in Shetreet, "Grey Area of War Powers," pp. 33–34.

24. Interview with Yitzhak Rabin.

25. Interview with Mordechai Gur. See also Peri, *Battles and Ballots*, p. 142.

26. Interview with Rafael Eitan.

27. Interview with Issar Harel.

28. *The Basic Law: The Army* enacted in 1976 was, of course, not in effect in 1954.

29. See Shetreet, "Grey Area of War Powers," p. 34.

30. Interview with Moshe Arens.

31. See Shetreet, "Grey Area of War Powers," pp. 39–41.

32. This is clearly stipulated in the Defense Reorganization Act (Goldwater-Nichols Bill) of 1986.

33. As mentioned, the Hebrew word *marut* conveys a sense of absolute subjection, which is not necessarily the case with *kafuf,* the Hebrew word for *subordinate.*

34. See note 19 of chapter 3.

35. See Shetreet, "Grey Area of War Powers," p. 40. See also Peri, *Ballots and Battles*, pp. 164–65.

36. Personal communication.

37. Peri, *Ballots and Battles*, pp. 141, 254.

38. Interview with Menachem Meron. There are several versions of what exactly transpired. For a detailed description of the incident, see Peri, *Ballots and Battles*, pp. 254–59.

39. Interview with Yitzhak Chofi.

40. See Hadar, "The Commanding Power of the Chief of Staff," p. 222.

41. *Laws of the State of Israel*, vol. 22, p. 263.

42. See Hadar, "The Commanding Power of the Chief of Staff," pp. 222–23.

43. For the publication requirements, see Section 41(b)(2) of *The Basic Law: The Government*. The requirements for ad hoc assumption are in line with general Israeli public law, as established by the Supreme Court.

44. Interviews with Chaim Yisraeli and Eitan Haber. See also Aharan Yariv, "Military Organization and Policymaking in Israel," in Robert J. Art, Vincent Davis, and Samuel P. Huntington, eds., *Reorganizing America's Defense* (Washington: Pergamon-Brassey's, 1985), p. 110; and Moshe Lissak, "Paradoxes of Israeli Civil-Military Relations," *Journal of Strategic Studies* 6, no. 3 (Sept. 1983): 6.

45. See note 9 of chapter 3.

46. Interview with Moshe Levy.

47. Interviews with Rafael Eitan and Chaim Yisraeli.

48. Interview with Mordechai Gur.

49. Interview with Chaim Bar-Lev.

50. Interview with Moshe Arens.

51. Interview with Ezer Weizman.

52. Interview with Yitzhak Rabin.

53. Interviews with Eitan Haber, Chaim Yisraeli, and Zeev Schiff.

54. The description of this affair is based on interviews with Yitzhak Rabin, Moshe Levy, and Eitan Haber.

55. Samuel P. Huntington, *The Soldier and the State* (New York: Vintage Books, Random House, 1957), pp. 177, 412.

56. This view is espoused by many students of civil-military relations in the United States.

57. See Sir Ewen Broadbent, *The Military and Government: From MacMillan to Heseltine*, Royal United Services Institute Defence Studies Series (London: Macmillan, 1988); and Jan Englund and Stephen Aubin, "The JCS and Congress: Lessons from France and Great Britain," *Comparative Strategy* 6, no. 3 (1987): 307.

58. Interview with Chaim Yisraeli.

59. See Peri, *Ballots and Battles*, pp. 80–82, 86–90, 151–55, 165–72.

60. Interviews with Chaim Yisraeli, Moshe Levy, Ezer Weizman, Yitzhak Rabin, and others.

61. Interview with Mordechai Gur.

62. Interviews with Aharon Yariv, Moshe Levy, and Moshe Arens.

63. Interview with Aharon Yariv.

64. Interview with Chaim Yisraeli.

65. Interviews with Shimon Peres, Ezer Weizman, Moshe Arens, and Rafael Eitan.

66. Interviews with Mordechai Gur, Moshe Levy, and Yitzhak Rabin.

5. *The Israeli System: Defense Organization*

1. Sir Ewen Broadbent, *The Military and Government: From MacMillan to Heseltine*, Royal United Services Institute Defence Studies Series (London: Macmillan, 1988), p. 3.

2. Martin Edmonds, *Armed Services and Society* (Boulder: Westview, 1990), pp. 171–72; Broadbent, *Military and Government*, p. 3.

3. Edmonds, *Armed Services*, p. 173. See John P. Lovell, "Civil-Military Relations: Traditional and Modern Concept Reappraisal," in Charles L. Cochran, ed., *Civil-Military Relations: Changing Concepts in the Seventies* (New York: Free, 1974), p. 12. See also Sweetman's discussion of the development of Britain's central defense organization in John Sweetman, ed., *Sword and Mace* (London: Brassey, 1986), ch. 2.

4. Edmonds, *Armed Services and Society*, p. 173.

5. Both Britain and Germany established the air force as a third independent service in the years immediately following World War I. The United States, on the other hand, did not create an independent air force as a third service until after World War II. During the Second World War, American air forces operated as part of the army and navy—the U.S. Army Air Corps and navy aircraft carriers.

6. See Edmonds, *Armed Services and Society*, p. 172.

7. For more on the COS Committee, see Broadbent, *Military and Government*, pp. 15, 17, 125–26; and John Sweetman, "A Process of Evolution: Command and Control in Peacetime," in Sweetman, *Sword and Mace*, p. 21.

Established in 1903 as the first permanent standing committee of the British cabinet, the CID was conceived as an advisory and consultative body. It was chaired by the prime minister and was to have a permanent secretariat. For a short history of the CID, see Yehuda Ben Meir, *National Security Decision Making: The Israeli Case* (Tel Aviv: Jaffee Center for Strategic Studies, 1980), pp. 54–56.

8. See Samuel P. Huntington, *The Soldier and the State* (New York: Vintage Books, Random House, 1957), pp. 317–19. See also U.S. Senate Committee on Armed Services, *Defense Organization: The Need for Change* (staff report) (Washington, D.C.: U.S. Government Printing Office, 1985), p. 139.

9. For the Canadian and Israeli cases, see Robert J. Art, "Introduction: Pentagon Reform in Comparative and Historical Perspectives" in Robert J. Art, Vincent Davis, and Samuel P. Huntington, eds., *Reorganizing America's Defense* (Washington: Pergamon-Brassey's, 1985), pp. xvii–xxii.

10. See Huntington, *Soldier and State*, p. 87. Note that the word *sovereign* refers here to either the head of state or the collective executive arm of the government.

11. See Trevor N. Dupuy, "Civilian Control and Military Professionalism: A Systematic Problem," *Strategic Review* 8, no. 1 (winter 1980): p. 41.

12. Art, "Introduction," p. xix. See also W. Harriet Critchley, "Changes in Canada's Organization for Defense: 1963–1983," in Art, Davis, and Huntington, eds., *Reorganizing America's Defense*, pp. 145–48.

13. See Ben Meir, *National Security Decision Making*, esp. pp. 36–38, 53–59, and 61–64.

14. See Art, "Introduction," p. xxii. For an excellent recent review of the formal aspects of civilian and military defense organization in Israel, see Aharon Yariv, "Military Organization and Policymaking in Israel," in Art, Davis, and Huntington, eds., *Reorganizing America's Defense*, pp. 108–29, esp. p. 114.

15. Section 1 of *The Israel Defense Forces Ordinance, Laws of the State of Israel*, vol. 1 (Jerusalem: Government Printer, 5708–1948), p. 15.

16. See Yariv, "Military Organization and Policymaking," p. 116. See also interview with Zeev Schiff.

17. Personal communication.

18. Interview with Moshe Levy.

19. Yariv, "Military Organization and Policymaking," p. 112. See also ibid., p. 114.

20. Interview with Moshe Levy.

21. Yariv, "Military Organization and Policymaking," p. 115.

22. Interview with Mordechai Gur.

23. See Moshe Lissak, "Paradoxes of Israeli Civil-Military Relations," *Journal of Strategic Studies* 6, no. 3 (Sept. 1983): 3.

24. See Yariv, "Military Organization and Policymaking," pp. 111, 112.

25. Personal communication.

26. See section 7 of *The Israel Defense Forces Ordinance, Laws of the State of Israel*, 1:16.

27. "Yishuv" was the name given during the mandate to the Jewish community in Palestine.

28. See Amos Perlmutter, *Military and Politics in Israel* (London: Cass, 1969), p. 80.

29. See Yariv, "Military Organization and Policymaking," p. 111.

30. See ibid., p. 111; Yoram Peri, *Between Battles and Ballots: Israeli Military in Politics* (Cambridge: Cambridge University Press, 1983), pp. 197–98; interview with Chaim Yisraeli.

31. See Lissak, "Paradoxes of Israeli Civil-Military Relations," pp. 3–4.

32. Interview with Yitzhak Rabin.

33. Perlmutter, *Military and Politics in Israel*, pp. 89–91.

34. Interview with Mordechai Gur.

35. Interview with Uzi Eilam.

36. Ibid.

37. Interview with David Ivri, *Yediot Aharonot* (in Hebrew), April 29, 1990, magazine sec., p. 4.

38. Interview with David Ivri.

39. For a discussion of the relationship between the CGS and the D-G, see "Defense Minister–Chief of Staff–Director-General" in chapter 6 and "Force Development" in chapter 7.

40. Interview with Chaim Yisraeli and Uzi Eilam.

41. Interview with Uzi Eilam.

42. Interview with Mordechai Gur.

43. See note 37 above.

44. Interview with David Ivri.

45. Interviews with David Ivri, Mendy Meron, Chaim Yisraeli, Zeev Schiff, Uzi Eilam, Yitzhak Rabin, and Moshe Arens.

46. Interviews with Mendy Meron, David Ivri, and Moshe Levy.

47. Interview with Moshe Levy.

48. Interview with General Hershko, *Bamachanah* (in Hebrew), April 5, 1989, p. 16.

49. Interview with David Ivri.

50. Interview with economic adviser Imri Tov, *Ma'ariv* (in Hebrew), June 12, 1990, financial magazine sec., pp. 12–14.

51. Interviews with Uzi Eilam and Avraham Tamir.

52. Interview with Avraham Tamir.

53. Interview with Uzi Eilam.

54. Interview with David Ivri.

55. Interviews with Moshe Arens, Yitzhak Rabin, Uzi Eilam, and David Ivri.

56. Interview with Moshe Arens, David Ivri, and Uzi Eilam.

57. Interviews with Zeev Schiff and Chaim Yisraeli.

58. Interview with Moshe Arens.

59. Interview with Yitzhak Rabin.

60. Interview with Moshe Levy.

61. This history of the development of strategic planning in Israel is based to a large

degree on an interview with Avraham Tamir, who headed the planning efforts of the IDF for over fifteen years (1966–1983). See also Ben Meir, *National Security Decision Making*, p. 123.

62. Interview with Uzi Eilam and David Ivri.
63. Interview with Moshe Levy.
64. Interviews with Yitzhak Rabin and Moshe Arens.
65. Interview with David Ivri.
66. *Ma'ariv* (in Hebrew), Oct. 26, 1990, sec. B, p. 5.
67. Personal communication.
68. Personal communication.
69. Peri, *Battles and Ballots*, p. 195.

6. Relationships Among the Key Actors

1. See Yehuda Ben Meir, *National Security Decision Making: The Israeli Case* (Tel Aviv: Jaffee Center for Strategic Studies, 1980), pp. 101–4.
2. Interviews with Shimon Peres and Issar Harel.
3. See Yoram Peri, *Between Battles and Ballots: Israeli Military in Politics* (Cambridge: Cambridge University Press, 1983), p. 137; interview with Chaim Yisraeli.
4. See Moshe Dayan, *Milestones* (in Hebrew) (Jerusalem: Edanim, 1976), pp. 422–23. See also Aharon Yariv, "Military Organization and Policymaking in Israel," in Robert J. Art, Vincent Davis, and Samuel P. Huntington, *Reorganizing America's Defense* (Washington: Pergamon-Brassey's, 1985), p. 124; and Peri, *Battles and Ballots*, pp. 136–37.
5. See Peri, *Battles and Ballots*, pp. 137–38; interview with Chaim Yisraeli.
6. Peri, *Battles and Ballots*, pp. 137–38.
7. Interview with Moshe Arens and Ezer Weizman.
8. Interview with Ezer Weizman.
9. Interview with Shimon Peres.
10. Interview with Chaim Bar-Lev.
11. Interview with Chaim Yisraeli.
12. Interview with Mordechai Gur.
13. Personal communication.
14. Personal communication.
15. Interview with Ephraim Poran.
16. Interview with Ezer Weizman.
17. Personal communication.
18. Personal communication.
19. Interview with Ezer Weizman.
20. Personal communication.
21. Interview with Yitzhak Rabin.
22. See Peri, *Battles and Ballots*, pp. 156–74.
23. Interviews with Chaim Bar-Lev, Mordechai Gur, and Rafael Eitan.
24. Interview with Moshe Arens and Moshe Levy.
25. Interview with Ezer Weizman.
26. Interviews with Zeev Schiff and Eitan Haber.
27. Interviews with Yitzhak Rabin, Chaim Yisraeli, and Meir Amit.

28. Interview with Yitzhak Rabin. According to Rabin, when Ben-Gurion was prime minister, the CGS would participate in cabinet meetings once or twice a year.

29. Interview with Zeev Schiff.

30. Peri, *Battles and Ballots*, p. 174.

31. Interviews with Ezer Weizman and Rafael Eitan.

32. Interview with Ephraim Poren.

33. Edward Luttwak and Dan Horowitz, *The Israeli Army* (London: Allen Lane, 1975), p. 134.

34. Interview with Chaim Yisraeli.

35. Interview with Moshe Levy.

36. Morris Janowitz, *The Professional Soldier* (New York: Free, 1960, 1971), p. 367.

37. Interview with Yitzhak Rabin.

38. Interview with Moshe Levy.

39. Interview with Mordechai Gazit.

40. Interview with Mordechai Gur.

41. Personal communication.

42. Interviews with Shimon Peres, Zeev Schiff, Chaim Yisraeli, and Ezer Weizman.

43. Interviews with Rafael Eitan, Moshe Levy, and Mordechai Gazit.

44. Interview with Mordechai Gur.

45. Personal communication. See also *Ma'ariv Special Supplement on Desert Storm* (in Hebrew), March 29, 1991. p. 3.

46. See Zeev Schiff and Ehud Yaari, *Intifada* (in Hebrew) (Tel Aviv: Shoken, 1990).

47. Interview with Mordechai Gur.

48. *Yediot Aharonot* (in Hebrew), June 15, 1990, magazine sec., p. 20.

49. Interviews with Ezer Weizman, Yitzhak Rabin, Moshe Arens, and Mendy Meron.

50. Interview with Chaim Bar-Lev.

51. Interviews with Moshe Arens and Moshe Levy.

52. Interview with Rafael Eitan.

53. Interview with Chaim Yisraeli.

54. Interview with Mordechai Gur.

55. Interviews with Moshe Levy, Ezer Weizman, Moshe Arens, and Yitzhak Rabin.

56. Interview with Moshe Levy.

57. Interview with Mordechai Gur.

58. Interviews with Ezer Weizman and Mordechai Gur.

59. Interviews with Zeev Schiff and Eitan Haber.

60. Interviews with Moshe Arens, Chaim Bar-Lev, and Yitzhak Rabin.

61. Interviews with David Ivri and Moshe Arens.

62. Interview with Mordechai Gur.

63. Interview with Shimon Peres.

64. Interviews with David Ivri and Uzi Eilam.

65. Section 3(c) of *The Basic Law: The Army, Laws of the State of Israel*, vol. 30 (Jerusalem: Government Printer, 5736–1975/76), p. 150.

66. Interview with Zeev Schiff. See also Peri, *Battles and Ballots*, pp. 89–90.

67. Interview with Chaim Bar-Lev.

68. Interview with Zeev Schiff. See also Peri, *Battles and Ballots*, p. 90.

69. Interview with Ezer Weizman.

70. Personal communication.

71. Interviews with Aharon Yariv and Yitzhak Rabin.

72. Interview with Yitzhak Rabin.

73. Interviews with Aharon Yariv and Chaim Yisraeli.

74. Interviews with Moshe Arens, Yitzhak Rabin, and Moshe Levy.

75. Interviews with Eitan Haber, Zeev Schiff, and Moshe Levy.

76. Interview with Chaim Yisraeli.

77. Interviews with Moshe Arens and Moshe Levy.

78. Interviews with Moshe Levy, Moshe Arens, and Menachem Meron.

79. Interviews with Moshe Arens and Moshe Levy.

80. Personal communication.

81. Interviews with Yitzhak Rabin, Moshe Levy, Eitan Haber, and Zeev Schiff.

82. Interview with Zeev Schiff.

83. Interview with Yitzhak Rabin.

84. Interview with Moshe Levy.

85. Interview with Yitzhak Rabin.

86. Interview with Zeev Schiff.

87. Interview with Yitzhak Chofi.

88. Peri, *Battles and Ballots.*

89. Interview with Moshe Levy.

7. Civilian and Military Involvement in National Security

1. Interviews with Rafael Eitan and Yitzhak Rabin.

2. Interview with Chaim Yisraeli.

3. For a detailed and dramatic recital of the intense struggle between the IDF general staff and Prime Minister Eshkol during the waiting period before the Six Day War, and specifically of the dramatic confrontation between the two at the IDF central command post on the night of May 28, 1967, see Eitan Haber, *Today War Will Break Out: The Memoirs of Brigadier General Yisrael Lior—Military Secretary to Levy Eshkol and Golda Meir* (in Hebrew) (Tel Aviv: Eidanim, 1987), pp. 157–224. For a lucid description of the valiant efforts of CGS David Elazar to convince Dayan and Meir to sanction a preemptive strike by the Israeli Air Force against Syria and Egypt on the morning of October 6, 1973, see ibid., pp. 11–31.

4. Jan Englund and Stephen Aubin, "The JCS and Congress: Lessons from France and Great Britain," *Comparative Strategy* 6, no. 3 (1987): 307.

5. Interviews with Yitzhak Chofi and Chaim Yisraeli.

6. For more on the Lebanon War, see the discussion later in this chapter, as well as Ehud Yaari and Zeev Schiff, *War of Deceit* (in Hebrew) (Jerusalem: Shoken, 1984); Shimon Shiffer, *Snowball: The Story Behind the Lebanon War* (in Hebrew) (Tel Aviv: Yediot Aharonot/Idadim, 1984); and Aryeh Naor, *Government in War* (in Hebrew) (Tel Aviv: Lahan, 1986).

7. See chapter 6.

8. For a detailed description of this incident, see Haber, *Today War Will Break Out*, ch. 19.

9. Interviews with Chaim Bar-Lev and Ephraim Poren.

10. Interview with Chaim Bar-Lev.

11. Interview with Rafael Eitan.

12. Haber, *Today War Will Break Out*, p. 332.

13. Interview with Aharon Yariv.

14. Shabtai Teveth, *Moshe Dayan: The Soldier, The Man, The Legend* (Boston: Houghton Mifflin, 1973), p. 261.

15. Interview with Yitzhak Rabin. See also Yitzhak Rabin, *The Rabin Memoirs* (Boston: Little, Brown, 1979), p. 113.

16. Interview with Yitzhak Rabin.

17. Interview with Yitzhak Chofi.

18. Interview with Chaim Bar-Lev.

19. Interviews with Chaim Yisraeli and Mordechai Gazit.

20. Interview with Ezer Weizman.

21. Interview with Eitan Haber.

22. Interview with Ezer Weizman.

23. Personal communication.

24. Interview with Eitan Haber.

25. Personal communication.

26. Interview with Zeev Schiff.

27. Interview with David Ivri and Zeev Schiff.

28. Graham T. Allison, *Essence of Decisions—Explaining the Cuban Missile Crisis* (Boston: Little, Brown, 1971), pp. 131–32, quoted in U.S. Senate Committee on Armed Services, *Defense Organization: The Need for Change* (staff report) (Washington, D.C.: U.S. Government Printing Office, 1985), pp. 305–6.

29. This case study is based on Shlomo Nakdimon, *Tammuz in Flames: The Story of the Bombing of the Iraqi Reactor* (in Hebrew), rev. ed. (Tel Aviv: Edanim, 1993), and on personal communications.

30. Samuel P. Huntington, "Organization and Strategy," in Robert J. Art, Vincent Davis, and Samuel P. Huntington, eds., *Reorganizing America's Defense* (Washington: Pergamon-Brassey's, 1985), p. 235.

31. Aharon Yariv, "Military Organization and Policymaking in Israel," in Art, Davis, and Huntington, eds., *Reorganizing America's Defense,* p. 127.

32. Amos Perlmutter, "The Dynamics of Israeli National Security Decisionmaking," in Art, Davis, and Huntington, eds., *Reorganizing America's Defense*, p. 131.

33. See Meir Pail, "Policy and the Military in the War of Independence, in Abraham Zohar, ed., *The Book and the Sword: David Ben-Gurion—State and Army* (in Hebrew) (Tel Aviv: Ma'arachot, 1988), pp. 31–39.

34. Interviews with Chaim Yisraeli, Aharon Yariv, and Eitan Haber.

35. Interviews with Menachem Meron, Chaim Bar-Lev, and David Ivri.

36. Interview with Mordechai Gur.

37. Interviews with Aharon Yariv and Zeev Schiff.

38. Interviews with Avraham Tamir and David Ivri.

39. Interviews with Avraham Tamir and Yitzhak Chofi.

40. Interview with Chaim Bar-Lev.

41. Haim Benjamini, "The Six-Day War, Israel 1967: Decision, Coalitions, Consequences: A Sociological View," *Journal of Strategic Studies* 6, no. 3 (Sept. 1983): 67, 77. See also ibid., pp. 71–72.

42. Interviews with Issar Harel and Chaim Yisraeli.

43. Interview with Aharon Yariv.

44. Interview with Mordechai Gur.

45. Interview with David Ivri.

46. Yechezkel Dror, "Ben-Gurion—A Civilian at the Head of the Military Establishment," in Zohar, ed., *The Book and the Sword*, pp. 52–53.

47. This case study is based on the sources in note 6 above and on personal communications.

48. Interview with Aharon Yariv.

49. Interviews with Aharon Yariv, Menachem Meron, and David Ivri.

50. Interviews with Aharon Yariv and Mordechai Gur.

51. Interview with Yitzhak Rabin.

52. See, for example, Zeev Schiff, "A Method of Canceling Projects," and Reuven Pedatzur, "The Arrow and the Lessons of the Lavie," *Ha'aretz* (in Hebrew), Aug. 8, 1990, p. B1.

53. Interviews with Mordechai Gur and Chaim Bar-Lev. See also *Ha'aretz* (in Hebrew), March 22, 1989, pp. 1–2.

54. Interview with Avraham Tamir.

55. Interviews with Yitzhak Rabin, David Ivri, and Eitan Haber.

56. Interview with Yitzhak Rabin.

57. Interview with David Ivri.

58. Interviews with Ezer Weizman, Mordechai Gur, and Eitan Haber.

59. Interview with Avraham Tamir.

60. See Schiff, "Method of Canceling Projects"; Emanuel Rosen, "No Way to Make Decisions," *Ma'ariv* (in Hebrew), March 22, 1989, p. 2; and Reuven Pedatzur, "Improvising in Shallow Waters," *Ha'aretz* (in Hebrew), March 23, 1989, p. B1.

61. Interview with Avraham Tamir.

62. Interview with Moshe Arens.

63. Haber, *Today War Will Break Out*, pp. 54–57, 68–70.

64. Interview with Mordechai Gur.

65. Interview with Menachem Meron.

66. Interview with Moshe Arens.

67. *Ma'ariv* (in Hebrew), March 23, 1989, p. 2.

68. Interview with Yitzhak Rabin.

69. This case study is based on a special report on the Lavie project by the Israeli State Comptroller in the *Thirty-Seventh Yearly Report of the State Comptroller's Office* (Jerusalem: Government Printer, 1987), pp. 1291–1325, and on personal communications.

8. Civilian Control Revisited

1. Interview with Mordechai Gur.

2. Amos Perlmutter, *Military and Politics in Israel* (London: Cass, 1969), p. 121.

3. *Ha'aretz* (in Hebrew), Dec. 20, 1988, p. 1.

4. Interview with Ezer Weizman; Yoram Peri, "Party-Military Relations in a Pluralist System," *Journal of Strategic Studies* 6, no. 3 (Sept. 1983): 50.

5. Yoram Peri, "Patterns of the IDF's Relations with the Political Establishment in

Israel," in Joseph Alpher, ed., *A War of Choice* (in Hebrew) (Tel Aviv: Hakibbutz Hameuchad, 1985), p. 36.

6. John E. Lawyer, "The Military Role in International Negotiations," *Air University Review* 31, no. 2 (Jan.–Feb. 1980): 27, 28.

7. For an example of military involvement in the armistice negotiations and the workings of the Mixed Armistice Commission with Syria, see Aryeh Shalev, *Cooperation Under the Shadow of Conflict: The Israeli-Syrian Armistice Regime 1949–1955* (in Hebrew) (Tel Aviv: Ma'arachot, 1989).

8. Interview with Mordechai Gazit.

9. Ibid.

10. Interview with Issar Harel.

11. Personal communication.

12. See Edward Luttwak and Dan Horowitz, *The Israeli Army* (London: Allen Lane, 1975), pp. 202–8. See also Moshe Lissak, "Paradoxes of Israeli Civil-Military Relations," *Journal of Strategic Studies* 6, no. 3 (Sept. 1983): 6.

13. Interview with Aharon Yariv.

14. Interview with Moshe Levy.

15. Interview with Mordechai Gur.

16. Interview with Moshe Arens.

17. For the five roles, see chapter 2 and note 41 there.

Appendix A. Theoretical Perspectives

1. See 2 Sam. 3.

2. See 1 Kings 2:5–6.

3. During the rebellion of Absalom against his father David, it was, of course, Yoav who commanded the troops loyal to the king in the crucial battle in which the rebel Absalom was killed. On learning that his son had been slain, instead of congratulating the army on its victory, David broke down weeping, mourning his lost son. It was Yoav who bitterly chided the king, vividly describing the disappointment and pain such behavior caused the soldiers, and it was he who warned the king of the grave damage to the army's morale that would result from this behavior. See 2 Sam. 18, 19.

4. Samuel P. Huntington, *The Soldier and the State* (New York: Vintage Books, Random House, 1957), p. 19; Morris Janowitz, *The Professional Soldier* (New York: Free, 1960, 1971), p. viii; John Sweetman, ed., *Sword and Mace* (London: Brassey, 1986), p. ix; see also David C. Hendrickson, *Reforming Defense: The State of American Civil-Military Relations* (Baltimore: Johns Hopkins University Press, 1988), p. 50.

5. Huntington, *Soldier and State*, p. 58. For a short overview of the new theory of war and of Clausewitz's writings, see Huntington, *Soldier and State*, pp. 55–58.

6. Samuel Huntington, foreword to Amos Perlmutter, *The Military and Politics in Modern Times* (New Haven: Yale University Press, 1977), p. ix; Martin Edmonds, *Armed Services and Society* (Boulder: Westview, 1990), p. 13. See Moshe Lissak, foreword to S. E. Finer, *The Man on Horseback* (Hebrew translation) (Tel Aviv: Ma'arachot, 1982), p. 9.

7. Huntington, *Soldier and State*, pp. 3, 7.

8. See Janowitz, *The Professional Soldier*; Edmonds, *Armed Services and Society*, p. 81.

9. David R. Segal and Janet S. Schwartz, "Professional Autonomy of the Military in

the United States and the Soviet Union," *Air University Review* 32, no. 6 (Sept.–Oct. 1981): 21, 25; Janowitz, *The Professional Soldier*, p. 367.

10. This characterization suffers, of course, from all the drawbacks of any generalization and is mentioned solely for didactic purposes. As mentioned previously, Huntington recognizes the importance of ideology—a social characteristic—in the development of civil-military relations. Finer also recognizes the importance of ideology. In his introduction to the Hebrew edition, he observed that two factors determine whether there will be a military coup in any given country: the structure and attitudes of society, on the one hand, and the structure and attitudes of the armed forces, on the other. Huntington, however, emphasizes throughout his work the importance of the level of military professionalism, while the major part of Finer's book is devoted to categorizing societies according to their levels of political culture and relating these levels to the various levels of military intervention.

11. See Samuel E. Finer, *The Man on Horseback*, 2d Enlarged. ed. (Middlesex: Penguin Books, 1976), pp. 78–80. See also Edmonds, *Armed Services and Society*, pp. 74–76.

12. See Amos Perlmutter and V. P. Bennett, eds., *The Political Influence of the Military* (New Haven: Yale University Press, 1980).

13. See ibid.; and Amos Perlmutter, *The Military and Politics in Modern Times* (New Haven: Yale University Press, 1977). See also Edmonds, *Armed Services and Society*, p. 84.

14. Perlmutter and Bennett, *Political Influence of the Military*, p. 13.

15. Ibid., p. 8.

16. Perlmutter, *Military and Politics in Modern Times*, pp. 4, 8. See also Perlmutter and Bennett, *Political Influence of the Military*, p. 13.

17. Huntington, foreword to Perlmutter, *Military and Politics in Modern Times*, p. xvi.

18. Perlmutter, *Military and Politics in Modern Times*, p. 32.

19. See *Encyclopedia of the Social Sciences*, s.v. "praetorianism," quoted in Perlmutter and Bennett, *Political Influence of the Military*, p. 199.

20. Perlmutter and Bennett, *Political Influence of the Military*, p. 13. See also Edmonds, *Armed Services and Society*, p. 84.

21. See Huntington, foreword, p. x.

22. See Perlmutter and Bennett, *Political Influence of the Military*, pp. 3–4. See also Edmonds, *Armed Services and Society*, p. 85.

23. Perlmutter, *Military and Politics in Modern Times*, p. 205.

24. See Perlmutter and Bennett, *Political Influence of the Military*, pp. 12, 21.

25. This point is made by many students of Israeli civil-military relations. See, for instance, Yoram Peri, *Between Battles and Ballots: Israeli Military in Politics* (Cambridge: Cambridge University Press, 1983).

26. Perlmutter points out that Israel has been more successful than China in the process of nationalization, depoliticization, and professionalization of the military (22–23). See also Peri, *Battles and Ballots*.

27. Perlmutter, *Military and Politics in Modern Times*, p. 14.

28. See, for instance, Amos Perlmutter, "The Israeli Army in Politics: The Persistence of the Civilian over the Military," *World Politics* 20 (1968): 606–43; Perlmutter, *Military and Politics in Modern Times*, ch. 9; and Amos Perlmutter, *Military and Politics in Israel* (London: Cass, 1969).

29. See also Yoram Peri, "Party-Military Relations in a Pluralist System," *Journal of Strategic Studies* 6, no. 3 (Sept. 1983): 46–63.

30. See Peri, "Party-Military Relations," p. 46. Peri's view confirms that it is not by chance that the only other country—besides Israel—that Perlmutter places in this category is Communist China.

31. Dan Horowitz and Moshe Lissak, "Democracy and National Security in a Protracted Conflict," *Jerusalem Quarterly*: 11–12.

32. Moshe Lissak, foreword to S. E. Finer, *The Man on Horseback* (Hebrew translation) (Tel Aviv: Ma'arachot, 1982), p. 10.

Index

military in, 18–20. *See also* Political processes
Draft system for IDF, 54, 176, 206n82
Dror, Yechezkel, 147–48
Drori affair, 71, 125
Dupuy, Trevor N., 10

Eban, Abba, 50
Edmonds, Martin, 7, 14–15, 76, 77, 188
Egypt, peace initiative of 1977, 147. *See also* Sinai
Ehrlich, Simcha, 60
Eilam, Uzi, 93
Eilon Moreh settlement: and nulled confiscations of land, 53–54; and supremacy of government over defense minister, 61
Eisenhower, Dwight D., 10–11, 19, 24, 25
Eitan, Rafael (former CGS): on access to prime minister, 116; advocate of strike on Iraqi nuclear reactor, 136; appointment as CGS, 122; approval of increasing presence of CGS at cabinet and MDC meetings, 112–13; approval of Sharon's objectives in Lebanon War, 155–56; on civilian control of operations, 128; decision against strike on Syrian anti-aircraft missiles, 141–42; on defense minister as representative of government, not commander in chief, 68; on former generals as defense ministers, 108–9; on latitude of emergency powers of IDF, xviii; operations without government authorization during Lebanon War, 62; recognition of subordination to prime minister, 57, 58; on relations between CGS, prime minister, and defense minister, 107; on subordination of defense minister to prime minister, 74
El Al aircraft protection, 146
Elazar, David (former CGS): appointment of, 122; meeting with prime minister on plan to cross Suez, 103, 107; memorandum to prime minister, 40, 64; recommendation for preemptive

strike on Syria, 129, 175; resignation of, 117; seizure of Golan Heights upon orders from defense minister, 65–66; suggestion for joint R-and-D unit, 92
Electoral politics. *See* Political/electoral processes
Emergency Defense Regulations (1945), 53, 98
Englund, Stephen, 129
Entebbe incident, 49, 59, 103, 113
Eshkol, Levi (former prime minister): doubling as defense minister, 70–71; force development decisions, 161; greater use of MDC, 31; influence over budget, 90; reaction to overstepping of authority by defense minister, 131; resistance to military pressure for war, 128–29
Europe, civilian control in, 2, 12
Executive branch of Israeli government, 3
Executive role for military, 25
Exports of military hardware, 89–90, 91

FADC (Foreign Affairs and Defense Committee) of Knesset, 46, 48–51, 59, 180
FA-HB (financial adviser-head of the budget), 91–92, 93, 182
FCH (field corps headquarters), 85, 86, 183; Apache helicopter purchase decision, 157
Field corps, 83, 86
Finance Committee of Knesset, 46–48
Finance Ministry and Lavie project, 163, 164–65, 167
Finer, Samuel E., 190, 218n10
Force development: case study–Lavie project, 161–68; examples of civilian control, 160–61; helicopter purchase decision, 157–58; increasing attention of media to, 158; lack of adequate civilian control of, 127, 156–61, 179; problems of procurement, 88–90, 91, 92, 93
Foreign Affairs and Defense Committee (FADC) of Knesset, 46, 48–51, 59, 180

Secret services, FADC subcommittee on, 50

Security considerations: lack of leaks from Knesset subcommittees, 51; limited public airing of defense issues, 48. *See also* Censorship

Security services: exclusion from study, 2; Shabak (General Security Service), xiii, 49, 101

Segal, David R., 11, 189–90

Settlements: active IDF involvement in, 6; Eilon Moreh and nulled confiscations of land, 53–54; IDF instigation of civilian pressure groups, 175; removal from Yamit, 133; Sabastia and settlers' resistence to forcible removal, 114–15, 169

Shabak (General Security Service), xiii, 49, 101

Shachak, Amnon, xiv

Shachal, Moshe, 61

Shamgar, Meir, 55

Shamir, Yitzhak: consideration for political implications of military appointments, 171–72; decision to not enter Gulf War, 114; disagreement with defense minister, 105; dismissal of Weizman for PLO contacts, 204n33; opposed to cancellation of Lavie project, 167; private meetings with DMI, 94; support for defense minister, 104; warnings to Saddam Hussein, xiii

Sharett, Moshe, 60, 100, 104, 106

Sharon, Ariel (former defense minister): acting aginst orders, 129–30; acting as diplomatic negotiator, 174–75; architect of Lebanon War, 148, 150–56; budget framework, 160; Dayan's attempt to dismiss, 125, 130; denied private access to prime minister, 104; direct orders to lower ranks, 65; expansion of planning staff to national security unit (NSU), 96; integration efforts, 92–93; micromanagement of military operations, 132, 133; operations without government

authorization during Lebanon War, 59–60, 62, 104; resigned in lieu of firing, 204n33

Shin Bet. *See* Shabak (General Security Service)

Shomron, Dan (former CGS): on Air Force relationship with IDF, 82; appointment of, 123; on defense minister as representative of government, 61, 62, 63; full cabinet review of military courts decision, 55; goal of cancellation of Lavie project, 166; private meeting with prime minister, xiv; reluctance to enter Gulf War, xiv, 113–14; resistance to using greater force against intifada, 114

Sinai Operation (1956), 146, 174

Sinai War, preparations without government knowledge, 60, 100

Sinai withdrawal: Begin's secret proposal for, 105; IDF compliance despite objections, 128

Six Day War, 128–29

"Small Plan" for Lebanon War, 152

Soldiers: consideration for morale of, 69–70; in revolutionary armies, 193; as "specialists in violence," 188

Soltan artillery gun, 160

State Comptroller's Office, 161

Strategic planning: case study–Lebanon War, 148–56; problem of partial integration of, 94, 95–97; recommendation for creation of department for, 183; weakness of civilian control in, 127, 143–48, 173–75, 179

Student kidnapping incident, 62

Study: basic theoretical premise of, 4; conclusions and recommendations, 178–83; interviews conducted for, xviii; perspectives, 1–8; scope and purposes, xv, 3, 194–95; theoretical model for, 3, 185–95

Subcommittees of Knesset: Foreign Affairs and Defense Committee (FADC), 46, 48–51, 59, 180; on IDF